ıts

Japan: Divic

W9-CUE-531

ny

General Editors:

Max Beloff

Former Gladstone Professor of Government and Public Administration in the University of Oxford

Gillian Peele

Fellow and Tutor in Politics, Lady Margaret Hall, Oxford

Titles already published

GOVERNMENT IN CANADA
Thomas A. Hockin

THE GOVERNMENT OF THE UNITED KINGDOM
Max Beloff and Gillian Peele

Forthcoming

GOVERNING FRANCE: THE ONE AND INDIVISIBLE REPUBLIC (*2nd edition*)
Max Hayward

Japan: Divided Politics in a Growth Economy

SECOND EDITION

J.A.A. STOCKWIN

Nissan Professor of Modern Japanese Studies, University of Oxford

W. W. NORTON & COMPANY

London *New York*

© 1975, 1982 by J.A.A. Stockwin

First American publication 1975
Second American edition 1982
Reprinted 1985

All rights reserved

W.W. Norton & Company, Inc., 500 Fifth Avenue, New York, NY 10110
W.W. Norton & Company, Ltd., 37 Great Russell Street, London WC1B 3NU

ISBN 0-393-95235-5

Printed in the United States of America

3 4 5 6 7 8 9 0

In memory of
J.M.H.W

Contents

Tables

Figure

Acknowledgements

The second edition of this book was completed while I was on study leave in Japan from the Australian National University during the first half of 1981. I should like to thank the Japan Foundation for financial support, the Institute of Social Science of the University of Tokyo for providing me with an affiliation on this and previous occasions, and to my head of Department at the Australian National University, Professor Jim Richardson, for encouraging my research. I owe a special debt to Professor Hayashi Shigeru in Tokyo, who has been a wise and generous counsellor to my family and myself for almost two decades. Many others have helped, directly and indirectly, and some without knowing it. These include Banno Junji, John Caiger, Hugh Collins, Sydney Crawcour, Peter Drysdale, Fukui Haruhiro, Aurelia George, John Hart, James Horne, Ishida Takeshi, Kawai Hidekazu, Richard Mason, Minagawa Shūgo, Nishihira Shigeki, Harry Rigby, Alan Rix, David Sissons, Rob Steven, Richard Storry, Watanabe Akio, John Welfield and Ian Wilson. My gratitude to the Australian National University – my academic home for over twenty years – knows no bounds. Lastly, I give thanks to my longsuffering family, who have added variety to the taste of Japanese politics with a seasoning of pottery, music and other pursuits.

Conventions

Throughout this book, Japanese names are given in their proper order, with the surname first and the personal name second. When, however, works written in English by Japanese writers are cited in footnotes, the order natural to English is preserved.

Editor's Introduction to the First Edition

The series of which this volume forms part is intended as a contribution to the study of contemporary political institutions in a number of countries both in Europe and in the rest of the world, selected either for their intrinsic importance or because of the particular interest attaching to their form of government and the manner of its working. Although we expect that most readers of such a series will be students of politics in universities or other institutions of higher or further education, the approach is not wholly that of what is now technically styled 'political science'. Our aims have been at once more modest and more practical.

All study of government must be comparative, in that the questions one asks about one system will usually arise from one's knowledge of another, and although we hope that anyone who has read a number of these volumes will derive some valuable general ideas about political institutions, the notion that politics is a suitable subject for generalization and prediction is alien to the empirical spirit that animates the series.

The authors are concerned with government as an important practical activity which now impinges upon the life of the citizen in almost every sphere. They seek in each individual country to ask such questions as how laws are made and how enforced, who determines and in what manner the basic domestic and foreign policies of the country. They seek to estimate the role not only of elected persons, presidents, ministers, members of parliament and of lesser assemblies but also of the officials and members of the armed forces who play a vital role in different ways in the different societies.

But government is not something carried out for its own sake; ultimately the criterion of success and failure is to be found in its impact upon the lives of individual citizens. And here two further questions need to be asked: how does a government conduct itself in regard to the citizen and what protection has he through the courts or in other ways against arbitrary action or maladministration? The second question is how the citizen can in fact make his influence felt upon the course of government, since most of the countries that will be discussed in these volumes claim to be democratic in the broadest sense. And this inquiry leads on to a discussion of political parties and the various interest groups or pressure groups which in modern states form the normal vehicles for self-expression by citizens sharing a common interest or common opinions. To understand their working, some knowledge of the role of the press and other mass media is clearly essential.

The study of such aspects of politics has recently been very fashionable and is sometimes styled the behavioural approach or the investigation of a political culture. But our authors have kept in mind the fact that while the nature of a country's formal institutions may be explained as the product of its political culture, the informal aspects of politics can only be understood if the legal and institutional framework is clearly kept in mind. In the end the decisions are made, except where anarchy or chaos prevails, by constituted authority.

We would like to feel that anyone suddenly required for official or business or cultural purposes to go to one of these countries hitherto unknown to him would find the relevant volume of immediate use in enabling him to find his way about its governmental structure and to understand the way in which it might impinge upon his own concerns. There is a great deal to be said for a guide-book even in politics.

Nevertheless no attempt has been made to impose uniformity of treatment upon these volumes. Each writer is an authority for his particular country or group of countries and will have a different set of priorities; none would wish to treat in the same way an old-established and highly integrated policy such as that of France or the United Kingdom and a vast and heterogeneous political society still searching for stable forms such as India.

Beloff

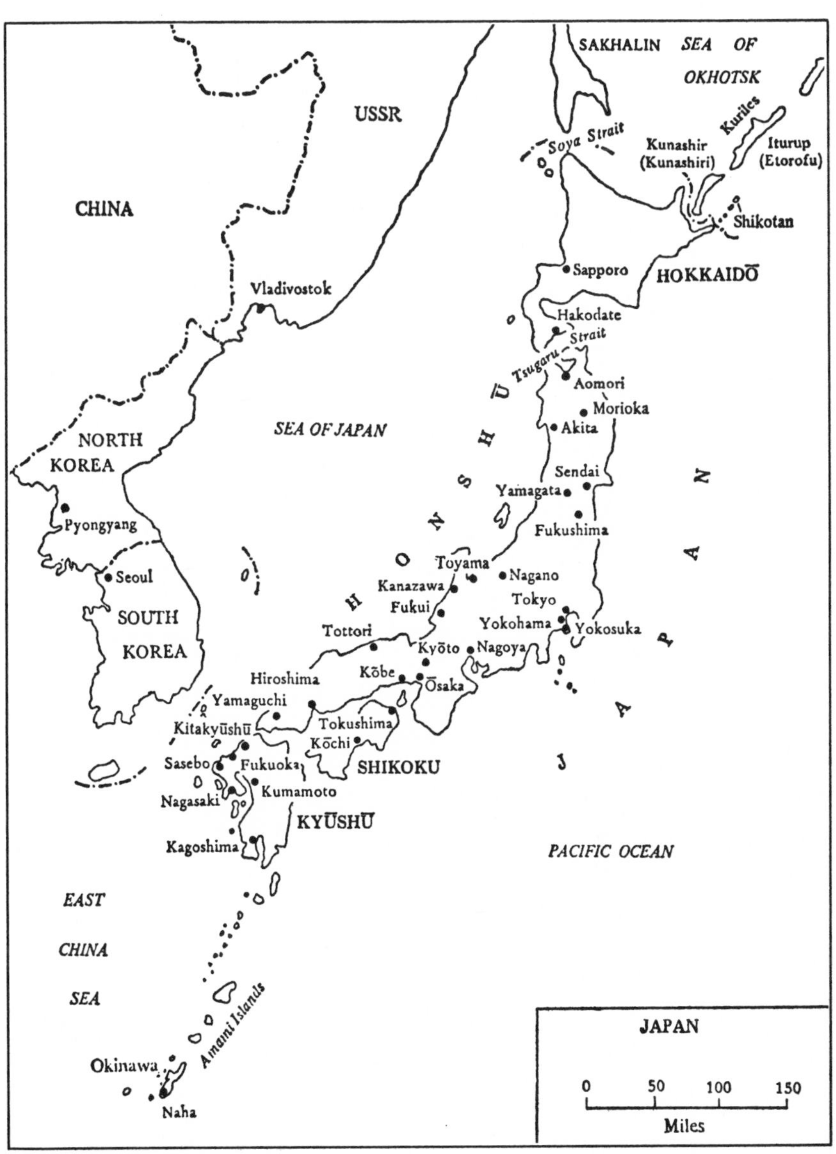
SAKHALIN
SEA OF OKHOTSK
USSR
Kuriles
Soya Strait
Kunashir (Kunashiri)
Iturup (Etorofu)
CHINA
Shikotan
Sapporo
HOKKAIDŌ
Vladivostok
Hakodate
Strait
Tsugaru
Aomori
Morioka
Akita
NORTH KOREA
SEA OF JAPAN
Sendai
Yamagata
Pyongyang
Fukushima
HONSHŪ
JAPAN
Toyama
Nagano
Seoul
Kanazawa
Tokyo
Fukui
SOUTH KOREA
Yokohama
Yokosuka
Tottori
Kyōto
Nagoya
Kōbe
Hiroshima
Ōsaka
Yamaguchi
Tokushima
Kitakyūshū
Kōchi
Sasebo
Fukuoka
SHIKOKU
Kumamoto
Nagasaki
KYŪSHŪ
Kagoshima
PACIFIC OCEAN
EAST CHINA SEA
Amami Islands
JAPAN
0 50 100 150
Miles
Okinawa
Naha

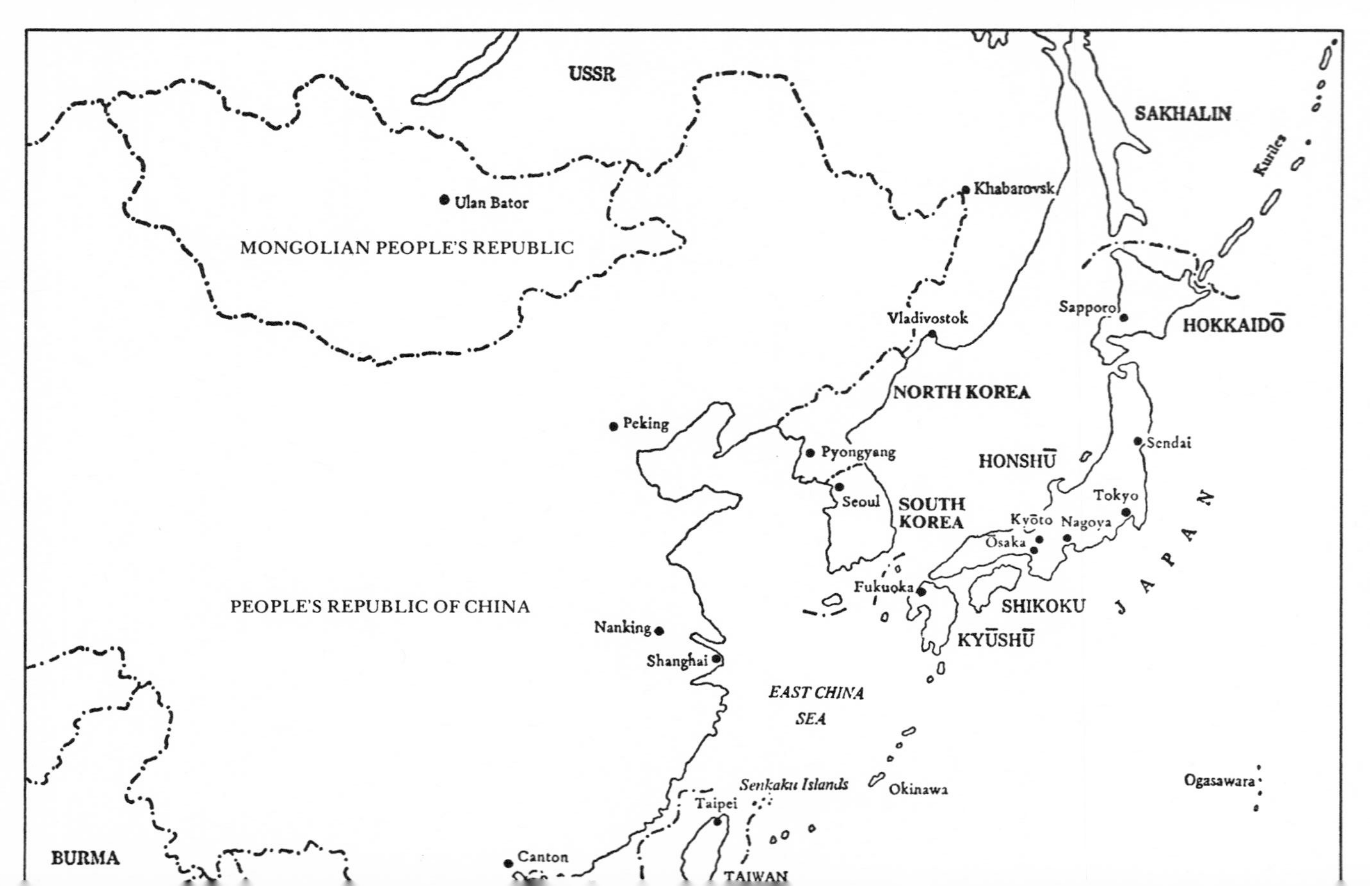

USSR
SAKHALIN
Kuriles
Ulan Bator
MONGOLIAN PEOPLE'S REPUBLIC
Khabarovsk
Vladivostok
Sapporo
HOKKAIDŌ
NORTH KOREA
Peking
Pyongyang
HONSHŪ
Sendai
Seoul
SOUTH KOREA
Tokyo
Kyōto
Nagoya
Ōsaka
JAPAN
Fukuoka
SHIKOKU
PEOPLE'S REPUBLIC OF CHINA
Nanking
KYŪSHŪ
Shanghai
EAST CHINA SEA
Senkaku Islands
Okinawa
Ogasawara
Taipei
BURMA
Canton
TAIWAN

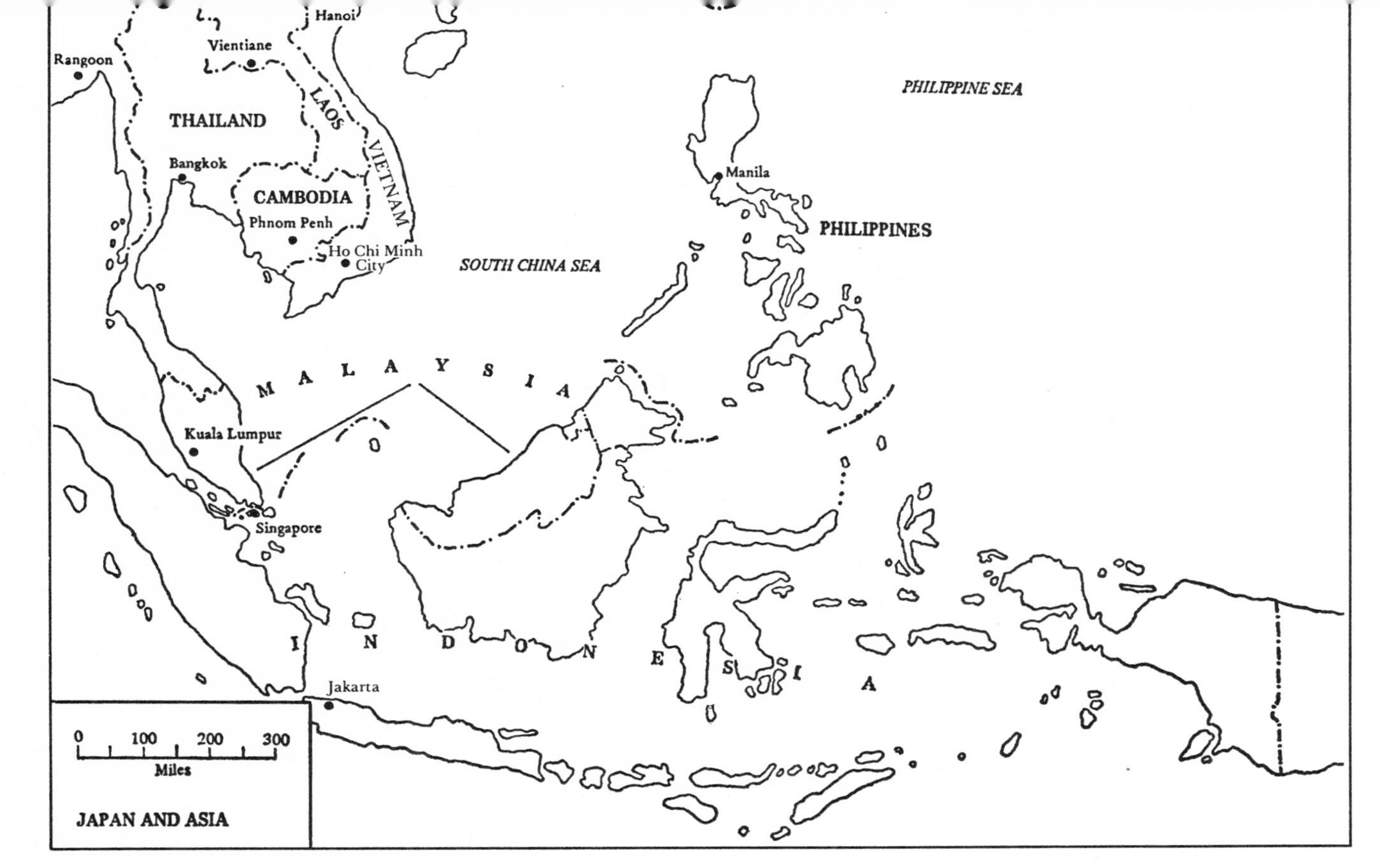
Hanoi
Vientiane
Rangoon
THAILAND
LAOS
VIETNAM
Bangkok
CAMBODIA
Phnom Penh
Ho Chi Minh City
PHILIPPINE SEA
Manila
PHILIPPINES
SOUTH CHINA SEA
MALAYSIA
Kuala Lumpur
Singapore
INDONESIA
Jakarta
0
100
200
300
Miles
JAPAN AND ASIA

1 Introduction

Despite the serious economic problems affecting Japan between 1974 and 1981, it was still the case that no other country had achieved such spectacular economic progress since the 1950s. Few would have dared to predict, after her defeat in 1945, that within a quarter of a century Japan would have created one of the three largest economies in the world. Already by the early 1970s only the United States and the Soviet Union had economies that in terms of gross national product were bigger than that of Japan. The resilience of the economy and its capacity to adjust rapidly to adverse circumstances were graphically illustrated by the fact that although economic growth turned negative for a year or so following the OPEC oil crisis of 1973–4, by 1975 steady economic growth had been resumed at a lower but still impressive level. Whereas between the mid-1950s and early 1970s the growth of GNP averaged an annual 10 per cent, between 1975 and 1980 it was averaging around 5 to 6 per cent per annum.

In some respects, it is true, Japan lagged further behind than her GNP would indicate. Social services, and that part of the economy known as the 'social infrastructure' (roads, sewerage, housing and the like), had been seriously neglected when compared with the attention given to them in other advanced economies. Gross neglect of the environment, particularly during the 1950s and 1960s, had caused some appalling tragedies. Living standards, though they had risen rapidly and continued to rise, were still probably rather lower than those of a few countries whose GNP was smaller, and were being affected by inflation. Moreover, the economy was exceedingly dependent on foreign supplies of oil (99 per cent of total requirements were imported), and heavily dependent on foreign countries for most other raw materials. As the cost of imported oil rose rapidly in the late 1970s and early 1980s, so the need to expand overseas markets further increased, and Japanese export drives were apt to cause difficulties with the United States, Europe and elsewhere. National security, in an economic as much as in a military sense, was a prime concern of Japan's policy-makers as the nation entered the 1980s.

Nevertheless, in many of these problem areas considerable progress had been made. Despite the patchy (but improving) state of social services, the expectation of life for both males and females at birth in Japan was (according to possibly arguable statistical assumptions) the highest in the world by 1980. Much was being done to improve the social infrastructure, especially in areas such as transport, though housing for much of the population was still expensive and of a relatively poor standard. Slower rates of economic growth and a tightening of regulations by Government had taken some of the pressure off the environment. By 1980, for instance, the required standards for exhaust pollution control in motor cars were practically the toughest in the world. External resource dependence was a most serious matter, particularly in respect of oil, but long-term plans were under way to reduce this dependence, both by effecting savings and by facilitating the use of substitutes for oil. For a decade the Government and industry had been seeking ways of diversifying sources of most raw materials, so that excessive dependence on any one country or region should be avoided. Diversification of markets was also a key aim of economic foreign policy.

The 1980s certainly looked like being a testing time for the Japanese economy, but while some of the more euphoric forecasts emerging from Western presses appeared exaggerated, the progress made was impressive, and there was even more reason to dispute such censorious judgements as that emanating from the European Community that the Japanese were a nation of workaholics living in rabbit hutches.

The reasons for the Japanese economic 'miracle' of the 1950s to 1970s have been quite widely studied by economists, who for the most part agree that there is no simple or single-factor explanation of it.[1] Yet although there may be dispute about the relative weights which ought to be given to each of them, it is clear that certain factors were particularly important.

Perhaps the most crucial is the high rate of productive

investment carried out by industry. As a percentage of GNP, fixed capital formation during the 1950s and 1960s was on average over 30 per cent (substantially more than any other comparable economy), and very little of it went into types of investment, such as housing, that were not directly productive.[2] This in itself, however, needs explaining, and the explanation is far from simple. A number of factors were involved. One was the extent to which Japanese industry over the period was willing and able to import foreign technology, purchased through licensing agreements, and develop it, incorporating improvements and adaptations. This had the twin advantages of minimizing research costs and enabling industry to incorporate the latest techniques developed overseas, without delay. Given also the willingness of businessmen to replace existing plant early (and this was no doubt initially connected with the fact that industry had had to start virtually from scratch with new equipment after the end of the Second World War), this resulted in an astonishingly rapid and sustained rise in productivity.

In its pursuit of growth, Japanese industry enjoyed what in retrospect seems like a uniquely favourable set of circumstances. The level of personal savings was extremely high, not so much because of any innate Japanese quality of thriftiness, as because the average individual needed to provide substantially for his own and his family's social welfare, as well as for his children's education. Channelled largely through the banking system, such savings provided industry with the funds for investment. Industry's bill for wages also remained moderate throughout the period, as productivity ran well ahead of wage increases. This was principally a result of the relatively low bargaining power of labour, which was organized for the most part in enterprise unions which in day-to-day bargaining with their employers would usually accept moderate wage settlements. Yet another factor was the buoyancy of Japanese exports, whose rate of increase was well in excess of the overall rate of growth of world trade. The free trading atmosphere of international economics in the 1960s was peculiarly favourable for the expansion of Japanese exports, and a number of key growth industries experienced fast growth in their export markets. These industries were largely those with high technology content, where productivity was rapidly rising and prices were highly competitive.[3]

Other factors may be mentioned more briefly. The work force was well educated and technologically skilled. There was a substantial pool of labour ready to be absorbed into industry from less productive occupations including agriculture. Taxation was moderate and defence spending low, while there had been 'windfall gains' from the Korean and Vietnam wars.

Finally, however, it is necessary to mention a factor of major and somewhat controversial significance, namely, the role of government in the expansion process. There has been some misunderstanding of the nature of the Government's role in economic management. It was not true, for instance, that the Government usurped the function of the industrialist to the point of making his day-to-day business decisions for him. The independent strength and purposiveness of the major Japanese companies is well known. Nevertheless, on many matters vitally affecting business conditions and the overall guidance of the economy, the Government occupied a key position. The Ministry of International Trade and Industry (MITI) took the initiative over a long period in relation to the pace of import and capital liberalization, and the purchase of foreign technology. Through 'administrative guidance' the nature and direction of an industry's investment programme, or the number of independent operators in a given industry, was capable of being influenced by government sources (particularly MITI). As we shall see later in the book, the important factor making such influence possible was the ability of government and industry to co-operate with each other, despite constant jockeying for position between different sections of both. In broad terms, the ability of government and industry to co-operate was premised upon the existence of stable conservative government, which predominated from the end of the Second World War. The long-term supremacy of the conservative business-oriented forces in Japanese politics was conducive in the circumstances of the time to sustained economic growth.

The economic environment of the 1970s was considerably more complex for Japan than that of the 1960s. Apart from the overriding problem of oil, which has already been mentioned, international trade as a whole was growing more slowly, wide fluctuations in the relative values of major currencies reflected a general mood of instability, and protectionist pressures had strengthened in several of Japan's major trading partners. Considerable progress had been made towards the internationalization of the Japanese economy, though the Government was reluctant to relax practices and alter institutional arrangements in such a manner as to render its economic policies less effective. Domestically, the intense wage-cost pressures which followed the 1973–4 oil crisis gave way to more moderate union demands, influenced by increased (though still relatively low) levels of unemployment and underemployment. Faced with reduced economic growth and an ageing population structure, firms were finding it harder to maintain intact the permanent employment system with its regular seniority increments for regular employees, so that various modifications of the system were making their appearance. One result of this was less harmonious labour relations in some sectors of the economy. Structural adjustment, however, continued apace, and productivity increases, though much lower than a decade earlier, were high relative to other advanced economies. Japan was now a world leader in many areas of technology, and rather than buying foreign patents, as she had largely done in the 1950s and 1960s, she was putting much greater resources than previously into her own research and development. The Japanese economy, in other words, was under much greater strain than it had been a decade earlier, but was also better equipped to withstand such strain.

When we turn, however, from economics to the broader field of politics, a substantially different logic is seen to apply in which conflicts and divisions abound, but consensus is laboriously reached or solutions are imposed. Japan is a seriously divided polity, although the divisions were partially concealed by a long period of conservative government. Vexed problems, left over from the Occupation period, or resulting from the forced pace of Japan's development, remained largely unresolved, and a way to their solution was by no means clear. There was thus a latent and sometimes overt tension in Japanese politics, even though in comparison with many other countries it was remarkably stable.

The juxtaposition of conflict and consensus, tension and stability, was probably the aspect of Japanese politics and government which was least easy to understand from the outside. A lack of general familiarity in the West with Japanese political traditions and practices meant that superficial and sometimes excessively alarmist analyses gained greater acceptance than they deserved. Politics in Japan was complex, and not easily reduced to a single formula. Problems of authority, participation, representation, cohesion and bureaucracy were at the centre of political discourse in Japan as in most other countries, and the solutions which emerged had much in common with those which were to be found elsewhere. On the other hand, the pace and discontinuities of Japan's development since the mid-nineteenth century imposed serious strains on her political life.

Over the past century Japan experienced two contrasting constitutions. The Meiji Constitution of 1890 was an ambiguous document which, after a reasonably promising start, ultimately failed to guide the course of social and economic change along a path either of liberalism or of political stability. The Constitution of 1947, virtually imposed upon a defeated nation by American Occupation forces, led to stable government and management of the economy consistent with the aim of economic growth. At the same time political forces outside the central decision-making orbit were often implacably opposed to existing authority, while constitutional and other political arrangements were matters of chronic division.

Japan in modern times experienced two periods of massive change, the first at the time of the Meiji Restoration of 1868, and the second following her defeat at the hands of the Allied powers in 1945. It was largely the radical change of direction brought about by these two 'revolutions' which led some Western writers to suspect that the Japanese character was particularly prone to adopt sudden massive shifts in political outlook without worrying unduly about the inconsistency of old and new approaches.[4] Thus, it was suggested, Japan could once more, in certain circumstances, radically change the direction of national policies from those of the period since the Occupation.

This, however, is not a particularly convincing argument, at least on the evidence of political events hitherto. Underlying the discontinuities of recent political history may be found a strong element of continuity. Breaks with the past are seldom complete, as a comparison of the habits, personnel and themes of Japanese politics before and after the Second World War will readily reveal. There is no counterpart in Japanese experience to the Bolshevik Revolution of 1917. Rather than the wholesale replacement of political leadership and radical reshaping of institutions and philosophies to which that event gave rise, political change in Japan even at its most radical point stopped short of a severing of links with what went before.

In part, this may well be largely a question of the character of political control in recent Japanese history. Despite the pace and scope of economic, social and political change since the middle of the nineteenth century, Japan never experienced anything resembling a revolution from below. Political activists from lower social strata at times acted as a catalyst for quasi-revolutionary changes (as in the case of the ultra-nationalist groups of young officers – many of peasant origin – who were active in the 1930s), but the political controllers, whether they were conservative or radical in outlook, always constituted a fairly self-conscious élite of people possessing high status in the society. This is as true of Japanese politics in the 1980s as it was in earlier periods, although the method of recruiting the élite is now substantially meritocratic. The politics of competing class-based parties, alternating in government, is a model that did not emerge as viable in Japan, even though in the postwar period the forms of party competition appeared to be based on the major premise that this was how the system ought to work. The reasons for this and the prospects for change will be explored in a later chapter.

Japan, it is sometimes remarked, is an oriental, not a Western, country. Some writers have argued that since the Japanese polity has a cultural context radically different from that of any of the major Western powers, one should not expect that polity to behave according to the normal expectations of Western political observers.[5] There is some truth in this, even though writers who press this point tend to forget that each Western polity also has unique elements in its political structure. On the other side it is arguable that Japan, as a modern industrial state, with a technologically skilled population, vast industrial output and a sophisticated network of communications, should have much in common politically with other similarly advanced states. *A priori*, it should have more in common with them than with less developed societies elsewhere in Asia, despite some cultural and social similarities with the latter.

It is important not to become bemused by this problem. As we have already hinted, Japan has a richness of political experience and tradition comparable to that of Britain, France or the United States. Japanese political culture is neither untouched by Western influences, nor a mere carbon-copy of any other political culture. The mere fact that Japan is an industrialized society does not mean that it is just the same as any other industrialized society, but neither is it unaffected by pressures common to all industrialized states. It should be possible to attempt an analysis of Japanese government and politics using a frame of reference which owes much to Western models. Since, however, there are significant features of Japanese social organization and cultural attitudes which *are* peculiar to Japan (or at least are not exactly replicated elsewhere) due attention must also be paid to these. Certain aspects of political behaviour and organization were undoubtedly formed in the mould of a social culture which emphasized group cohesiveness and local loyalties. Other aspects can be illuminated if one realizes that parts of the traditional culture held achievement in high esteem. The group, however, rather than the individual, was and is widely regarded as the engine of achievement, although by the early 1980s the accuracy of this generalization was under attack in some quarters.

Neither the dynamism of the Japanese economy, nor the persistent fragmentation of political life into cliques and factions can be properly understood without an awareness of the social context (including an appreciation of the extent to which it is changing). The whole nature of decision-making is profoundly affected by social and cultural norms which are recognizably Japanese, even if to an extent they have their counterparts elsewhere. Once again, however, this is true of politics in any state one cares to name. There is a mixture of influences, social, cultural, political and economic, which has to be analysed in depth in order to gain some understanding of how the system works, has worked, and is likely to work in the future.

In any case it would be wrong to suggest that cultural peculiarities are the only thing which have given an element of uniqueness to Japanese political patterns. Since the nineteenth century the nation's economic circumstances have also had a profound effect upon its politics.

The contrast between the 1890 and 1947 constitutions indicates that it has been far from easy to find a satisfactory framework for the operation of politics in Japan. Now one (though only one) of the reasons for this is that the priority given to the task of solving the problem of national economic backwardness has dictated expedients which have led to illiberal political practices and arrangements.

The challenge of economic backwardness has by now been substantially overcome (although vulnerability in respect of oil supplies and supplies of other raw materials remains), and by this token the Japanese political experience tells a story of spectacular success.[6] Whatever the successes and failures of Japanese economic management over the past century, one thing that is certain is that national economic imperatives have crucially shaped the character of the polity and the perceptions of political leaders. Many of Japan's leaders perforce developed certain habits of mind and certain kinds of political arrangement adapted to the governing of a resource-poor nation, dependent upon making the best of meagre natural advantages, so as to survive in a competitive economic and political environment. These economic imperatives, reinforced, it must be added, by straightforward power considerations, have probably been as important as the social and cultural background in promoting basic continuities in Japanese politics.

In one sense economic pressures have tended to work in a similar direction to traditional social characteristics of the Japanese people. The natural poverty of the nation, coupled with its geographical and historical isolation, have served to foster a strong sense of national vulnerability and even inferiority. This in turn tended to facilitate a sense of cultural uniqueness and group-togetherness, which was seized upon by thepolitical leaders of the Meiji period (1868–1912) as a means of cementing nationalism, including national purpose and national discipline. Only since the emergence of an increasingly affluent society and a more internationally oriented economy in the 1960s and 1970s have forces been set in motion which could radically alter in a more relaxed direction the style of exercising power and the extent of political participation. Even here we are witnessing determined resistance by the 'old guard'.

There are two particular aspects of continuity in Japanese politics which are significant in this context. One is the habit of close co-operation between government and business, which has led to a unique blend of private enterprise and political direction. Although the extent of this in the most recent period and indeed also in the Meiji period has sometimes been exaggerated,[7] it is none the less true that Japanese industrialization was begun largely on government initiative, and political leaders continued to involve themselves closely in its progress.

The second area of continuity is the great influence of government bureaucracy in political decision-making. Essentially this was part and parcel of the doctrine of a strong Executive enshrined in the Meiji Constitution of 1890. The power of the bureaucracy, however, remains strong in practice under the 1947 Constitution, even though its relative position has been somewhat attenuated. The idea that the Executive should be strong, which not even the American Occupation was able to transform, may also be traced to a deep-seated instinct among government officials that the economy, despite its superficial advances, was too vulnerable to risk political relaxation.

The economy, however, has grown so rapidly in recent years that talk of economic vulnerability in the old sense is anachronistic, although the problem of energy and raw material supplies has yet to be overcome, if indeed a 'solution' is possible. Issues have become more complex, and between 1976 and 1980 the political system went through a period of marked instability, with the ministerial party only barely maintaining a parliamentary majority. Even though the 1980 general elections spectacularly restored conservative dominance over the national Diet, relationships between the electorate, pressure groups, political parties, the Diet and the government bureaucracy were undergoing considerable change. Japanese politics was becoming if anything more dynamic, and the constellation of forces within government, though heartened by its electoral victory and by a conservative mood in the electorate, needed to exhibit fine political judgement if it was to retain fully effective power on a long-term basis. Whatever form the distribution of political power might assume in the future, the adaptability of the present system was being continuously tested.

2 Historical Background

From the perspective of the 1980s it is difficult to imagine that a little over a century ago government in Japan was conducted according to the principle of preserving the *status quo* intact whatever the cost. For nearly two and a half centuries (the Tokugawa period) the Japanese people were, by deliberate government policy, virtually isolated from contact with the outside world, frozen socially into rigid social strata and governed, much like the feudal societies of Europe in the Middle Ages, by local *han* (clans) which were self-supporting and self-governing, but owed allegiance to the central government.

The Bakufu, as the chief power centre was called, was itself a remarkable institution. In origin a military government, headed by a Shōgun (Generalissimo) and having its immediate power base in a coalition of various *han* situated largely in the northern and eastern parts of the country, it was accorded legitimacy throughout Japan. Other *han*, principally in the southern and western regions, were regarded by the Bakufu as potentially less loyal, but were kept in check by a comprehensive set of restrictions designed to reduce to a minimum their physical capacity to create trouble. The Tokugawa period, which brought peace after centuries of recurrent civil war, was founded in the perception that social, economic or political change, as well as foreign influences, were likely to be highly destabilizing. Therefore it was determined that all of these things should be kept to an absolute minimum. The Tokugawa regime succeeded in creating a 'utopian' society – 'utopian' in the sense of a total order which was not supposed to evolve.[1] All elements in that order were to be maintained intact so that the order itself should not collapse. Draconian social, economic and political controls were felt by the regime to be fully justified if they contributed to that end.

Ironically the final collapse of the regime in the 1860s bore out the apprehensions of its rulers about the destabilizing character of piecemeal relaxation of controls. Once foreigners had been allowed access to Japan and some of the controls over the southern and western *han* had been lifted, the overthrow of the Bakufu and the collapse of the utopian order it had cherished came swiftly. This is not to say however, that, had the controls been retained, things would have continued indefinitely as before.

Many of the conditions for change had been maturing over the long Tokugawa peace. The rigid hierarchical divisions of *daimyō* (feudal lords, one in charge of each *han*), *samurai* (warrior-administrators), peasants, artisans and merchants (in that order) bore less and less relationship to economic reality. Despite the fact that the merchants had the lowest formal status, they had accumulated wealth and were the creditors of many of the *samurai*. The *samurai* had become in many cases, and for a variety of reasons, disgruntled and impoverished. Moreover, peace had brought a degree of national prosperity, which happened to favour the 'outer' (i.e. southern and western) *han* rather more than the Bakufu itself, thus upsetting the delicate balance of power. There was also a slow but steady spread of education and commercial institutions during the Tokugawa period, so that the country was not entirely unprepared for a period of modernization and innovation once the old regime was overthrown.

The 1850s and 1860s were a period of increasing instability, precipitated by the pressures which several Western nations were bringing to bear with a view to opening up Japan to commercial intercourse with the outside world. Whether internal change or external pressure was the most crucial cause of the eventual change of regime is hard to say, because of the extent to which the various trends and events interacted with each other.[2] What is important is that once the old Tokugawa regime was overthrown (in 1868) the politics of the *status quo* was swiftly replaced by the politics of radical innovation. The new rulers had little compunction about discarding most of the shibboleths of the former regime, even though they did not claim to be acting in the name of a radically different ideology. It may be noted in passing that nothing of the sort happened in China until much later (1911) and that as a consequence China found it considerably harder than Japan to lay the foundations of a modern state.

What is termed the 'Meiji Restoration' in 1868 was the event that most obviously marks the transition from the old regime to the new. As was suggested above, the transition could well be regarded as a revolutionary one. Nevertheless, as the term 'Restoration' suggests, the new leaders themselves were concerned to emphasize their links with the past. They were 'restoring' the imperial institution to its rightful position which the Shōguns had usurped centuries earlier. And yet, in the interim, there had been no break in the imperial line. An emperor, though quite powerless, continued to reside in Kyōto, and the Shōgunate continued to acknowledge that its own legitimacy ultimately derived from him. In a country where indirect rule was accepted as fairly normal, this state of affairs caused little surprise until the grip by the Bakufu on the affairs of state began to falter.

It was only comparatively late in the process of turmoil and agitation which culminated in the Meiji Restoration that the imperial institution came to be championed seriously as a substitute for the Bakufu. Previously many of the revolutionary leaders had been seeking ways of strengthening the Shōgun and his government in their struggle to ward off the danger of foreign penetration.

However, once the Bakufu had been overthrown,[3] the newly 'restored' emperor proved to be a powerful weapon in the hands of the revolutionary leaders. As a symbol of the legitimacy of their newly established regime, the emperor was a powerful support for them in the enactment of a range of bold and adventurous reforms. As the most recent in an ancient and unbroken line of sovereigns, he could be manipulated into the supreme symbol of nationhood, and in practical terms could be used as an instrument of the centralizing and modernizing which the new leaders proceeded to take upon themselves.

As a revolution, which it undoubtedly was, the Meiji Restoration of 1868 has some surprising features, at least when viewed with the experience of revolutions in Western countries in mind. First of all, the revolutionary leaders came for the most part from the ranks of the *samurai*-administrators who had held effective power at the local level in the old regime. It was not, in Marxist terms, a 'bourgeois–democratic' revolution, since the merchants, no doubt because of their low formal status, took no active part. Essentially it was a revolution carried out by dissident elements of the old ruling class: a revolution from above, not from below. Geographically speaking, however, there was a genuine upset of the *status quo*. Apart from a handful of former court nobles from Kyōto, the rulers of the new Japan hailed largely from the southern and western *han* of Satsuma, Chōshū, Tosa and Hizen, which had always been regarded with suspicion by the Bakufu. Despite the fact that the *han* were abolished as administrative units shortly after the Meiji Restoration, Japan's key political and military leaders were still being identified with these four areas (especially Satsuma and Chōshū) for another forty years.[4]

The second remarkable feature of the Meiji Restoration and its aftermath was the extraordinarily ambivalent attitude that the new leadership took towards change. On the one hand they proclaimed the necessity of bringing Japan into the modern world through a crash programme of Westernizing reforms, which they proceeded to put into practice with gusto. On the other hand most of them professed to be against dilution of the spiritual essence of the Japanese people, which later came to be formulated in the term *kokutai* (national polity). They tended to harbour what in retrospect seems the curious illusion that wholesale social, economic and political reforms along Western lines could leave the Japanese people fundamentally untouched in their 'spiritual' values. The fallacy inherent in this view probably accounts in part for alternating phases of Westernization and reassertion of national values that characterized Japanese history from the Meiji Restoration until after the Second World War.

What principally motivated the Meiji leaders themselves in this regard can best be described as nationalism. Initially, from the 1850s, incensed by the failure of the Bakufu to withstand foreign pressures, they took the extreme nationalist stance enshrined in the slogan, 'Expel the barbarian'. Later, when the futility of trying to rid the country of foreign influences without the material means of doing so became apparent to them, they had the foresight and flexibility of mind to embrace the very enemy they had sought to expel. A new slogan, 'Strong nation and powerful army', became the order of the day, and even if the long-term consequences of making Japan 'strong' were not fully appreciated, the programme itself had rapid and remarkable success.

The sweeping reforms of the early Meiji period included the abolition of the *han* and the creation of *ken* (prefectures), which formed the principal local unit in an increasingly centralized system of local government. A system of universal conscription removed the old *samurai* monopoly of the right to bear arms and formed the base for the creation of an army with truly national loyalties. Universal primary education was introduced as a matter of priority, and a number of universities and other secondary and tertiary educational institutions were set up. The first steps were taken towards industrialization, with the Government in several cases setting up an industry on its own initiative and later handing it over to private entrepreneurs. The taxation system was completely restructured, and the Government proceeded to obtain much of its revenue from a land tax, the effect of which was to produce a surplus for industrialization at the expense of the rural interest. Reforms to the legal system were also initiated, although these did not come to full fruition until much later, when the Government was determined to abolish the principle of extraterritoriality, whereby foreigners were able to be tried in their own courts for offences committed on Japanese soil.

So far as central government was concerned, the Meiji leaders were content to work for some twenty years on the basis of temporary and *ad hoc* administrative arrangements. This was the period in which they were both consolidating their grip on power and seeking to put their indelible stamp upon events.[5] Formal constitutional arrangements could therefore wait. Meanwhile pressures for the wider sharing of political power were building up in some quarters, and embryo political parties made their appearance during the 1870s. The government leaders reacted to and against these developments, and when they finally brought in a constitution in 1889 (effective 1890) it was found to contain severe restrictions upon effective sharing of political power.

Nevertheless the Meiji Constitution is a landmark in Japan's modern political development. In part, it represented a policy of the Meiji leaders that Japan should have at least the forms of a modern Western-type state. Significantly, they were the most attracted by the constitutional practices of Bismarck's Prussia. Although their motives here were by no means uniform, there is little reason to believe that they saw the Constitution other than as formalizing and thus perpetuating substantially the same sort of regime as had obtained hitherto. That is, the emperor (meaning in practice his advisers) should retain effective power, the newly created popular assembly should have only a consultative role, and the political parties should be an impotent opposition rather than a potential alternative government. In practice, as we shall see, things did not quite work out like that, and the government leaders, to an extent at least, found themselves imprisoned by constitutional forms of their own making. It has been argued that their later reluctance, despite these difficulties, to suspend or otherwise grossly to override the Constitution derived from the same determination to be seen as an equal of the Western powers which had inspired so many of the reforms from 1868 onwards.[6]

The Meiji Constitution established an Imperial Diet (parliament) consisting of two houses, a House of Peers, which was composed of members of the imperial family, the orders of nobility created after the Meiji Restoration and imperial nominees, and an elective House of Representatives (articles 33–4). The House of Representatives was not to be seen as the more effective house, each having equal powers of initiating legislation (article 38),[7] and the House of Peers had the right of veto over legislation initiated in the House of Representatives (article 39).[8]

The position of the Diet as a whole, however, was severely limited by the superior status and powers of the emperor, although these were not always easy to pin down in practice. Thus the emperor was 'sacred and inviolable' (article 3). In him resided sovereignty (not, of course, in the people), although he was to exercise it in accordance with the Constitution (article 4). It was the emperor who exercised the legislative power, though with the consent of the Imperial Diet (article 5), who gave sanction to laws (article 6), had considerable powers over the duration of Diet sessions (articles 7, 42, 43) and dissolved the House of Representatives, this leading to new elections (articles 7, 45).

Moreover, the emperor was able to issue imperial ordinances for a wide range of purposes when the Diet was not sitting (articles 8, 9), although they were to be submitted for the Diet's approval subsequently, at its next session. Since the Diet was expected to sit for only three months in any year (although prolongations of a session, and also extraordinary sessions, could be held by imperial order), the scope for the imperial ordinance power was obviously considerable. *Ex post facto* review of such ordinances by the Diet was unlikely to be very effective.

It goes without saying that the powers attributed to the emperor by the Constitution were not expected to be exercised by him as a personal ruler. The preamble stated that the ministers of state, on behalf of the emperor, should be held responsible for the carrying out of the Constitution (preamble, para. 6). They were also specified as imperial advisers who were 'responsible' for their advice, while the counter-signature of a minister of state was required on '[a]ll Laws, Imperial Ordinances and Imperial Rescripts of whatever kind' (article 55). The ministers of state, however, were not alone in tendering their 'advice' to the emperor. He could also consult a separate body, called the Privy Council, which was then required to 'deliberate on important matters of State' (article 56). Moreover, in practice an extra-Constitutional body called the Genrō (Elders) – of which more will be said later – occupied a key position of power at certain periods, while the chiefs of staff of the armed services had what was termed 'independent access' to the emperor on purely military matters, and certain members of the Imperial Household Ministry occupied positions of great influence at certain times.

The situation of the ministers of state, as well as their relationship with the Imperial Diet, contained a number of uncertainties and anomalies. The Constitution deliberately contained no reference to the term 'Cabinet', and Prince Itō Hirobumi,[9] in his Commentaries on the Constitution of which he was the leading author, specifically rejected the doctrine of collective cabinet responsibility as derogating from imperial sovereignty. Moreover, there was no provision in the Constitution stating that ministers had to be members of the

Diet, nor that they needed to be answerable specifically to the Diet.

On both of these issues there was much subsequent controversy, which the extreme ambiguity of the Constitution did little to help solve. The traditionalists continued to support the principle of what were termed 'transcendental' cabinets, whose ministers were neither Diet members nor dependent upon a Diet majority, while those more progressively inclined wanted 'responsible' Cabinets, which among other things would have to resign if defeated on the floor of the House. Something like a British-style relationship between Cabinet and Parliament had been established by the 1920s, but such a fundamental liberal principle enjoyed only a brief flowering at that time.

The working of the Meiji Constitution in practice did not entirely bear out the expectations of the Meiji leaders. The House of Representatives proved anything but docile, and the political parties, which despite their recent origin had already accumulated some experience in regional assemblies, fought hard against the principle of transcendental cabinets. Successive governments applied a variety of weapons, constitutional and otherwise, in an attempt to confine the parties to an advisory role. These included frequent dissolution of the House of Representatives, large-scale bribery at elections and the use of article 71 of the Constitution to override opposition by the parties to the governmental budgetary policies.

This last issue is of particular significance. Article 71 reads: 'When the Imperial Diet has not voted on the Budget, or when the Budget has not been brought into actual existence, the Government shall carry out the Budget of the preceding year.'

On the face of it, this presented any government with a cast-iron method of nullifying party objections to government policy in the crucial area of budgetary policy. However, this would have been the case only where the size of the budget did not substantially change from year to year. In a period of rapidly rising government expenditure, such as occurred from the outset of the Sino-Japanese war in 1894, the parties had in their possession a weapon of considerable effectiveness.[10]

The use they actually made of this weapon provides us with a fascinating test of party–Government relationships at this period. It also illuminates a much longer-term characteristic of

Japanese politics, namely the equivocal nature of both conflict and compromise between governments and oppositions.

In the 1890s the electoral franchise was confined to about one per cent of the population of Japan. This meant in effect that a high proportion of the Diet members elected in the early general elections represented the landlord interest upon which fell most heavily the burden of the land tax, used by the Government as the main means of financing its 'strong nation and powerful army' policies. This undoubtedly accounts for the vehemence with which parliamentarians in the mid-1890s called on the Government to retrench its spending; and the threat of forcing the Government to carry on with the budget of the previous year was a powerful one. It is therefore doubly interesting that by the end of the decade the government leaders had succeeded in breaking the deadlock by a series of deals with Diet members and leading party men, which gave them an entrée into the councils of government while allowing the Government to maintain its fiscal policies more or less intact.[11]

The Meiji 'oligarchs' – the powerful and creative political leaders of pre-Constitution days, who continued to dominate governments through the 1890s – were ultimately forced to step down into the arena of party politics themselves. When Prince Itō founded the Seiyūkai Party in 1900 with a membership largely of established party politicians, he was pointing the way to a new style of politics, different indeed from what he himself had envisaged in his Commentaries on the Constitution. By going along with this and subsequent arrangements, however, the parties were gaining a limited right of participation in decision-making at the expense of their ability to present forthright and effective opposition. Henceforth, the line between government bureaucrats and party politicians was a thin one, as it has remained to this day.

One weakness which the political parties continued to manifest to their very great cost was the considerable venality of party politicians. Their propensity for entering into advantageous 'deals' with outsiders, and their consequent liability to being 'bought', made it particularly difficult for the parties to maintain cohesion or internal unity of purpose. It is probable that this was related to group norms in Japanese society, which will be discussed in chapter 3. At the same time it was undoubtedly also related to the ambiguities inherent in the Constitution itself. According to that document, sovereignty resided in the emperor, but the emperor did not rule personally, and it was not at all clear who *was* supposed to. The enthusiasm of the authors of the Constitution to ensure a powerful executive and a weak legislature led them to downgrade even the position of the Cabinet, by providing rival centres of power and inveighing against the principle of collective Cabinet responsibility. The emperor 'cult', which they assiduously promoted as a means to national discipline, also tended to force overt criticism and opposition under the surface, where it was more likely to become immersed in factional intrigue.

Japanese politics during the first two decades of the twentieth century was thus essentially an affair of balancing élites. Cabinets, political parties, top bureaucrats, the House of Peers, the Privy Council, the emperor's personal advisers in the Imperial Household Ministry, the army top brass and certain big business combines were all jockeying for power in a situation where it was unclear where power really lay. Even that is an over-simplification, because separate elements within each of these élites were playing a power game of their own.[12] For a time, overall direction of key decisions was in the hands of the small group of elder statesmen previously referred to as the Genrō. This group, which never consisted of more than seven people, furnished senior Cabinet ministers from among its own ranks until the turn of the century, when it retired more into the background. It still, however, continued to make important decisions, particularly when the choice of a new prime minister, or a matter of war and peace, was at stake. The influence of the Genrō had markedly declined by the end of the First World War, when their 'meddling in politics' was much resented by younger politicians.[13]

The Genrō, though anachronistic, had at least functioned as ultimate political co-ordinators and setters of guidelines. By the 1920s there had taken place a substantial broadening of the base of political participation, but the locus of power at the top remained unstable. The suffrage was broadened by stages, and encompassed all males over twenty-five years of age by 1925. Party Cabinets became the rule, and transcendental Cabinets appeared to be a thing of the past. The parties came to be closely aligned with big business, and even embryo socialist parties began to contest elections.

The instability of this arrangement, however, soon manifested itself. There was a rapid turnover of Cabinets, much corruption and jockeying for power. Despite their ascendancy, the parties still had to contend with the other élites sanctioned by the Constitution. The same Cabinet which brought in universal male suffrage also introduced a 'Peace Preservation Law', designed to give the police more power to harass the left wing.

During the 1930s the power of the political parties ebbed rapidly as the armed forces came to play a more and more commanding role in the affairs of state. The process can be dated at least from the Manchurian 'Incident' of September 1931, when a gross act of insubordination by the Kwantung Army stationed in Manchuria was apparently connived at by the army command in Tokyo, and went unpunished and uncorrected by the civilian Government. Japan proceeded to take over the whole of Manchuria and set up the puppet state of Manchukuo.[14] Subsequently politics in Japan was punctuated by a series of political assassinations and attempted *coups*, the most serious of which, the February 'Incident' of 1936, resulted in the deaths of several members of the Cabinet. Although those directly responsible for these crimes were not admitted to positions of power, their actions helped elements in the army high command increasingly to take over the reins of government.[15]

The reasons for this reversal of previous trends are extremely complex and can only be briefly summarized here. Five main factors command attention.

The first is social and economic. The world depression bore particularly hard upon the Japanese peasantry, and provided fertile soil for right-wing radicalism. Since the army recruited a high proportion of its younger officers from farming areas, ultra-nationalist agitation spread easily within the armed forces and, given the delicate political balance of power in government circles, had a pervasive political effect.

The second is international. This was the age of economic protectionism and a fascist example in Europe. Both politically and economically the international situation was very fluid, and this seems to have had destabilizing effects upon the perceptions of some Japanese leaders. Some others, who were basically liberal, were eliminated by assassination.

The third relates to ideology and indoctrination. Since the Imperial Rescript on Education in 1890, emperor-worship had been officially sanctioned as the keystone of a national ideology, thus blurring in people's minds the true location of decision-making. It was therefore easy for ultra-nationalist fanatics in a period of national crisis to gain wide support for acts of insubordination and even of revolution taken in the name of loyalty to the emperor. It was easy for them to pillory members of the existing Establishment as corrupt and disloyal.

Fourthly, as we have seen already, the constitutional arrangements which had prevailed since the Meiji period contained an unsettling element of ambiguity. The attempt by the Meiji oligarchs to prevent the supremacy of the legislature by a series of checks and balances had merely served to obscure the effective location of sovereignty. It is perhaps remarkable that, given this obscurity, a fairly liberal interpretation of the Constitution had become orthodox by the 1920s. This was the 'organic' theory, which stated that the emperor, far from being an absolute ruler, was organically dependent upon the other 'organs of state'. This did not constitute a 'liberal-democratic' theory of the Constitution along Western lines, and indeed Minobe Tatsukichi, the Professor of Constitutional Law at Tokyo Imperial University who had originated the 'organic theory', publicly opposed the new Constitution introduced during the American Occupation. Nevertheless, in the context of the times, the theory could readily be used to justify relatively liberal political arrangements.[16] On the other hand, with the ascendancy of militarist politics from the early 1930s, the organic theory was overturned, Minobe was dismissed from his post, and an 'absolutist' school, which maintained that the emperor was above the state, and therefore not dependent upon or accountable to other state 'organs', became the new orthodoxy.

Finally, the special position of the armed forces calls for comment. Ever since the leaders of the Meiji Restoration had proclaimed the slogan, 'A strong nation and a powerful army', priority had been given to military preparedness. Indeed, the armed forces had fought in a number of wars, and had inflicted defeat upon Russia in 1906. Reference has already been made to the independent access to the emperor enjoyed by the chiefs of staff of the armed services. Although this was supposed to be restricted to what were termed 'purely military' matters, it proved on a number of occasions to be a useful means of bypassing the Cabinet on sensitive issues. Another convention (not in the text of the Constitution, but adopted some time afterward) was that the minister for the army and the minister for the navy in any Cabinet should be serving officers of the highest rank in their respective services. In the 1930s this brought about the collapse of several Cabinets which were reluctant to let the armed forces have their own way. The resignation of one of the service ministers would be followed by a refusal by the army (or navy) to provide a substitute from its ranks, and thus the prime minister would be forced to tender his resignation.

For these reasons, among others, Japan went through a chaotic period of 'dual government', with the civilian and military arms pursuing uncoordinated though not always unrelated strategies. By the late 1930s, and especially from the outbreak of war in China in 1937, the character of Japanese politics had undergone a profound transformation. Ideologically, virtually all parts of the system had assimilated a militant nationalist ethic, even though the ultra-nationalist army officers who had participated in the February 1936 'Incident' and other similar instances of bloodletting were little more than a catalyst. Recent research has indicated that it is seriously misleading to regard the parties as defeated defenders of the 'liberal' norms of the 1920s, and the armed forces and other 'reactionary' groups as the victors. With some exceptions of relatively minor significance, party politicians were enthusiastic about many of the developments taking place. Even after all existing parties were disbanded in June and July 1940, to be replaced by the Taisei Yokusankai (Imperial Rule Assistance Association) sponsored by Prince Konoe, party politicians continued to play an important role in the total political structure, and indeed they went on politicking in ways that were familiar to them.[17] In April 1942, with war raging in the Pacific, the Tōjō Government even held general elections for the House of Representatives. The vast bulk of successful candidates were from a list of those 'sponsored' by the Government, but a small number of unsponsored candidates were also elected.

Politics in Japan during the Pacific War have been described as 'totalitarian'. Whether or not that overused term is appropriate, the regime bent its energies to the task of mobilizing the population for total war. Functional groups (business organizations, labour unions and the like) were made organs of State, a network of 'neighbourhood associations' did the Government's bidding at the local level, and the Kempeitai (Thought Police) were pervasive. Under wartime pressures, the involvement of the State in most areas of the life of the people became entrenched. Multiple linkages between government and industry, encompassing habits of regular and close consultation, were a legacy of the 1930s and the wartime period of the 1940s which was transmitted through the time of Occupation to the Japan of the 1950s and 1960s.[18]

3 Social Background

Many postwar Western writers on Japanese society have regarded group loyalty as its most salient feature. Indeed Ezra Vogel has recently gone further and commended what he sees as the group-based, disciplined and goal-oriented norms and practices of Japanese society as worthy of emulation in the United States.[1] Sugimoto and Mouer have criticized Vogel, as well as influential Japanese writers such as Nakane[2] and Doi[3], for their 'holistic' tendencies, that is, for their alleged stereotyping of the Japanese people in a way that ignores both differences between various parts of the society, and change over time.[4] Instead, they argue that a model of Japanese society based on conflict and exploitation may be just as convincing as a model emphasizing group co-operation and disciplined striving for common goals.

We do not have space to analyse this controversy in detail, but wish to make three points about it, which are fundamental to the argument of this book. The first is that in Japanese society and politics consensus and conflict are not mutually incompatible. If the individual feels strong loyalty to the group of which he is a part, then he may be inclined to regard other groups with coldness or even hostility. There is no necessary theoretical reason why a society in which group feeling is strong should exhibit a general pattern of social cohesiveness, and indeed there are many group-based, anti-individualistic societies in the world which as a whole are anything but socially cohesive.

Secondly, however, Japan has developed social and political institutions which go a long way to explaining why Japanese society is indeed in many respects remarkably cohesive. In education, law enforcement, employment and other areas, there is ample evidence that complex and sophisticated means are used to ensure the maximum social consensus and to minimize deviance. A well-known example is that of gun control.

Gun laws in Japan are so tight that private gun ownership is rare. In this way an instrument of social conflict – the gun – is virtually eliminated from society (though not from law enforcement agencies) by institutional means.[5]

This undoubtedly indicates a talent for organization and for the creation of a broad consensus, as many writers have pointed out. Also, however, as has been cogently argued by some of Vogel's critics, it may well involve a considerable degree of social coercion and restriction of individual freedom.[6] It is at this point that the balancing of social costs and benefits requires value judgements. In some cases (freedom to own a gun against freedom to walk the streets in safety) the value judgement is an easy one, but it is much more difficult where the costs and benefits of social cohesion accrue differentially to separate sections of the population. As we shall see later in the book, Japan's industrial structure is based on a highly differentiated system of benefits as between permanent employees of large powerful firms, and those working for small undercapitalized establishments. In that the dynamism of the Japanese economy has arguably been dependent on these differentials of status, security and income, there is a difficult problem of value to be resolved.

Thirdly, the maintenance of social and political cohesion in a society where group loyalty is strong requires careful accommodation of rival group interests. Where opposition is weak, this is compatible with a dynamic and efficient outcome of decision-making processes, but where opposition is strong and intransigent, immobilism and stalemate can result.

It is with these thoughts in mind that we shall embark on a brief account of some aspects of Japanese society. It is important to bear in mind that we are not trying to provide a single unvariable model, but merely to indicate some patterns that have manifested themselves in Japanese society in the recent and not so recent past.

It is often remarked that collectivist norms in Japanese society are based on ways of thinking derived from the Japanese family; and although this is an over-simplification, since the family itself has never manifested completely uniform patterns throughout the country, it is certainly important to understand some features of what may be termed the 'traditional' family –

a kind of model which has been used in many 'quasi-family' situations, and has wide political ramifications. In part, this may result from the fact that 'traditional' family patterns were reinforced officially under the prewar legal system, so that the paternalistic family was held up by the state as a desirable social model to be preserved and emulated. Although the legal status of the family was radically changed after the war, the processes of social evolution have naturally been more gradual.

The traditional family structure in Japan contains some very interesting peculiarities. The basic unit is the *ie* (house, or household), the perpetuation of which is regarded as supremely important.[7] So far as the traditional system was concerned, it was not the individual who was the focus of social importance, but the *ie* to which he belonged. The *ie* was strongly male-oriented and paternalistic. In its internal relationships it was hierarchical, with the bonds between father and son being accorded the greatest symbolic and practical importance. Relations between those of comparable status, such as siblings or husband and wife, were regarded as less significant. The head of the household was granted supreme respect, but the obligations between the head and the other members of the *ie* were not simply a one-way affair, but contained a strong element of mutuality.

Paradoxically, however, despite the great emphasis placed upon the status of the head of the household and upon family continuity, succession was not necessarily patrilineal. The perpetuation of the family line was regarded as much more important than the perpetuation of the blood line. In order that continuity of the *ie* be preserved, adoption of a non-blood successor was quite common.

What was at stake was the succession to the headship of the family. The head of the *ie* was the man who was in charge. A new head might take over when the existing head retired or died. (If the previous head had retired he could still continue to live on in the family as a member having a subordinate role, though high status.)

Succession to the family headship could take place essentially in three ways – through consanguinity (obviously much the most common), by fosterage (the adoption of a male heir in childhood), and by the adoption of an adult male successor.[8]

The third method calls for some explanation. If there were no male child then a son-in-law might be adopted, in order to marry a daughter of the family. The son-in-law was likely to be a second, or later, son of another family, so that his original family had no problems with its succession. The son-in-law would then take the name of the family into which he had been adopted and would relinquish the name with which he was born. If an *ie* had no children, than a married couple could be adopted to carry on the family name, usually from among close relatives.[9]

Some anthropologists regard it as logical to treat marriage in the traditional Japanese situation as in all instances a case of adoption.[10] Thus if, as most normally happened, a woman married a man from another family and adopted his surname (or more strictly, the surname attached to that *ie*), she could be regarded as having been adopted into that family. But equally well, a male might be adopted into a family, in order eventually to take over the responsibilities of headship, in circumstances such as those mentioned above. Although the first alternative was obviously the most common, it would be a mistake to regard the other alternative methods of perpetuating a family as in any way departures from a social norm. They were quite usual should the circumstances require them, though in recent years they have become increasingly uncommon.

The whole system was symbolized by the fact that whoever was adopted (whether bride, bridegroom, male child or already married couple) was, according to the terms of the prewar family code, formally removed from the family register of his or her original family and entered into the register of his or her adoptive family.

This was not a 'joint' family on the Indian or Chinese model, and it was rare for married brothers or sisters to live in the same *ie*, except temporarily. Siblings had unequal status, the key status difference being that between the one who was to succeed to the headship of the *ie* and the rest, who would not. The latter were expected to break away and to form separate stem families of their own. In the rural areas of prewar Japan the system was legitimized with the legal principle of primogeniture, which had the salutary effect of preventing an infinite subdivision of agricultural holdings. In the postwar legal code primogeniture was abolished, but it lives on to some extent in the countryside as a social norm. Indeed, in most parts of rural Japan, even eldest sons have left for work in towns and cities, leaving many farms to be cultivated by old people. Before the war, despite the operation of these safeguards against families becoming too large, loose hierarchical networks of kinship ties, known as *dōzoku*, were commonly met with especially in northern areas of Japan.

There are a number of highly significant political implications of the traditional Japanese family system.

We have seen that direct kinship relations, though important, were subordinated to the primary aim of assuring the continuity of a corporate group called the *ie*, which could easily incorporate non-blood as well as blood relationships. It was also however extensible in a figurative sense to situations where actual family ties were not involved at all. In Nakane's words, 'The piety and loyalty shown by Japanese dependants towards the father was in the nature of that shown to the leader of a kind of economic corporate group, but combined with family sentiment.'[11] It is this extension of patterns of family behaviour to non-family situations which needs to be understood in order to make sense of much Japanese political behaviour. Later in this chapter we shall devote some space to discussing specific examples of what may be called 'figurative extensions' of the traditional family system.

Some further implications may be noted. It is important to realize, for instance, that the system in its traditional form was anti-individualistic, and based on the vertical ties of hierarchy rather than horizontal ties of equality. A marriage between members of two families was in one sense a marriage between two families (rather than between two individuals); but at the same time the membership of the two families was quite exclusive, and *dōzoku*-type links, though they might be quite important, in no sense amounted to a coalescence of separate nuclear families into one larger group. The hierarchy was usually quite clear.

Nakane argues that this system, especially in its extension to non-family groups, even today does not permit social pluralism, because it means that there are few cross-cutting relationships. People belong to one group and one group only, which combines elements of family and work. As she puts it, '... groups become independent of each other with no elaborate or constant network cutting across the different groups, in the way that Hindu caste networks cut across various villages'.[12] As she also argues, 'This type of social organisation provides an excellent basis for development of an effective state administrative system able to extend down to the household level.' Nakane's model, however, suggests a uniformity of social pattern that is somewhat exaggerated in contemporary Japan.[13]

It is sometimes suggested that, because traditional Japanese social relationships were not based on formal contract, they provided no obstacle to personal exploitation. That exploitation of inferiors by superiors is typical of Japanese social organization even today is widely argued, especially by Japanese writers themselves.[14] The rationale behind this argument is that where group aims predominate, and relationships are based on personal feeling rather than any form of contract, those at the top have little to stop them from ruthlessly exploiting those below. On the other hand, given the importance of *ninjō* (literally, 'personal feeling') in the context of intra-group relationships, some restraint would appear likely to be imposed. This is because *ninjō* implies not only personal affection between the group members, but also a considerable degree of mutual obligation.[15]

Notions of obligation were highlighted by the social anthropologist Ruth Benedict in her pioneering work on Japanese society, *The Chrysanthemum and the Sword*, which was intended as a guide to Japanese behaviour for Americans occupying Japan after the war.[16] She concentrates on the concepts of *on* and *giri*, which she likens to Western-style debt repayment conventions, with the difference that they cover a far broader range of activity and relationships than the purely financial. According to her analysis, *on* could also be translated as 'love' or 'devotion', generally to a hierarchical superior. She speaks of *on* as a set of obligations passively incurred, since every Japanese conceives himself as a 'debtor to the ages and the world'. *On* can be received from the emperor, one's parents, one's lord, one's teacher, and from all the contacts in the course of one's life.[17]

It is now widely accepted that this analysis was too extreme. Dore, for instance, comments that: 'This ethic would have been explicitly acknowledged by the samurai of the Tokugawa period if he had read any of the books of moral exhortation which were written for him and if he in any way resembled the characters of contemporary fiction and drama.'[18]

Benedict also talks of *giri*-type obligations, which, according to her, are more specific repayments of favours received, with time limits upon repayment. Dore remarks that this is not materially different from the act involved in the statement, 'We really ought to go and see Auntie Mabel when we are in London. She's a bit of a bore, but she will be upset if we don't.'[19] Nevertheless, it would appear to be true that there is a difference of degree between the scrupulousness with which Japanese pursue matters of mutual obligation, even today, and the way in which they are pursued in the West.

In this writer's view, however, Benedict places too much emphasis on patterns of obligation as such, whereas what should be given primacy is rather the general patterns of interaction within and between groups. Thus, for instance, Benedict stresses the unwillingness of people to accumulate excessive obligations because of the burdens of repayment which this places upon them. Conversely, they are said to be unwilling to do favours to other people unless it is absolutely necessary (or unless they are already indebted to the other party), so as not to burden the other person with excessive debt repayment. Without doubting the accuracy of this observation, at least for the period in which it was written, one may well describe it as a symptom rather than a cause. There is plenty of evidence that it is the surviving vigour of group consciousness, and the tendency for groups to remain jealously independent of each other that gives rise to such punctiliousness about inter-personal obligations.

It is sometimes said that the Japanese have a view of ethics which is 'situational' rather than universal. Although it is uncertain how far this remains true today, behaviour within groups, and between group members and outsiders, can still show singular contrasts. This has obvious implications for politics, in predisposing people to act according to special relationships rather than impartially.

Another concept used to describe an aspect of group orientation in Japan is *amae*. Defined by Doi (in its verbal form *amaeru*) as 'to depend and presume upon another's benevolence',[20] it would seem to indicate a noteworthy Japanese cultural trait. A desire to depend on somebody else, expressed both as a desire to belong and a desire to have a dependent relationship, are lumped together by Tsurumi as 'dependent collectivism'.[21] Political behaviour that is 'dependently collectivistic' is, as we shall see, still a significant feature of Japanese politics. As with Nakane, however, so with Doi there is a tendency to overstate the sociological significance of a single pattern of behaviour.

One important aspect of dependence upon a collectivity is a preference for the reaching of decisions by the method of consensus. The alternative method, of accepting the view of a majority against that of a minority, tends to be disliked on the grounds that it leaves some members of the group dissatisfied and is therefore potentially disruptive. It is also felt to expose the individual to an uncomfortable assertion of his actual views, whereas the final responsibility for a decision should be collective. The practice of consensus decision-making, on the other hand, involves a process of the adjustment of initially differing views, so that everyone having a part in the decision can in the end subscribe to it knowing that his views have been taken into account. This has vital implications for practically all facets of government in Japan. Of course, if consensus proves impossible to attain, the consequences may be serious, and may include extreme expressions of hostility and frustration on the part of those who feel that their views have been ignored or rejected.

In our discussion so far we have concentrated on the crucial collectivist aspect of Japanese society. This is something which, while it is now often praised in the West, generally speaking, Japanese intellectuals regard as a malign influence upon political life. They tend to see it as inevitably leading to the corruption attendant upon close personal ties between 'bosses' and 'henchmen' and, because of 'dependent collectivism', to the weakness of the individual in the face of bureaucratic government. Whether and to what extent charges such as these are really justified will be examined later.

Another social characteristic of the Japanese which is frequently remarked upon, especially by foreigners, is the achievement ethic, which appears to be well developed in modern Japan. The rapid growth of Japanese industry since the Second World War could not, it is frequently suggested, have taken place without a single-minded determination to succeed on the part of a great many people in high and low positions. Comparisons have been made between the role of the achievement ethic in Japanese economic growth and the Puritan ethic in the development of Western capitalism. Whether it is psychological factors of this kind which have proved effective, or whether technical economic factors working in Japan's favour should be accorded more weight is highly debatable. Nevertheless, the desire to achieve must certainly be regarded as a vital (though hardly unique) feature of the social outlook of modern Japan.

Herman Kahn has popularized a song said to have been sung at regular intervals by workers at the factories of the Matsushita Electric Company.[22] Robert Cole quotes the example of workers from a shoe factory who march in demonstrations at the weekends, largely as a release from the tensions of working a sixty-hour week, but refuse to organize a union because they talk easily with the boss and they feel that a union would retard the progress of the company towards a successful and competitive position in the market.[23]

These examples may possibly suggest to the unwary reader that all Japanese workers have a single-minded devotion to their companies, and will normally sacrifice their own interests to promote the company interest. This however would be to neglect the considerable degree of union militancy that does exist in various sectors of the Japanese economy. Perhaps more importantly, it neglects the extent to which, in the industrial situation as it exists at present, the interest of the worker and the interest of the company do in fact coincide. With the firm being the provider of many important welfare services and bonuses for its staff, it is in the direct interest of the workers in that firm not to sabotage the capacity of the firm to provide those services. Since most labour unions are even now enterprise unions, there is a strong tendency for the union to put the interests of the firm as a corporate entity high in its list of priorities, even if it is simultaneously putting pressure on the employers.

This shows that the emphasis on achievement in Japanese society is closely connected with the attachment to groups (on a quasi-family model), which we have already discussed. According to Vogel, groups in Japanese society value competence on the part of their members very highly, but primarily in so far as it contributes to group goals.[24] This suggests a crucial difference between the achievement ethic in the Japanese context and the Puritan ethic in the West, namely that the incentive to achieve is a collective one, rather than a question of rugged individualism. (Here again, however, it is important to realize that while collective achievement remains a potent motivating force in many sectors of industry, the individualistic values of home, car and leisure have also made substantial inroads into people's lives.)

We have spoken already of 'figurative extensions' of the Japanese family system. What was meant by this is that the traditional family has served as a kind of model for other types of social or political grouping not necessarily involving direct family ties. Bearing in mind what we have already said about the family itself, let us examine a number of these figurative extensions in turn.

The emperor system from the Meiji period until 1945 is an obvious case in point. It was part of the genius of the Meiji leaders that they were able to project the norms of small face-to-face groups in scattered communities on to a national level in the interests of building national cohesiveness. The language used to describe the relations between the emperor and his subjects was deliberately chosen with the norms of the Confucian family in mind.[25]

Another example is the so-called *oyabun–kobun* relationship, which emerged in the chaotic conditions of the labour market during the Occupation, and drew the interest of some American administrators.[26] The meaning of the term can be grasped if we understand that *oya* means 'parent', *ko* means 'child', and *bun* means 'standing in the place of', or 'quasi'. Thus a literal translation would be a 'quasi-parent–quasi-child' relationship. A more familiar term in English might be a 'boss–henchman' group, although this possibly understates the degree of quasi-familial affectivity to be found in Japanese instances of the type. Nevertheless, fairly close parallels may be found in some non-

Japanese gangster and criminal organizations. The southern Italian *mafiosi* immediately spring to mind.

In conditions of acute job scarcity such as prevailed during the Occupation a labour boss, or *oyabun*, would farm out his *kobun* (perhaps fifty or a hundred of them) to prospective employers, and typically would himself collect their wages, distributing them according to his own criteria of fairness, need and loyalty. Interestingly enough, the overall pattern of *oyabun-kobun* systems allowed for considerable variety of operation in practice. Usually the most vital factor was the personality and degree of competence of the *oyabun*. His group could be highly authoritarian and even exploitative for his own benefit or, at the other extreme, it could be based on principles of genuine co-operation and mutual assistance.

As the labour market returned to normal in the 1950s, so the *oyabun-kobun* groups gave way to company-controlled methods of recruitment. The groups fairly rapidly retreated to the criminal fringe and to certain particularly traditional artisan occupations.

Nevertheless, the term *oyabun-kobun* is commonly encountered in contemporary descriptions of Japanese politics, particularly those appearing in the Japanese press. Its use signifies that a fictive-parent status is being attributed to a certain prominent or powerful political individual, while his coterie of personal followers (*kobun*) are demonstrating family-like loyalty to their *oyabun*. It is of course significant that the press often castigates this kind of political behaviour as both old-fashioned and reprehensible. At the same time the frequency with which such descriptions appear indicate that the patterns persist, even though the context may have markedly changed.

Another closely related usage is the ubiquitous term *batsu*. Given a variety of prefixes, the term signifies 'clique' or 'faction', with overtones of some sort of quasi-familial relationship. It will be appreciated that the term tends to be used vaguely and loosely, and too much should not necessarily be read into it when used by Japanese.

Let us, however, examine some specific usages.

In descriptions of Japanese government from the Meiji period to the Second World War the terms *hanbatsu* and *gunbatsu* are not infrequently encountered. *Hanbatsu*, sometimes awkwardly translated 'clan-clique', means that remarkable group of leaders from the south-western *han* which largely engineered the Meiji Restoration and continued to control the reins of national power for the following forty or fifty years. The looseness of this usage is indicated by the fact that these men frequently differed among themselves, had no single acknowledged leader, and all operated from their own power bases. They are referred to as *batsu*, essentially because they nearly all came from a particular region and kept sufficient cohesiveness, despite their differences, to maintain their grip on the central organs of decision-making.

Gunbatsu, which means 'military clique', is likewise an inexact term. There were, for instance, many divisions within the armed forces during the 1930s. Nevertheless, the concepts of group loyalty and exclusiveness were powerful features of the armed forces during that period, and their 'cliquishness' was manifest from the Manchurian Incident onwards.

A contemporary term of wide application is *habatsu*, which is usually translated into English as 'faction'. There is little difference in connotation between the two parts of this word, so that *ha* and *batsu* mean almost the same thing, and the two together are mutually reinforcing. In party politics it is common to see *ha* attached to the surname of a leading politician, so that Suzuki-ha can be translated as 'Suzuki faction'.

One should however use the translation 'faction' with caution because of the connotations it has acquired in Western (particularly Anglo-Saxon) political thought since Madison.[27] A classic definition of 'faction' by Harold Lasswell holds that factions are ephemeral, lack permanent organization, tend to concentrate on a single issue and are in 'agreement with the larger group on essentials, while differing on details of application'.[28] This is in line with a negative evaluation of factional activity as self-seeking and disruptive of a larger, principled, unity.

Such a definition is hard to apply to the Japanese case if we are to equate *habatsu* with faction. *Habatsu* are often long-lasting, comparatively well organized, and may even be the focus of loyalties which are prior to loyalties to the larger group. It may well be more accurate, therefore, to regard political parties as coalitions of self-standing and independent-minded *habatsu*, rather than quintessentially cohesive bodies threatened from time to time by selfish factional disruption. This point will be pursued in greater depth in later chapters. It may be noted in passing that the party-faction relationship in Japanese politics appears to have more in common with Indian patterns than with those of Britain, Australia or even the United States.[29]

The Japanese do not confine *habatsu* to political parties. They are regarded as fairly ubiquitous phenomena within government ministries, industrial firms and even in schools of wrestling and flower arrangement. What these various phenomena have in common is that personal connections (*kankei*), often of a quasi-familial kind, are utilized for the purposes of advancement, or even simply so that the individual can gain personal identification in a group milieu.

A related term is the *gakubatsu*, which may be translated as 'academic clique'. A more colloquial translation might be 'old school tie'. Broadly speaking, this relates to two closely connected things, the narrow streaming process of Japanese education, especially at top levels, and the apparent importance of personal connections made at university in the course of a political, administrative or business career.

The extent of the élite streaming process may be seen in the fact that between 1949 and 1959, some 79 per cent of senior civil servants had attended the prestigious Tokyo University. The figures ranged between 95·7 per cent for the Ministry of Education to 42·9 per cent for the Ministry of Communications.[30] The dominance of the Tokyo University *gakubatsu* over the government bureaucracy has somewhat declined in recent years, as the reputation of other universities has increased, but it still remains much the most frequent Alma Mater of senior civil servants. It should however be remembered that entry to Tokyo University is through a highly competitive examination, and that merit is a highly significant (even if not the only) factor affecting subsequent careers. Moreover, with so many senior civil servants coming from the same tertiary institution, one might surmise that the advantages conferred thereby within the service itself are scarcely those of an élite within an élite.[31] At the same time, the whole system exemplifies the importance of personal connections made and consolidated at the various stages of an individual's career, and also the narrowness of the path he must walk if he is to succeed.

The type of *batsu* which is perhaps best known to the outside world is the *zaibatsu*. This is defined by Eleanor Hadley as a 'family-dominated combine', a 'combine' being 'a complex of corporations displaying unified business strategy arising primarily out of an ownership base'.[32] On this definition one should, strictly speaking, use the past tense. The prewar *zaibatsu* were each headed by a holding company whose main function was to exercise control by holding stock, and this holding company in turn was controlled by a single family. Moreover, the big prewar *zaibatsu* had interests across virtually the whole range of the Japanese economy. In postwar Japan the term *zaibatsu* has largely given way to *keiretsu* (which could possibly be translated as 'organizational linkage'). The similarity or otherwise between the *keiretsu* and the old *zaibatsu* is a matter of controversy, as is their political impact, which will be discussed in chapter 8. Here it may be noted that, although the attempts of the American Occupation to break down *zaibatsu*-type concentrations of economic power were only partially successful, the *keiretsu* are much looser structures than their predecessors, while control by a single family through a holding company has more or less disappeared.

Finally, mention must be made of what is often called 'paternalism' within industrial firms. The general pattern of employment is still much affected by the practice of permanent employment for the worker within one firm, by enterprise unions, and by extensive fringe benefits designed to cement the loyalty of the work force to the firm. Somewhat paradoxically, this pattern is especially tenacious in some of the largest and most powerful firms, whose internal organization is necessarily bureaucratic and impersonal. Workers in such firms however are conscious of themselves as members of an industrial élite, and are presumably anxious to retain their privileges by demonstrating their loyalty to their companies. Lower rates of industrial growth and a harsher economic climate from the mid-1970s onwards have made it harder for firms to maintain the permanent employment system, but it still remains a widespread form of employment.

The picture of Japanese society we have drawn in this chapter has necessarily been much oversimplified. We have not attempted to quantify the social changes which have been under way as a result of industrialization, the shift of population to the cities, and widespread affluence. Our purpose was the limited one of giving a framework of understanding of the social context in which politics and government are conducted. It should be obvious already that political life in Japan must be profoundly affected by this social context, even though many other influences are important as well. In conclusion, we may attempt a general statement of the kind of problems which Japanese social norms present for the conduct of politics and government.

Japanese governments since the Meiji period have been able to mobilize group cohesiveness and dedication to the achievement of group goals. For the most part they have succeeded in channelling the energies of a highly motivated society along constructive paths, although a period of disruption in the 1930s led to a disastrous war.

At the same time – as indeed was graphically demonstrated in the political chaos of the 1930s – in a society whose fundamental unit is a group based on the model of a traditional type of family, the problem of co-ordination from the centre can be extremely difficult. The constant jockeying for power by small groups within larger units, signified by political factionalism, may be consistent with a high degree of overall political stability, provided that certain conditions are met. The most important of these is that there should be a generally accepted and unambiguous set of guidelines for the legitimate exercise of power. This was in part lacking under the Meiji Constitution, and contributed to the collapse of the system.

Where such guidelines exist political instability should be easier to avoid, even though, as in postwar Japanese politics, there is more or less constant factional struggle. The political stability which has predominated in Japan since the 1950s has been premised upon a 'mainstream' alliance of conservative politicians, senior public servants and leading businessmen, and upon the continuance of economic growth. Factional struggles within the Opposition have generally proved more disruptive than factional conflict within the government forces themselves.

From the standpoint of the early 1980s we can say that while the demands upon government from the outside have in certain respects increased, and while group conflict and accommodation remain a constant feature of Japanese politics, radical destabilization of the orderly processes of politics and administration has for the most part been avoided. The period 1976–80 was a difficult one for the political Establishment because of the position of near parity with the ministerial party that the Opposition parties had between them attained in the National Diet. As was suggested at the beginning of this chapter, the relative stability and effectiveness of political institutions was instrumental both in mobilizing the integrative and in minimizing the politically disruptive implications of group-centred social norms.

4 The American Occupation

The Allied Occupation of Japan (1945–52) raises acute but fascinating problems for the student of politics and government. Normally, the political scientist is at a disadvantage in comparison with his colleagues in the natural sciences because he cannot conduct experiments. In a limited sense, however, the six and a half years of rehabilitation and tutelage which the Japanese people underwent at the hands of the United States[1] may be seen in retrospect as a kind of experiment. It is true that, strictly speaking, 'experiment' is the wrong word, since the crucial concept of 'control' was inapplicable. What happened in Japan between 1945 and 1952 was unique, and it is of course quite impossible to apply the standard scientific techniques of changing some of the variables while holding others constant, since history is always unrepeatable, and in retrospect unmanipulable.

Nevertheless, in a less strict sense the analogy is sound. In Japan up to 1945 political and social institutions, practices and habits of mind had developed largely without direct interference from outside, and were derived essentially from indigenous experience. At certain periods, notably that immediately following the Meiji Restoration, foreign ideas and experience had been eagerly sought; at other times such importations had been consciously resisted, but Japanese themselves had always been in control.

With the Occupation however Japanese national sovereignty was temporarily suspended, thus facilitating the introduction of a staggering range of reforms which the Japanese had little chance of resisting and only a limited opportunity of modifying, at least until the Occupation forces had withdrawn. Full sovereignty[2] was then handed back to a Japanese government, which was able to do just as it liked with the reforms which had been coercively or persuasively introduced. What the Americans in effect did therefore was to interfere, temporarily but massively, with what one might consider the normal working of the Japanese state, and then discharge the 'patient' after his course of treatment. The 'patient' might fully recover or he might suffer a relapse, but this would become fully evident only after he had been on his own for a period without medication. The 'doctor', in any case, was unlikely to be on hand again, nor would he be acceptable to the 'patient' should anything go wrong.

The experimental data which this whole exercise provides for the political scientist are considerable, although by no means easy to use. One cannot know, for instance, what would have happened if Japan had never been defeated, or had been defeated but not occupied, although one can make intelligent guesses about the way things might have gone. And yet, without such knowledge one cannot say for certain how much influence on events the American reforms actually had. Without, for instance, knowing whether the Japanese of their own free will would have rewritten the Meiji Constitution, it is difficult to make definitive judgements about the wisdom of introducing a brand new constitution, as was done in 1946–7.

Again to evaluate the Occupation means making at least a rough separation of things for which the Occupation was directly responsible from those whose origin lay elsewhere. To take a simple and somewhat crude example, it could be argued that political stability in Japan from about 1960 was premised upon the high rate of economic growth being experienced at that period. Was political stability therefore an achievement with which the Occupation experience had nothing to do? Here one might argue that, while economic growth should be seen as the mainspring of political stability, it was also true both that the Occupation contributed some of the groundwork for economic growth, and that there was a further base for political stability, namely the workable framework of political institutions for which in considerable part the Occupation was responsible. To complicate matters, however, two further factors need to be introduced.[3]

First, as the Occupation recedes in time, so the likelihood

increases that new or recent factors increase in significance. To take our example about political stability, the fact that the LDP between 1976 and 1980 was close to losing its parliamentary majority was something that bore only a tenuous connection with the Occupation reforms some twenty years previously.

Secondly it could well be argued that the sort of political stability attained in the 1960s was not entirely a good thing, that it was achieved at the expense of democracy. This takes one into the realm of political value judgements where no general agreement is likely between different observers, and yet any evaluative analysis of the Occupation is almost bound to make such value judgements in one way or another.

It is possibly as a result of the acuteness of the problems of perspective that no really definite study of the Occupation as such has yet appeared in English.[4] Much of the writing about it which has been done (especially in works appearing at the time or shortly after) had focused strongly on a descriptive and rather narrowly institutional approach, being concerned for instance with the operation of the Occupation's bureaucracy and its interaction with the organs of the Japanese Government, or with a description of the content and pattern of acceptance of the various reforms, or with analysis of the Constitution.

Another focus which has been attempted from time to time is the ethical one, posing such questions as whether the Americans were morally justified in occupying Japan or, having done so, whether they were morally justified in embarking on an imposed programme of wholesale reform. Some of the more polemical writing which appeared at the time, though it was not concerned mainly with the ethics of the operation as such, raised serious doubts about the morality of General MacArthur's highhandedness and the style of rule which obtained under his command.[5]

Although institutional-descriptive and ethical questions of this kind are inevitably involved in any analysis of the Occupation, the focus of this chapter will be rather different. An attempt will be made to answer a number of questions relating to what, essentially, the Americans were trying to achieve and to how far, and for what reasons they were successful in achieving it. To put it at its crudest: did the Occupation work?

The first question to be asked then is what were the basic

aims, the underlying political philosophy, of the Occupation authorities; what was their notion of a desirable polity? This is relatively easy to determine with some degree of confidence. The task of determining how far they were successful in these aims is more difficult.

The second question is how far the Americans were sensitive to the peculiarities of the Japanese environment, and whether their efforts at reform reflected such sensitivity. Clearly, if they were wrong in important respects about the way Japanese society and politics worked, then the direction of their reforms was likely also to be misconceived. How far, in other words, were their reforms likely to prove viable in a specifically Japanese context?

Thirdly, to what extent have the reforms survived the return of independent government in 1952? Some reforms were quickly reversed, others were retained and some have been modified over the succeeding period. The fate of the various parts of the Occupation's programme has been bound up with the vicissitudes of Japanese politics, but retention or rejection of a given reform can be seen as some indication at least of its suitability.

Finally, what are the long-term, as distinct from the short-term, implications of the Occupation programme? To answer this question necessitates the separation of cause from effect in areas where that may be exceedingly difficult. It involves the crucial question of perspective, and cannot be answered definitively until the post-Occupation period has been extensively covered. Nevertheless, a preliminary attempt will be made.

The underlying philosophy of the Occupation was predictably liberal and democratic. Although different sections of SCAP[6] differed in their degree of enthusiasm for some of the more democratic reforms, and although reforming zeal was more marked in the earlier than the later stages of the American presence, it seems that most people in authority assumed that it was desirable to reform Japanese institutions, and hopefully ways of thinking, in a direction that would make them conform more or less with Western democratic norms.

Given this overall aim, it is hardly surprising if the Americans involved in the Occupation tended to think in terms of American norms of democratic government. This caused some problems, as we shall see later, because the institutional framework inherited from prewar Japan was in certain respects more European than American in character, and no attempt was made to substitute for it an American-style presidential system based on the separation of powers, as was done in the Philippines. Thus, whereas the political relationships between Executive and legislature that emerged from the Occupation were much closer to the British model than to the American, it was still implicit in the Occupation 'philosophy' that Parliament should control and limit the power of the Executive in a day-to-day sense, rather after the superseded ideal of British liberalism in the mid-nineteenth century. Similarly, the reactions of the Occupation authorities to the extensive links which rapidly developed between the resurgent labour union movement and left-wing parties reflected an American lack of familiarity with a phenomenon familiar enough to anyone brought up in Europe or the British Commonwealth.

Perhaps the best way to consider the 'philosophy' of the Occupation is to examine what reforms were actually implemented. The initial programme of the Occupation is often labelled one of 'demilitarization and democratization'. Demilitarization need not long detain us. The armed forces were speedily demobilized and disbanded, and subsequently the controversial article 9 (the 'pacifist clause') was written into the Constitution. (This is a major issue in contemporary Japanese politics, and will be treated extensively in chapter 10.)

'Democratization' in the Japanese context meant essentially two things. The first was the establishment of popular sovereignty both in theory and in fact. One of the prerequisites for this was that the vagueness of the Meiji Constitution about the location of sovereignty should be effectively eliminated. According to the Meiji Constitution, sovereignty rested with the emperor, but since the emperor in practice did not rule, the effective location of sovereignty was a shifting thing, depending upon the balance of power at any one time between the various political élites. This phenomenon of dual (or multiple) government, whereby the armed forces in particular had been able to exercise uncontrolled power by virtue of their independent access to the emperor, was inimical to the principle of clarity in the location of sovereignty, and it was to this task of clarification that the Americans addressed themselves.

A number of the main reforms may be grouped under this heading. The clarification of sovereignty and its firm location in the people, through a popularly elected National Diet to which Cabinet was directly responsible, was their principal purpose.

The position of the emperor was radically changed. He was persuaded to renounce his divinity on 1 January 1946, a matter of great psychological importance to the people. From 'Head of State', he became merely 'Symbol of the State and of the unity of the people, deriving his position from the will of the people, with whom resides sovereign power'. The word 'symbol' apparently meant little to many Japanese at the time, although the status of the emperor has since gained widespread acceptance.[7] All his special powers (exercised, in practice, by his advisers) were taken away, including those which could be exercised in time of emergency. His functions as listed in the new Constitution were purely ceremonial.

The peerage was abolished except for the immediate royal family, and with it the House of Peers was eliminated. Although SCAP seems originally to have intended a unicameral legislature, the House of Peers was in fact replaced by a 'House of Councillors', which was elected, though on a different electoral system from the House of Representatives. It had limited powers of delaying legislation.

The armed forces were completely eliminated, and therefore could no longer be a factor in politics. The attempt to make this situation permanent was enshrined in article 9 of the Constitution, but this has not prevented the subsequent establishment of substantial armed forces, now known as the Jieitai (Self-Defence Forces), whose constitutional status nevertheless remains doubtful. Perhaps in anticipation of such a development, the Occupation authorities saw to it that the principle of civilian control was strongly emphasized. Also, it was specifically provided by the Constitution that 'The Prime Minister and other Ministers of the State shall be civilians' – an apparently superfluous article if there were to be no armed forces of any kind.[8]

In addition to the removal of the emperor and the armed forces from effective political participation, the Privy Council, the Imperial Household Ministry, the Genrō and the senior statesmen were also abolished for this same reason, that they disputed the legislative and executive power of the Diet and the Cabinet.

It was further stipulated in the Constitution (article 68) that the prime minister and a majority of his ministers should be Diet members (MPS). In practice very few ministers indeed have not held a seat in the Diet. Moreover, the prime minister was to be chosen by the Diet from among its own members (article 67). Thus a convincing victory was won over the old principle of 'transcendental Cabinets'.

The principle of collective Cabinet responsibility to the Diet, absent from the Meiji Constitution (where the term 'Cabinet', as distinct from 'ministers of state', was nowhere mentioned), was enshrined in article 66, which also clearly and unambiguously vested executive power in Cabinet, though its authority was confined to the execution of legislation enacted by the Diet.

Similar clarity in the location of sovereignty was aimed at in the famous article 41, which states that: 'The Diet shall be the highest organ of state power, and shall be the sole law-making authority of the State.' The various articles of the Constitution relating to the Diet sought to reinforce this supreme position. Thus its power over the budget was assured (article 60), as well as over finance (articles 83–91), and the provision of the Meiji Constitution, that if the government's budget was rejected by the Diet the budget of the previous year could come into force, was dropped.

It can be seen that what these reforms had in common was the intention to produce a Diet/Cabinet system, essentially on the British model, with clear lines of responsibility and an unambiguous statement of where sovereignty actually lay. A further set of reforms, however, may be seen as having a separate but complementary aim, namely that of broadening and democratizing participation in politics. The relationship between what have here been singled out as two separate sets of reforms lay in the desire to establish a political system in which the political views and interests of the broad mass of the population should be represented through a government whose lines of responsibility were clear. This desired situation was in turn contrasted with the state of affairs prevailing under the Meiji Constitution, where not only was the political say of the population at large restricted in a variety of ways (restricted suffrage, officially sanctioned social norms inculcating submissiveness to the state as enshrined in a semi-divine emperor, police suppression of 'dangerous thoughts', and so on), but the power relationships existing among the political élite (or élites) were fluid, ill-defined and, as it turned out in the 1930s, dangerously unstable.

The following reforms may be seen as largely or in part connected with the aim of broadening the base of independent participation in politics.

The suffrage was increased to include women, who had never been enfranchised under the prewar system, and the minimum age for voting was lowered from twenty-five to twenty.

Labour unions and other independent groups were given official sanction and were encouraged to put forward their views and exert pressure on the Government without being required to express their views in terms of the interests of the State, as had tended to be the case before the war.[9]

Left-wing political parties, whose existence had been precarious since their formation in the mid-1920s, were granted complete freedom to organize and were given active encouragement by some sections of SCAP as a potential nucleus of an alternative government to the various conservative groups. Communist leaders were released from prison, where they had languished in some instances since the late 1920s, and a vigorous Communist Party was formed, as well as a Socialist Party, which was electorally much more successful than the Communists.

A wide range of civil liberties was written into the Constitution, and this has ensured, among other things, almost completely untrammelled freedom of expression for the mass media, which are rarely inhibited from criticizing government action.

Partly in order to enable 'new blood' to flow freely through the political arteries, a large number of politicians were excluded for the time being from all participation in public life. This 'purge' edict extended broadly through the ranks of politicians, former military men, businessmen and bureaucrats, and cleared the way, for instance, for Yoshida Shigeru, a former Foreign Ministry official with no previous political experience, to become a highly forceful and successful prime minister over much of the ten years following Japan's defeat.[10]

Following on article 62 of the Constitution – 'Each House may conduct investigations in relation to government, and may compel the presence and testimony of witnesses, and the production of records' – a Diet standing committee system was set up, and has become in effect the main forum for parliamentary debate. This represents perhaps the most significant departure from the British model of parliamentary procedure and the closest adherence to the American, since the system of Congressional committees was the model upon which it was based. Here again, the aim in part seems to have been to avoid narrow cliquishness in decision-making, and throw open the decision-making processes to a wider audience.

In order to destroy what were regarded as excessive concentrations of economic power, legislation was introduced to break down into their constituent units the *zaibatsu*, or family-based combines, which were an important element in the Japanese economy of the 1920s and 1930s. Whatever the wisdom or otherwise of this reform, and whatever the degree of success in implementing it, it was undoubtedly conceived as a measure of economic democratization, in that economic power (and so, presumably, to an extent at least, political power) was to be distributed more broadly and more evenly.[11]

Parallel to the programme of economic deconcentration was a measure designed to bring democracy to the countryside, namely the land reform. Rural landlordism, especially absentee landlordism, had been a potent source of discontent during the depression of the rural economy in the 1930s, and the effect of the land reform was, by placing a ceiling of three *chō* (1 *chō* = about $2\frac{1}{2}$ acres)[12] on individual land holdings, to create a relatively egalitarian peasantry of small farmers. This is often regarded as the most unequivocally successful of the Occupation reforms, although its legacy is not without its problems today. Ironically enough, by removing previous sources of discontent from the countryside, it has provided a solid base of support for conservative politicians. This, reinforced by a continuing electoral gerrymander and government support for rural industries, has greatly strengthened the position of conservative parties in postwar Japan.[13]

Another area of reform which the Occupation authorities saw as an exercise in broadening the base of political participation (rather on the American model) was in local administration. Whereas previously, local government had been firmly in the hands of the Home Ministry, and most important positions were appointive, not elective, the Occupation abolished the Home Ministry and set up in its place the Local Autonomy Agency (later Ministry) with greatly truncated powers. Substantial powers were placed in the hands of local authorities, and most of the relevant positions were made elective.[14]

In two particular areas of administration – police and education – a drastic form of decentralization was carried out, with the aim of taking responsibility in these key sensitive fields away from the central government and putting it into the hands of the newly elective local authorities. This, however, was only one aspect of the 'democratization' of the education system. Syllabuses were substantially revised to remove the emphasis on nationalist mythology and to replace it by a far more internationalist orientation. The prewar 'ethics' courses were abolished. Moreover, the whole structure of the education system was revamped, and at the tertiary level the number of institutions offering full degree courses was greatly increased.

Some would argue that the Occupation's attempts at administrative decentralization were unfortunate; and so far as police and educational administration is concerned, the decentralizing measures were put into reverse fairly soon after the Occupation ended. In the long term, however, local politics has enjoyed a vigorous and healthy growth, particularly since the appearance of citizens' movements from the 1960s.

Finally, substantial reforms of the judicial system were introduced. These included an attempt to reduce the influence of the Ministry of Justice over the courts and to increase that of the Supreme Court, and a revision of the civil code.

Perhaps the most surprising reform in this area was the provision for periodic popular referenda on the suitability of Supreme Court judges. This curious innovation may be seen as an attempt to extend the principle of democratic participation to a point where it would appear to conflict with the independence of the judiciary. (In practice however the referenda have always resulted in heavy votes of approval for the

Supreme Court judges.) Another area in which a concern with checks and balances potentially conflicted with the principle of a single locus of sovereignty was the introduction of judicial review by the Supreme Court of the constitutionality of legislative and official acts. Here again, in practice the power has been sparingly used.[15]

Speaking very broadly, the reforms which have been most highly regarded by moderate or liberal Japanese and by similarly inclined outside observers are: the constitutional establishment of popular sovereignty; the elimination of the emperor institution as a political force and the clarifying of relations between the prime minister, Cabinet and the two Houses of the national Diet; extension of the suffrage; guarantees of rights and freedoms, including freedom of speech and of political activity; encouragement of interest groups; and especially the land reform. Others, in particular some of the educational reforms, decentralization of local government, the 'peace clause' of the Constitution and the anti-trust measures, receive much less unanimous commendation.

Each of these requires more extensive treatment in the light of more recent developments, and this we shall give later in the book. Here, however, we shall confine ourselves to a brief examination of a selection of reforms, in each case raising the questions mentioned earlier. These, it will be recalled, were the following: What was the 'philosophy' of the Occupation? How far were the reforms suited to the Japanese context, both theoretically and in practice? To what extent have the reforms survived the end of the Occupation? And what are their long-term, as distinct from short-term, implications?

We shall take the land reform as our first example, for two reasons – firstly because it is the single reform most widely hailed as successful, and secondly because of the magnitude of the problems it appears to have created in the long term.

The 'philosophy' of the land reform seems to have been the early American democratic ideal of the independent small farmer, which was apparently close to General MacArthur's heart, despite its obsolescence in contemporary American agriculture.[16]

The reform was also premised upon an analysis of the role of peasant discontent and the agricultural family in the rise of militarism in the 1930s. Peasant discontent, according to the argument, resulted from economic depression, over-population and inequalities of tenure. These factors combined to make the armed forces popular in the countryside. The armed forces provided social mobility for under-privileged and under-educated rural youths, while the expansionist aims of the army sounded good to an over-populated peasantry. The army and the peasantry thus became allies in their intense dislike of the urban rich and of foreigners, and in this atmosphere ultra-nationalist indoctrination and control were able to flourish.

Thus, a rather nineteenth-century ideal about the virtues of small independent farmers and an analysis of Japanese agriculture stressing social and economic inequalities as well as hierarchical and communal patterns of social interaction came together to justify a very radical reform.

The administration of the land reform was also conducted by land committees elected by and from among the local farmers, which gave the locals considerable experience in administration. They for the most part conducted their affairs smoothly, and a much more egalitarian and participatory pattern was quickly established in the countryside. Moreover, the compensation which was to be paid to the landlords for the loss of their land was soon eroded by the rampant postwar inflation, and thus their political power was largely broken.[17]

Although the philosophy behind the land reform was outdated in American terms, it happened to work well in terms of the realities of Japanese rural society at the time. In any case, moves to reduce tenancy had been made before the war, but without sufficient means of enforcement. The American reform was bold, radical and largely suited to the social needs of the time. The Americans also pursued the reform single-mindedly during the Occupation, unlike their record in anti-trust policy and other areas.

The land reform survived the Occupation and, as MacArthur wanted, the countryside became populated by independent small farmers. Two things, however, have happened since the Occupation ended. Agricultural productivity has rapidly increased, to the point where the ceiling on the size of land holdings is proving increasingly anomalous. There has also been a rapid movement of population from the country to the cities and towns, as industry has continued to develop in scope and sophistication. The country therefore now has a serious dearth of young people willing to carry on the family farms. In the circumstances the economics of large-scale capitalist farming are increasingly attractive, but the ceiling on land holdings is still an inhibiting factor.

The political effects have been somewhat ironic. The farming areas have been made into territory safe for the conservatives by the substantial elimination of the social tensions and inequalities which used to be associated with tenancy. The conservatives have been able shrewdly to consolidate their hold by expensive agricultural price support schemes, and by their reluctance to correct a marked rural bias in the electoral system. The influence of the Nōkyō (Agricultural Co-operative Associations), linked together nationally in a huge corporate structure, has become pervasive.[18]

A Marxist could well argue that the land reform, by removing the seeds of social conflict from the countryside, had merely succeeded in postponing real change. On the other hand it can be argued that, without some outside agency such as the Occupation, land reform would not have been accomplished because of the determined resistance it would have met from the landlords. By contributing to political stability the land reform has (according to this second view) in the long run facilitated other major changes which ought to be welcomed.

In contrast with the land reform, the programme of administrative decentralization has often been seen as one of the least successful of the Occupation reforms. It appears to have been based on a philosophy (or, more modestly, a tradition of thought) which saw elective local government as a vital element in grass-roots democracy.

Unfortunately, the thinking behind this set of reforms incorporated an equation of American and Japanese conditions in the postwar period which was unwarranted. For one thing, the geographical dispersion of centres of population in the United States lent itself to genuine local autonomy, whereas in Japan the mass of the population was concentrated along a narrow strip of coast, and thus more prone to centralized administration. Historically too the Japanese and American experiences could scarcely have been more different. Whereas the constant extension of the 'frontier' by independent-minded citizens was a key part of the American experience, progress in Japan since the Tokugawa era had been intimately bound up with a process of centralizing most aspects of administration. In many ways the centre could be regarded as more progressive and modern than the periphery, even though the extension of its rule could well be felt by many as oppressive.

There were also practical reasons why the decentralization of responsibility for education and the police in particular did not work. The most important was that inadequate finance was provided, so that they rapidly became an intolerable financial burden for local authorities. Moreover a tradition of local autonomy was not something that could be created overnight. In the case of the locally elected boards of education, where there was no tradition of participating in educational decisions, most of those elected to the boards turned out to be teachers. So far as the police were concerned, the operation of an efficient police force on a national scale proved highly problematical when the responsibility was spread among a multiplicity of impecunious and unevenly motivated local bodies.

These particular reforms were speedily reversed by Japanese governments after the Occupation had come to an end. Although their undoing was resisted by the Opposition parties on the grounds that they were part of an intended full-scale 'reverse course', it is arguable that they were reversed principally because they did not work in contemporary Japanese conditions.

On the other hand, the great increase in elective positions which the Occupation brought about has for the most part survived its demise. Passin's argument that this reform led to a 'cancerlike growth of elective positions, . . . a kind of overloading of the political communication circuits',[19] is questionable in the light of developments in local government and politics from the late 1960s. Rather, the political structures at the local level set up during the Occupation ultimately facilitated the vigorous expression of local interests and points of view, and thus provided a crucial counterweight to the centralizing tendencies of Tokyo (see chapter 11). In this as in other cases the success or failure of the reforms carried out under American auspices in Japan between 1945 and 1952 hinges upon their long-term effects. These, however, are notoriously difficult to distinguish from effects having little or nothing to do with the Occupation itself.

Finally, it is in the area of reforms to the basic structure of central government as enshrined in the 1947 Constitution that some of the most interesting questions lie. The Occupation's philosophy here can broadly be characterized as 'democratic', though as we shall see in the next chapter a 'radical phase during 1945–6 and to some extent into 1947 was followed by an increasingly 'conservative' phase from 1947–8 onwards. It was presumably principally the desire to see a more democratic Japan that led to the whole series of reforms that we have listed under the heading of 'political participation'.

At the same time the Occupation authorities correctly diagnosed as a dangerous weakness of prewar Japanese government, the lack of co-ordination between the various arms of government, and especially the independent political power of the armed forces. This was translated into a question of sovereignty, and an attempt was made both to remove the ambiguities of the Meiji Constitution on this matter and to place the new Constitution firmly on the foundation of popular representation, by proclaiming the existence of popular sovereignty.

Popular sovereignty, however, meant more than a proclamation in the preamble to the new Constitution. It was deemed necessary to eliminate the possibility of 'dual government', and to ensure that the channels of legitimate representation and authority should be clearly and unambiguously defined. In a sense, the elimination of dual government was in tune with the philosophy of the conservative later stages of the Occupation, when American policy shifted from relative sympathy with labour unions and moderate Socialists to support for the consolidation of power at the centre under conservative politicians such as Yoshida Shigeru. Dower has argued that it was the Occupation's later stages that were most formative for the kind of centralized political system that reached maturity following the formation of the Liberal Democratic Party (LDP) in 1955.[20] There is much to agree with in this argument, though both the short- and long-term effects of the early Occupation reforms need also to be kept in mind. In particular, these reforms facilitated a great expansion of activity by a wide range of interest groups with which the government must constantly consult.

The constitutional implications of eliminating dual government are of particular interest. It was easier to reconcile a single line of authority and responsibility with a British-type fusion-of-powers theory than with American-style notions of the separation of powers. Where Parliament is elected by the people, Cabinet is chosen from among the members of Parliament (in practice by a majority party or parties), the prime minister leads the Cabinet, government departments each have a member of the Cabinet at their head, and legislation is introduced by the Government (broadly defined) into Parliament, which it can normally control because of its majority, then the lines of authority and responsiblity are fairly clear.

It was probably a correct assessment that this style of government was more likely to solve the problems raised by Japan's ambiguous constitutional tradition than any system based primarily on the separation of powers. The party-based Cabinets of the 1920s – the era of Japanese liberalism before the war – approximated to the British model, even though their status was uncertain and their powers incomplete. Conversely, the 'transcendental' Cabinets of the Meiji period, which appeared again in the 1930s, looked rather more like the American president in his relations with Congress, although of course Congress has always commanded far more independent influence than did the Japanese Imperial Diets of the 'transcendental' eras.

In choosing, therefore, a system for Japanese government based on the fusion of powers, the Occupation authorities seem to have been both in tune with Japanese political needs,[21] and to have facilitated the eventual emergence of a conservative, centralizing political order which also permitted the development of powerful interest groups. At the same time, as we have seen, elements having more in common with the separation-of-powers theory crept into the reforms at various points. The extensive Diet committee system – based on Congressional committees – is a relevant case. Another example is the Supreme Court's power of judicial review. Moreover, as we have seen, some Occupation officials seem to have expected the Diet to act more independently of the Cabinet than a familiarity with British or British Commonwealth patterns would have led them to expect. They thought, for instance, that the Diet and not the Cabinet would have the final say on when the Diet was to be dissolved, whereas practice (and an ambiguity in the Constitution) dictated the opposite.[22]

These reforms have survived without amendment, at least to the letter of the Constitution. The Americans, in any case, ensured that constitutional revision would be difficult.[23] Subsequent events have tended to strengthen the executive against the legislature in a way that would hardly be unfamiliar to those acquainted with a long period of hegemony by a single political combination in a fusion-of-powers system.[24] The hitherto unbeatable supremacy of the LDP since 1955, together with a strongly entrenched bureaucracy, has given Japan continuous and effective government at a time when this was no doubt urgently needed. Whether the national Diet will in the future become stronger *vis-à-vis* the executive remains to be seen. Perhaps a better guarantee, however, of genuinely democratic government would be the alternation of parties in power, with an opposition capable of taking office and also providing effective, non-revolutionary rule.

Whether or not this is in prospect will be discussed in later chapters. However, what the Occupation 'experiment' appears to have demonstrated above all is that a nation with sophisticated political traditions of its own, a strong economic and social base and a sense of nationhood is likely to be easier to 'reform' than a nation not possessing these attributes. Considering the rather hit-and-miss nature of the Occupation's efforts, they have so far been crowned with remarkable success.

5 Political Chronicle 1945–81

In this chapter we shall attempt to chronicle the main political developments from the end of the war until the present. Space demands selectivity, and this will in no sense be an exhaustive treatment. Political change has been complex and multi-faceted, so that it is possible only to indicate major trends and crucial turning points.

The major reforms of the Occupation have been analysed in chapter 4. Here we shall supplement that discussion by outlining in roughly chronological order the major political developments of that period before going on to the scene following independence.

Nearly all the principal reforms of the Occupation were carried out between 1945 and 1948. The atmosphere was reminiscent of periods of revolutionary change. Japanese governments were subject to the authority of SCAP and had little choice but to act within the boundaries of SCAP policy directives, even though discretion could be exercised in certain areas.

The first postwar Prime Minister was a general and cousin of the Emperor, Prince Higashikuni Naruhiko, who was appointed to the post on the day following the emperor's surrender broadcast. He lasted less than two months, and in October 1945 was replaced by Baron Shidehara Kijurō, a former diplomat regarded as relatively liberal and international in orientation.

The brief life of the Shidehara Government (October 1945–May 1946) coincided with the initiation by SCAP of a number of its key reforms including the introduction of the new Constitution, the original text of which was announced on 6 March 1946. Treated formally as a revision of the Meiji Constitution, it was debated by the House of Representatives between June and August 1946 and by the House of Peers until October, was formally promulgated by the emperor in November and came into effect the following May.

The way in which the new Constitution was brought in is even now a highly controversial issue, and will be dealt with in more detail in chapter 10. Suffice it to say here that General MacArthur was not satisfied with the various drafts submitted by the Shidehara Government towards the end of 1945 and into 1946, on the grounds that they remained within the spirit of the Meiji Constitution. In February 1946 he ordered the Government Section of SCAP to prepare a radically new draft (to be known as the GHQ draft), which was done in secret and completed to an extremely tight schedule. The way in which the Shidehara Cabinet was prevailed upon to 'present a draft' based upon the GHQ draft meant that, whatever the Constitution's intrinsic merits, its origins were tainted with the suspicion of American coercion and duplicity.

The main effects of the new Constitution on the system of government have already been discussed in chapter 4. Little has yet been said, however, about article 9, the famous 'pacifist' or 'peace' clause. This clause has been of such momentous importance for Japan's foreign policies and domestic politics that we shall quote it here. It reads:

> Aspiring sincerely to an international peace based on justice and order, the Japanese people forever renounce war as a sovereign right of the nation and the threat or use of force as means of settling international disputes.
>
> In order to accomplish the aim of the preceding paragraph, land, sea, and air forces, as well as other war potential will never be maintained. The right of belligerency of the state will not be recognized.

It remains uncertain whether this article (which incorporates some highly significant watering down of the original GHQ draft – see chapter 10) was MacArthur's own idea or was suggested to him by Shidehara.[1] The controversy is more than a mere historical curiosity, and touches upon the relationship between anti-war feeling and nationalism in contemporary Japan.

Another issue that gravely affected the conduct of politics in the Shidehara period was the purge which began in January 1946. It should be remembered that the Meiji Constitution still functioned, and in many respects continued to be interpreted under illiberal wartime rules. Thus the Shidehara Cabinet was 'transcendental' in the old sense, consisting largely of former bureaucrats. When the political parties began to revive, as they did rapidly with the demise of the monolithic Imperial Rule Assistance Association, into which they had been assimilated in 1940, the Cabinet was not immediately beholden to any combination of them. Moreover, the parties soon found themselves decimated by the rather inflexible provisions of the purge edict, and they had to enter the 1946 general election campaign with for the most part untried candidates.[2]

An ironic effect of the purge, crucial in its long-term significance, was that former career bureaucrats were enabled to consolidate their power by entering the vacuum formed when a high proportion of existing party politicians were purged from political life. Certainly these ex-bureaucrats had to step down into the party political arena in order to do so. It is easy, however, to see a parallel here with the compromises made between career bureaucrats and party politicians at the turn of the twentieth century. In both cases the result was that political parties gained access to the central process of decision-making; but at the same time, those whose careers had been made in the bureaucracy came to take a leading role in the inner councils of the parties.

This situation was in part also an outcome of the first postwar general election to the House of Representatives, held on 10 April 1946, and the political arrangements which followed it. In that election the Liberal Party (Jiyūtō), led by the veteran party politician Hatoyama Ichirō, won the largest number of seats (141 seats out of 464), but not enough to become the majority party on its own. The other main conservative party, the Progressive Party (Shimpotō), had suffered much more catastrophically from the purge than had the Liberals, and despite having previously been the party with the most seats was able to win only 94 seats in the 1946 election. Negotiations for a coalition of Liberals and Progressives were already under way when Hatoyama was suddenly removed from the scene by being purged. In the difficult situation which followed this rather dubious action by SCAP, the Liberal Party found a new and surprising leader in Yoshida Shigeru, a former career diplomat who had been Foreign Minister in the Shidehara

Cabinet, but who had no previous connections with a political party.

This was a fateful decision. Yoshida at the time was sixty-seven years old, and had followed a similar career pattern to Shidehara. He was to remain Prime Minister, with one break of about seventeen months, for the next eight and a half years. At least until the Occupation ended he was able, for a number of reasons, to dominate the Liberal Party in a way that few political leaders have managed to do before or since.[3] He provided strong and individualistic leadership at a time when a prime minister, sandwiched between the Occupation authorities and a complex political environment, was in a position of great delicacy. He also nurtured a small band of younger politicians, similarly of bureaucratic origin, who were to play a leading role in politics for many years after his retirement. Although it was not until the 1949 election that former central government bureaucrats became numerically significant in the conservative parties,[4] the unexpected elevation of Yoshida to the prime ministership in 1946, like the forming of the Seiyūkai Party in 1900 by Itō Hirobumi, was to facilitate that partial fusion of government bureaucracy with party that has been so characteristic of Japanese politics in the modern period.

In 1946, however, implications such as these were not yet clear. The first Yoshida Government was an unstable coalition of Liberals and Progressives with a bare majority in the House of Representatives. The reformist programme of the Occupation was in full swing and the Government found itself as a conservative coalition being leaned upon to introduce a series of radical reforms. The economic situation was chaotic, inflation was rampant, and the labour union movement, which had been recently revived, was increasing in militancy. A general strike was planned for 1 February 1947 but was banned by SCAP at the last minute. This was an early sign of changing priorities on the part of the Occupation.

After a hectic and insecure year in office Yoshida agreed to hold new elections in April 1947, though under revised rules.[5] The results were a remarkable success for the Japan Socialist Party (JSP),[6] which increased its representation from 92 to 143 seats and its percentage of the vote from 17·8 to 26·2 This put it ahead of the two main conservative parties, the Liberal Party with

131 seats and the Democratic Party (Minshutō – the Progressive Party under a new name) with 121. A complicated series of manœuvrings between and within the various parties led to the formation of a new coalition government under a Socialist Prime Minister, Katayama Tetsu. Participants in the coalition were the JSP, the Democratic Party and the small People's Co-operation Party (Kokumin Kyōdōtō), which had 29 seats in the Diet and was moderately conservative in orientation. For a time it seemed as though a four-party coalition might be formed, including also the Liberals, but this broke down after Katayama had refused the Liberal Party demand to expel certain left-wing members from his party. (He did however agree to exclude them from cabinet office.)

In retrospect, the circumstances and timing of its first and only experience of government office was most unfortunate for the JSP. Apart from the frustration of coalition government, Katayama had to face the fact that his own party was a coalition of several factions with long prewar pedigrees. This was true of the conservative parties as well (especially the Democratic Party, which underwent a bewildering series of fissions and fusions in the first postwar decade). With the Socialists, however, personal factionalism was accentuated by paralysing ideological differences.

Divided over the merits of such issues as nationalization of industry,[7] the Government lacked the initiative to handle the day-to-day crises that beset it. Finally, in February 1948, Katayama announced his resignation and the Government fell. After various possible coalitions to replace it had been explored, it was succeeded by a government of virtually the same composition, but with the Democratic Party leader, Ashida Hitoshi, at its head.

The Ashida Government proved scarcely more capable than its predecessor of maintaining its own cohesion, and it resigned in October 1948 following the arrest of Nishio Suehiro, a leading figure of the JSP right wing, on suspicion of breaking the law regarding campaign contributions.

The 'opening to the left' had resulted in fiasco, and as a result Yoshida's Liberal Party (now called the Democratic Liberal Party, or Minshu Jiyūtō) took over. New general elections were called for January 1949, and they resulted in an absolute majority of seats for the Democratic Liberals (264 out of 466 seats and 43·8 per cent of the total vote). The Socialists were routed, seeing their representation fall from 143 to 48 seats (with only 13·5 per cent of the vote), and the Democratic Party also lost heavily, sinking from 121 seats to 69 (15·7 per cent of the vote).

Genuine ideological differences within the centre-left Governments of the 1947–8 can be seen as a major reason for their failure. But while the differences within the JSP were essentially between Marxist and non-Marxist Socialists, in the Democratic Party there were serious divergences of attitude towards the new Constitution and the programme of the Occupation in general. Progressives and traditionalists were pulling in a variety of directions, and the whole situation was exacerbated by personal factionalism.[8]

Another problem for the coalition Governments was that they coincided with a gradual change in priorities by the Occupation. With the development of Cold War tensions in Europe, the enunciation of the Truman doctrine and Communist advances in China, both General MacArthur and the United States Government began to see the position of Japan in a different light. Rather than a conquered enemy to be set on the true road of democracy and peace, Japan was coming to be seen as a potential ally in a worldwide struggle against 'International Communism'.

Other factors also contributed to the Occupation's change of tack. The slowness of economic recovery in Japan was proving an unwelcome drain on the pockets of the American taxpayer, and such things as the *zaibatsu* dissolution programme and the demands being made for reparations by various Allied powers[9] were clearly contributing to economic uncertainty and lack of initiative. The labour union movement was proving strongly militant, and as we have already seen SCAP was moved to ban the proposed general strike in February 1947. Communist influence within the labour unions also increasingly came to worry Occupation authorities, who responded by encouraging non-Communist (though often Marxist-influenced) groups to combat Communists' attempts at takeover. (The foundation of the Sōhyō Federation of trade unions in 1950 was the culmination of such efforts.)

Other measures included severe restrictions, imposed in 1948, on the right to organize and conduct union activities for workers in public enterprises, and a virtual halt to the *zaibatsu* dissolution programme, in order to enable Japanese industry to become once more competitive on world markets. A somewhat drastic austerity programme of 'sound economics', drawn up by a Detroit banker called Joseph Dodge, became the basis of the so-called 'Dodge line', which dominated economic policy in the latter half of the Occupation. This had the effect of stabilizing the economy and virtually halting the rampant postwar inflation, but it also added to the sense of disillusionment and betrayal by the Americans which was widely felt within the labour unions and left-wing parties. This was to be a lasting legacy of the Occupation's change of tack, and contributed to the bitter left-wing anti-Americanism of the post-Occupation years.

It is particulary interesting that for some considerable time the changes were practically confined to aspects of domestic policy. The idea that Japan should once more maintain armed forces in any shape or form was late in coming. Indeed, as late as March 1949 General MacArthur was talking about Japan as the 'Switzerland of the Pacific', and thus precipitated a debate within Japan about the viability of neutrality as the basis of post-independence foreign policy.[10]

The outbreak of war in Korea in June 1950 (coming less than a year after the Communist victory in China) was the event which finally persuaded MacArthur to change his mind. He speedily authorized the formation of a 75,000-man National Police Reserve, which would supplement the now decentralized police forces and do something to fill the vacuum caused by the movement of American troops from Japan to Korea. He followed this up with a New Year broadcast on 1 January 1951 (after the Chinese had entered the Korean War), in which he suggested that Japan might consider some measure of rearmament. He did not call for any change in the 'peace clause' of the Constitution. The effect, however, was to throw the 'peace clause' into the centre of political controversy, where it has remained ever since.

By 1950 it had become fairly clear to both Americans and Japanese that the Occupation had lasted long enough. The initial reformist impetus had changed, as we have seen, to one of consolidation and even in some cases to a reversal of earlier reforms. Resentments at the absence of national independence were growing, and the whole exercise was in danger of turning sour. The status of Japan, however, had become embroiled in international politics, and the prospects for a peace treaty which all the former Allied powers would sign were dim.

The Americans therefore determined to obtain the best settlement possible in the circumstances, and began negotiation for what became known in Japan as a 'Partial Peace'. These efforts resulted in the San Francisco Peace Treaty, signed by all the former Allies except the Soviet Union, Poland and Czechoslovakia, India, Burma and Yugoslavia.[11] Neither the People's Republic of China nor the Republic of China (Taiwan) were invited to the peace conference, but Japan shortly afterwards signed a separate peace treaty with the latter.

Largely at American insistence, the Peace Treaty was a favourable one for Japan. Although she renounced claims to her former imperial territories, no restrictions were placed on the development of her economy and her trade, nor was she obliged, as some Japanese had earlier feared, to retain any of the Occupation reforms if she should choose not to.

On the same day that the Peace Treaty was signed, the United States and Japan signed a bilateral security pact which was to provide for a continuation of an American military presence in Japan after independence. The question of the security relationship between these two countries was to prove a matter of delicate controversy between Tokyo and Washington, and also in Japanese domestic politics.

Closely involved also was the question of Japanese rearmament. In his talks with Japanese leaders in the early part of 1951, John Foster Dulles, representing the Truman administration, had strongly urged upon Yoshida that Japan should rearm on a massive scale, to the extent of building a 350,000-man army. Yoshida, realizing the disastrous economic and political consequences that this could have, resisted, and was apparently supported by General MacArthur in his stand.[12] Nevertheless, the Security Treaty contained a clause to the effect that the United States would maintain forces in and about Japan '. . . in the expectation . . that Japan will itself increasingly assume responsibility for its own defense against direct and indirect aggression, always avoiding any armament which could be an offensive threat. . . .'[13] Subsequent negotiations were to lead to the formation of the Self-Defence Forces (Jieitai) in 1954, at very much lower strength than had been envisaged by Dulles.[14]

The peace settlement of 1952 and the attendant issue of rearmament had a traumatic effect upon the left. The existing ideological divisions within the JSP were greatly exacerbated by the injection of brand new questions of foreign policy and defence. In October 1951, shortly after the San Francisco Peace Treaty, the Party split right down the middle into two separate Socialist parties, of left and right. Between them, however, riding a wave of anti-war and anti-Government sentiment, they were able to retrieve the ground lost in the 1949 election, until by 1955 they jointly held 160 seats in the Lower House.[15] The Communists, were not so successful. Having won 35 seats with nearly 10 per cent of the vote in 1949, they saw their Lower House representation wiped out entirely in 1952. In January 1950 the Party's leadership had been severely criticized by the Cominform for its 'lovable' image, and was enjoined to embark upon a militant anti-American struggle. The Party's leadership was purged on Occupation orders, and a period of confusion, extremism and factional conflict followed. The JCP did not begin to recover substantial electoral support until the 1960s.

The conservative parties were also beset by factional conflict, largely of a personal nature. While Japan was still under the Occupation, Yoshida was able to maintain virtually undisputed power by virtue of the electoral successes of the Liberal Party (especially in the 1949 elections), his cordial relations with MacArthur and the absence of credible rivals to him within his own party. His reputation was of an aloof, somewhat autocratic party leader, who kept his party under control through a number of former bureaucrats owing direct personal allegiance to himself.

However, once the Occupation was wound up and those former party politicians who had been purged were free to return to political life, his supremacy came under increasing challenge. Hatoyama, who had been purged when about to form an administration in 1946, returned to political life with a sense of burning resentment against Yoshida, who now refused to step down in his favour despite an understanding that he would do so when Hatoyama was released from the purge. The return of Hatoyama and other ex-purgees to the political arena was something which Yoshida's style of leadership proved ill-equipped to deal with, and after two Lower House elections (October 1952 and March 1953) in which the Liberals did badly,[16] and after a series of scandals in 1954 involving government subsidies to the shipbuilding industry, Yoshida finally stepped down in December 1954, to be replaced as Prime Minister by Hatoyama.

The Reformist Party (Kaishintō), as the Democrats were now called, would not have been able to form a government had not the Hatoyama faction of the Liberal Party defected and joined them in November 1954, thus creating the Japan Democratic Party (Nihon Minshutō). This party did well in the Lower House elections of February 1955, as did the two wings of the Socialist Party, while the Liberals lost further ground.[17]

The stage was now set for a much clearer polarization of political forces between right and left than anything that had been seen hitherto. In October 1955 the two Socialist parties were reunited after a series of long and difficult negotiations. Partly under pressure from business interests, which feared further socialist advances at the polls and a possible socialist government, the Liberal Party and the Japan Democratic Party merged one month later to create the Liberal Democratic Party (Jiyūminshutō, or Jimintō).

This may be seen in retrospect as a crucial turning point in postwar Japanese politics. Despite the persistence of acute factional rivalries, the Liberal Democrats were able to avoid further defections and to consolidate their position as a hegemonic ruling party. Socialist unity, on the other hand, was to prove more fragile, and despite a gradual shift of the preference of the electorate towards the left, the JSP was unable to maintain its impetus of the mid-1950s. Some observers initially hailed the events of late 1955 as signifying the establishment of a two-party system, but the implication that government office should alternate between the two parties was not to be realized.

Hatoyama proved a weak Prime Minister and, having negotiated an agreement for restoration of diplomatic relations with the USSR,[18] was succeeded in December 1956 by Ishibashi Tanzan, who resigned because of ill health two months later. He in turn was succeeded by a former member of Tōjō's war Cabinet and Class 'A' war criminal, Kishi Nobusuke, in February 1957. Kishi was in many ways an extraordinary choice for Prime Minister, and although he clearly had great administrative ability he proved a divisive figure, attracting criticism and distrust both for his wartime background and for many of his policy initiatives. This was to culminate in the Security Treaty Crisis of May–June 1960.

If the period 1952–60 was one of transition in party politics, it was also one of acute polarization of opinion. The policies of successive conservative governments were often lumped together under the term 'reverse course'. From the government side, the Occupation reforms were subjected to critical scrutiny, and attempts were made to dismantle or emasculate those which were most objectionable. From the Opposition side (which in this context meant the left-wing parties, labour unions, academics and much of the mass media) fears were expressed that each new piece of government legislation was part of a planned programme of putting the clock back to the prewar era.

The main areas in which reform was desired or actually implemented by governments were police administration and powers, labour unions, educational administration and the content of courses, defence and the Security Treaty, and the Constitution.

Police administration and powers, evoking memories of the prewar period in which the police had been an instrument of political control, were a particularly sensitive issue. In 1954 the Yoshida Government introduced a new Police Law which effectively recentralized police administration. In 1952 a Subversive Activities Bill, largely directed against the Communist Party, was passed by the Diet, but a Police Duties Law Amendment Bill, introduced by the Kishi Government in 1958, did not fare so well. This bill, designed among other things to give the police enhanced powers of controlling demonstrations, met a concerted barrage of criticism within and outside the Diet, and eventually was allowed to lapse.[19]

Post-Occupation governments continued the restrictive attitudes towards labour unions which had been initiated during the latter half of the Occupation, especially with the restrictions on the union rights of government workers imposed in 1948 and amendments to the postwar Labour Union Law which were passed in 1949. Following prolonged strikes in the coal and electricity industries which took place in 1952, a Coal and Electricity Strike Control Act went into the statute books in 1953. Labour union membership, which had risen very rapidly in the early part of the Occupation, then stagnated for some years, in part as a result of government policies. The labour unions themselves, after Communist attempts to control them during the Occupation had largely failed, nevertheless retained much of their radicalism during the 1950s. The Sōhyō Federation, formed in 1950, split in 1954 into a radical wing (still called Sōhyō) and a smaller moderate wing (Zenrō, later called Dōmei). Relations between the labour unions and the socialist parties remained close.

Education policy was another highly contentious area, in which the conservatives were particularly concerned to reverse some at least of the policies initiated during the Occupation. In 1956 the Hatoyama Government introduced legislation to recentralize educational administration. The local boards of education ceased to be elective and came to be appointed. The Ministry of Education, under separate legislation, acquired powers of vetting and authorizing school textbooks. In 1958 the Ministry of Education began to use a teachers' efficiency rating system, which was bitterly contested by the Teachers' Union (Nikkyōsō) and other groups, partly on the grounds that it was likely to be used for political ends. Another issue was that of curricula, occasioned particularly by the introduction of 'ethics' courses into schools in 1958. With their memories of what 'ethics' had meant before the war, members of the Teachers' Union and others attacked this also. Relations between the Ministry of Education and the Teachers' Union (which was strongly Marxist-orientated) became strained to say the least.

Defence and the Security Treaty were the most celebrated area of controversy. Although the Yoshida Government successfully resisted Dulles's demands for massive rearmament by Japan, it authorized the formation of a modest military force known euphemistically as the 'Self-Defence Forces' and in 1954 signed the Mutual Security Assistance Agreement (MSA) with the United States. It was left, however, to Kishi to negotiate a revision of the original Security Treaty of 1951. His attempts to do so triggered Japan's worst political crisis since the war, leading ultimately to his resignation. Anti-war feeling at this period was still strong, and the Socialist Party campaigned on a platform of 'unarmed neutralism'. Any attempt by the Government, therefore, either to improve the national defence capacity or to consolidate its defence relationship with the United States, was bitterly resisted by the left.

Campaigns against American military bases in Japan were a feature of the politics of the period, and a movement against nuclear weapons, known as Gensuikyō, was able to tap a vast reservoir of anti-nuclear sentiment in a nation which had undergone – to quote a phrase which gained currency at the time – 'nuclear baptism'. Gensuikyō originated in a housewives' petition after a Japanese fishing boat had been showered with radioactive ash from an American test at Bikini atoll in 1954. In the 1960s it became a political battleground between the Communist and Socialist Parties and also between the two sides in the Sino-Soviet dispute. It consequently lost much of its appeal, but annual rallies continued to be held every August at Hiroshima.

Finally, the Constitution was not surprisingly a major field of contention. The Hatoyama Government came to power with a policy of initiating Constitutional revision, and in July 1956 a bill passed the Diet providing for a Cabinet Commission to Investigate the Constitution. The Commission began to function in August 1957, by which time Kishi, who also wanted Constitutional revision, was prime minister. The socialists and their allies refused to participate in the Commission, which despite this proved not to be the solidly revisionist body that many had feared. The Commission reported finally (and voluminously) in 1964, but by that time pressure for revision had receded and no action was taken. The attitude of the Opposition to the whole issue (but especially to article 9, the 'peace' clause) is summed up in a JSP campaign slogan used in the 1960s: 'The Constitution protects you; we protect the Constitution'.

The Security Treaty revision crisis of May-June 1960 was the most serious political fracas since the end of the Occupation. It produced mass demonstrations and riots on an unprecedented scale, led to the cancellation of a state visit to Japan by President Eisenhower, precipitated the fall from office of a Japanese prime minister (but not his party), and seriously strained relations between Japan and the United States. On the other hand, Japan obtained a Mutual Security Treaty which in several respects was an improvement on the old one; and some saw the crisis itself as a realization of democratic participation in the political process. Following the crisis, moreover, Japan entered a period in which political stability was markedly greater, and the temperature of politics noticeably lower, than it had been in the 1950s.

Very briefly, what happened was this. In 1958 the Kishi Government began negotiations with the Eisenhower administration for a revision of the 1951 Security Treaty to make it more acceptable from the Japanese point of view. Essentially, Kishi was trying to increase Japan's independence of action under the Treaty without reducing the value of the American defence commitment or committing Japan to excessive defence responsibilities. To a very considerable extent, he succeeded in this aim.[20]

The left-wing Opposition for the most part objected to the Treaty in any shape or form, and saw revision as perpetuating a dangerous 'military alliance' with the United States. In February–March 1959 a People's Council for Preventing Revision of the Security Treaty was formed, to co-ordinate activities. The left at this time was encouraged by the success of the campaign to block the revision of the Police Duties Law Amendment Bill in 1958, where mass demonstrations by unionists, students and others had been a big feature. Their morale was also given a boost by the March 1959 verdict of the Tokyo District Court in the Sunakawa case, which held among other things that the presence of American troops in Japan was incompatible with article 9 of the Constitution (see chapter 10). The decision, which cast grave doubt on the constitutionality of the Security Treaty (and also of the projected revised Treaty), was reversed by a decision of the Supreme Court in December of the same year.

During the earlier stages of the movement against revision of the Treaty, it was fairly limited in scope and in the number of people involved. The Socialist and Communist Parties, the Sōhyō trade union federation and the student movement Zengakuren were the main participants, with some support from academics and the mass media. It was these elements which were largely involved in demonstrations which broke into the Diet compound on 27 November 1959 and which unsuccessfully attempted to prevent Kishi from leaving Haneda airport on 16 January 1960 in order to sign the revised Treaty in Washington.

In May and June 1960, however, a series of events occurred which broadened the base of the movement to previously uncommitted or apolitical people. It so happened that, as the Diet debates on the Treaty were nearing completion, international tension rose dramatically with the U2 incident and the breakdown of the planned summit meeting between Eisenhower and Khrushchev. This gave rise to acute fears of Japan being dragged into an international conflict by virtue of her security links with the United States. Eisenhower's world trip was now likely to include only anti-Communist capitals and not Moscow, as had been planned. The symbolism, for the left, was highly unpalatable. Meanwhile, Kishi was faced not only with a continuous series of hostile demonstrations, but also with constant obstruction of Diet proceedings by the Opposition parties. Moreover (and this in a sense was the most crucial point) he could not count on the unswerving loyalty to him of several of the intra-Party factions. While his own factional alliance was loyal, some factions were decidedly equivocal in their support and others were openly hostile and criticized his policies incessantly, no doubt with the expectation that one of their leaders would be able to replace him as prime minister.

Kishi's first tactical defeat was when he failed to have the Treaty passed by the House of Representatives by 26 April. If it had been passed by that date, then it would have been ratified by the House of Councillors without further action on 26 May, and without the necessity of formally extending the regular session.[21] The consequences of this failure were compounded by what in retrospect seems a most unwise decision, namely to invite President Eisenhower to Japan for 19 June, on the assumption that the Treaty would have been formally ratified by that date. This meant it had to pass the Lower House by 19 May.

When 19 May arrived and the Treaty still had not passed the Lower House, Kishi decided on drastic action. He called police into the Diet to remove Socialist MPs and their male secretaries who were physically preventing the Speaker from calling a vote on the extension of the session, and then, late at night with only Liberal Democratic members present and with many of them unaware of what was planned, held two votes in quick succession, the first to extend the session and the second to ratify the Treaty.[22]

To public apprehension about the Treaty was now added a widespread fear that Kishi was subverting basic parliamentary procedure and even democracy itself. The obstructionist tactics of the Socialists (such as imprisoning the Speaker) were regarded more leniently. There followed a month of serious crisis, with a mounting series of demonstrations and strikes. On 10 June Eisenhower's press secretary was mobbed in his car by a crowd of demonstrators and had to be rescued by helicopter. Things came to a head on 15 June, when a massive demonstration outside the Diet led to an invasion of the Diet compound and pitched battles with police. There were many injuries and one girl student was killed. The next day Kishi cancelled the Eisenhower visit on the ground that he could not guarantee the President's safety. The revised Security Treaty duly passed the House of Councillors on 19 June, and four days later Kishi announced his resignation. The LDP did not split, although it came close to it. The demonstrators all went home.

The suddenness with which the 1960 Security Treaty crisis was over suggests that the causes of it were temporary rather than rooted in the long-term political situation. It is true that there were some disturbing instances of political violence in the aftermath of the crisis.[23] The next few years, however, were relatively calm and uneventful. Ikeda Hayato, who followed Kishi as President of the LDP and thus Prime Minister, was also of bureaucratic background and was a protégé of Yoshida. Government remained in the hands of a predominantly conservative and business-oriented political party.

Ikeda, nevertheless, succeeded in projecting an image very

different from that of his predecessor. Following a more conciliatory approach to Opposition susceptibilities, and what he termed a 'low posture' (*tei shisei*) in his foreign and domestic policies, he received a wide measure of popularity. Deliberately, he played down contentious political issues such as revising the Constitution and defence co-operation with the United States, and concentrated on the more rewarding area of economic growth. By the early 1960s the Japanese economy had already moved to the stage of ultra-high growth rates, and Ikeda was able to gain considerable political advantage from this by issuing a long-term economic plan for 'income doubling' over a ten-year period. He made genuine efforts to restore the normal working of the Diet, the reputation of which had been seriously damaged by the events of the previous months. He also concentrated on gaining Japan full recognition as an advanced industrial nation. Japan became a member of the Organization for Economic Co-operation and Development in 1964. Perhaps as a reflection of these efforts, the LDP did well in Lower House general elections held in 1960 and 1963.

For a time the conciliatory approach taken by the Ikeda Government met its due response in more moderate policies by the Opposition. The Socialist leader Eda Saburō, newly risen to prominence, promoted a policy of 'structural reform', which was reformist rather than revolutionary in its implications. His grip on the party organization was fragile, however, and by 1965 he had been replaced by leaders of a more extreme and doctrinaire stamp.

For the Socialist Party the 1960s were an unhappy decade. Whereas in the mid-1950s it was confidently expected in many quarters that the JSP would continue to gain in electoral strength until it would be able to form a government in its own right, by 1960 its support appeared to have ceased growing when it had the allegiance of about one-third of the voters. Party unity, forged with much difficulty in 1955, did not prove durable. In 1959 a right-wing group led by Nishio Suehiro (prominent in the Katayama and Ashida Governments of 1947–8) broke away in protest against the Party's drift to the left[24] and formed the middle-of-the-road Democratic Socialist Party (DSP). The DSP did not do particularly well at the polls,[25] but its defection destroyed the ideological balance within the JSP, and made it easier to run that Party from the extreme left than from the centre or right.

The JSP was also poorly organized and heavily dependent upon labour unions affiliated with the Sōhyō federation. This left the way open to other groups with an eye to the organization of discontent to poach on the Socialists' traditional bailiwick. Two such groups became significant during the 1960s. One was the Sōka Gakkai, a proselytizing neo-Buddhist sect which was having astonishing success in attracting members from the ranks of unorganized workers, small shopkeepers and middle-aged housewives in the cities.[26] In the late 1950s it began sponsoring candidates for election to the Diet and in 1964 founded a new political party, the Kōmeitō, which campaigned on a platform of 'cleaning up' political corruption and paying attention to the problems of the little man. The party was highly disciplined and able shrewdly to organize its base of support, and the high point of its success was at the 1969 Lower House general election, when it won 47 seats. The other rising force on the Opposition side was the Japan Communist Party, which was rapidly recovering from its setbacks in the 1950s and developing a more independent, even nationalist, line in relation to Moscow and Peking. It also paid great attention to organization, strove to project a 'soft' image and was becoming an important political force, especially in the major cities.[27] The JSP, on the other hand, suffered a major defeat in the 1969 election, by losing 50 seats and sinking to a total of 90.

As Prime Minister, Ikeda had to cope, like his predecessors, with challenges to his position from rival factions within the LDP. In July 1964 he quite narrowly avoided defeat in a party presidential election by his factional rival Satō Eisaku. In November of the same year Ikeda had to resign because of ill health, and Satō replaced him as Prime Minister.

Satō Eisaku, the younger brother of Kishi Nobusuke (see chapter 3, note 3), was another former bureaucrat and protégé of Yoshida, and was to remain in office until June 1972 – a record time. Satō presided over a period of rapid economic advance, which by the late 1960s had placed the Japanese economy ahead of that of West Germany and into third place behind the United States and the Soviet Union in terms of gross national product. Japan was becoming a major force on the world scene, though her economic influence was hardly matched by political initiative.

Satō was a cautious Prime Minister, though somewhat more right-wing and less inclined to be conciliatory to the Opposition than Ikeda. His most tangible achievements, but also his most notable setbacks, were in the field of foreign policy. Thus in 1965 he finally concluded a treaty with the Republic of Korea, paving the way for close economic links between Japan and that country. In 1970 he gained the agreement of the United States Government for indefinite extension of the Security Treaty, and thus avoided a repeat performance of the 1960 crisis, which had been widely predicted. In November 1969 President Nixon agreed to return Okinawa to Japan, and this duly took place in May 1972, thus defusing an issue with which the Opposition was making great play.

Satō's cautious attitude to the Vietnam war and to any extension of Japan's defence responsibilities also probably paid political dividends.[28] Vietnam was an issue which once more raised the temperature of politics in the late 1960s, and again polarized the Opposition from the Government. The Opposition, however, was now divided into several separate parties, and was therefore less effective.

The years 1968 and 1969 saw a flare-up of violence on university campuses which for a time confronted the Government (and of course the universities themselves) with a serious situation. Educational and political issues became inextricably confused as the student bodies were increasingly radicalized. Finally the Government, after waiting for some time until public opinion was beginning to tire of the student radicals, introduced a Universities Control Bill (August 1969) which had a dramatic effect in bringing things back to normal.

The final year of the Satō era was, however, much more seriously troubled. The startling success of Japanese exports to the United States caused a sharp reaction in that country and President Nixon's economic measures of August 1971 were designed, among other things, to force Japan to revalue her currency. Following a confused reaction from the Japanese Government, the currency was duly revalued by 16·8 per cent in December of the same year. The announcement in July of President Nixon's coming visit to the People's Republic of

China, which was not communicated to Japanese officials in advance, was similarly traumatic. These two initiatives by President Nixon were referred to as the 'Nixon shocks', and precipitated a great deal of rethinking of Japan's basic international position. Satō was unwilling (or unable) to take real initiatives on China, whereas the mass media were virtually at one in urging a drastic change in China policy, and in calling on Satō to step down if he could not produce one.

Towards the end of Satō's prime ministership there was also mounting pressure for a rethinking of economic priorities to give more attention to the problems of environmental pollution (particularly severe in Japan's crowded cities), welfare and living conditions, and less to economic growth for its own sake. A rise in support for Opposition candidates in the big cities was a symptom of the problems which a rapid growth of affluence had brought and governments had yet to solve.

A return of nationalism in various forms also drew widespread attention. Perhaps its most extreme manifestation was the quixotic suicide in November 1970 of the celebrated novelist Mishima Yukio, after calling upon members of the Self-Defence Forces to rise up against their equivocal status under the Constitution.[29] The appointment in 1970 of a rather flamboyant LDP faction leader, Nakasone Yasuhiro, as head of the Defence Agency was also seen as evidence of a more positive attitude towards defence. The extent of this change, however, tended to be exaggerated in the foreign press.

In July 1972 Satō was replaced as Prime Minister by Tanaka Kakuei, a man of limited formal education and no bureaucratic background, who had made his career in business and in the party machine. The tide of disillusionment with Satō was probably what robbed his preferred successor, Fukuda Takeo – a man of similar background and perceptions to himself – of the succession.

Tanaka immediately took bold initiatives in two directions. He moved at once to recognize the People's Republic of China, which meant severing formal ties with the Republic of China on Taiwan. He also produced a plan for the 'Reconstruction of the Japanese Archipelago', which involved dispersal of industry and population to areas of the country away from the existing big cities. Although criticized on the ground that it would 'spread pollution', this plan appeared to be in tune with current trends of opinion. Meanwhile the economy, which had been in recession at the time of revaluation, recovered its former momentum.

General elections for the House of Representatives were held in December 1972. The Liberal Democrats were returned with a slightly reduced majority, but the Communists made spectacular gains, and the Socialists recouped some of the ground lost in 1969, at the expense of those of the centre (Kōmeitō and DSP). The Communist achievement of 38 seats even surpassed its previous high point in 1949.

Despite its relatively auspicious start, the Tanaka regime soon ran into serious difficulties. With the economic recovery came unprecedentedly high rates of inflation, which in part reflected international inflationary trends. The publication of the Prime Minister's decentralization plan was followed by an extraordinary boom in land prices, especially in those areas earmarked for future development. Because of economic and political pressures, the scheme had to be shelved for the time being.

A similar fate befell an attempt by Tanaka in April 1973 to replace the multi-member constituency system for House of Representatives elections with one largely based on single-member constituencies. Motivated by fears of defeat in the 1974 House of Councillors elections, Tanaka seems to have calculated on obtaining through electoral reform the two-thirds majority in the Lower House necessary to override rejection of government bills by the Upper House. In the event, however, he was not politically strong enough or skilful enough to force the bill through against a determined Opposition. Tanaka's handling of this issue apparently disillusioned many of his supporters in the LDP, while in the country at large his initially high popularity sank to alarmingly low levels.

The Arab–Israeli war of October 1973 and the achievement by OPEC of a massive increase in the price of oil precipitated what came to be known in Japan as the first 'oil shock'. Although early fears of a catastrophic interruption in oil supplies did not materialize, the threat of such an interruption forced Japan to move from a neutral to a pro-Arab position in her policy towards the Middle East, against the wishes of the US

Government. The price increase, however, could not be dealt with so easily. Oil imports tripled (and ultimately quadrupled) in price at a time when inflationary pressures had been allowed to build up within the economy. The wholesale price index for December 1973 was 29 per cent higher than it was a year previously, and retail prices were rising fast, fuelling wage demands by trade unions.

The political impact was far-reaching. Tanaka reshuffled his Cabinet in December and brought in his rival Fukuda as Finance Minister to stabilize the economy. Rather than high growth and ambitious reconstruction programmes, economic stabilization now became the order of the day, even though it represented a drastic reordering of Tanaka's own priorities. Real economic growth declined from 9·7 per cent in fiscal 1972–3 (April to March), to 5·3 per cent in fiscal 1973–4, and down to −0·2 per cent in fiscal 1974–5, the first example of a negative growth rate since the postwar period.

An anti-Establishment mood became detectable within the electorate. The media publicized alleged hoarding of consumer goods by industrial firms at a time when panic buying had created acute shortages of several basic items. The popular image of business suffered as a result, and further deteriorated when huge sums of money were poured into the LDP campaign for the House of Councillors elections of July 1974, and some firms put pressure on their employees to support certain LDP candidates. Against expectations, the election results showed a marked swing to the Opposition, leaving the Government with a majority of only seven seats over the Opposition as a whole. Shortly after the elections, both Fukuda and another faction leader, Miki Takeo, resigned from the Cabinet.

The Prime Minister's tour of Southeast Asian capitals in January 1974 was marred by anti-Japanese demonstrations in Jakarta, Bangkok and elsewhere. Although local political issues were involved as well, the anti-Japanese theme was dominant enough to cause some rethinking in Japan about the role and behaviour of Japanese firms in the region.

Following the July elections, the monthly journal *Bungei Shunjū* in October carried an article exposing dubious financial dealings in which Tanaka was allegedly involved.[30] Initially ignored by the daily press, it was accorded prominent coverage after foreign correspondents began reporting the accusations. In November Tanaka resigned as party President and Prime Minister. The reasons for his resignation remain a matter of controversy, and are still canvassed by newspapers and journals fascinated by the personality of Japan's most colourful contemporary politician.[31]

The succession to Tanaka was a delicate matter. As in 1964, when Ikeda had resigned because of illness, the Party preferred a quiet sounding-out of party views to the divisive mechanism of a presidential election. The party elder Shiina Etsusaburō, entrusted with the task of canvassing views, judged that to appoint either of the leading contenders, Fukuda and Ōhira, risked disrupting the Party. He therefore opted for a compromise candidate, Miki Takeo, three times previously a candidate for party presidency, leader of a small faction on the left of the LDP, and able to project himself as untainted with the kind of 'money politics' that had so damaged Tanaka's reputation.

Miki took office in December with one unusual advantage and an important disadvantage. On the one hand, having had office thrust upon him rather than having campaigned for it, he had few political debts to repay when making Cabinet and party appointments. On the other hand, not having constructed a factional alliance he found it difficult to persuade other factions to back him in his legislative proposals, particularly since a number of these were more 'progressive' than the party was normally used to. For a few months in 1975 he actually tried to rely on votes from Opposition parties in support of bills opposed by the right wing of the LDP. Even so, much of his legislation failed to pass the Diet. His attempt to strengthen the Anti-Monopoly Law against opposition from big business and its sympathizers in the LDP was largely a failure, although an emasculated version of the bill did eventually pass the Diet. A rare success was ratification of the Nuclear Non-Proliferation Treaty, long after its signature in 1970.

In February 1976 a sub-committee of the US Senate Foreign Relations Committee heard evidence from the Deputy President of the Lockheed Corporation that several million dollars had been given in bribes to unnamed politicians in Japan and elsewhere in order to influence aircraft contracts. This admission caused a sensation in Japan, and the 'Lockheed scandal' came to dominate the nation's politics for the rest of the year, as well as straining relations with the United States. As the media entertained the public with ever more lurid details of Lockheed's alleged subversion of Japanese decision-makers all too willing to be subverted, the outlines of the story became well established. Lockheed, it was alleged, had used three main avenues for the channelling of money into Japan: the Marubeni Corporation, All Nippon Airways and an ultra-rightist political activist called Kodama Yoshio. The unsavoury nature of Kodama's past record, and the allegation that his contacts with LDP politicians were sufficiently intimate to make him a worthwhile intermediary for Lockheed, added to the morbid fascination which the affair held for the Japanese public. It also drew public attention to the problem of 'structural corruption' – the fact that the cost of running political campaigns was so great that politicians found it hard to avoid becoming tainted with corruption.

Miki, unlike some of his predecessors in similar circumstances, allowed the official investigators a free hand to probe as deeply into the affair as they wished. In a sensational move, Tanaka was arrested in July and made to answer charges about his part in the affair. Though quickly released and still a member of the Diet (he later resigned from the LDP), he had to face protracted court proceedings which were still continuing in 1981. Miki, politically weak from the time he became Prime Minister, was from mid-1976 fighting for his political life, as factions other than his own sought to have him replaced. His attempts to uncover the whole truth about the Lockheed affair were proving embarrassing as the list of those suspected of involvement grew longer. Miki's only effective weapon was an implied threat to take his faction out of the Party if he were to be deposed. Had he done so, the LDP would no longer have had the numbers to govern alone. In fact a group of six Diet members led by Kōno Yōhei did defect, and formed the New Liberal Club (NLC) in June 1976. But although they did well in the House of Representatives elections in December, their number was too small to affect the composition of the Government.

Before the elections twenty new metropolitan seats had been added in order somewhat to redress the population imbalance between city and country seats. The LDP did badly but just managed to retain a clear majority with the help of Independents. The centre parties did well but the left (especially the Communists) lost ground. The LDP lost control of a number of Lower House Diet committees, thus complicating its legislative task. An era of Government–Opposition 'parity' (*hakuchū*) had begun and was to last until June 1980.

Following the elections Miki finally agreed to step down, and was replaced by Fukuda, who was accepted by the Party without overt dissent. The Fukuda Government began to feel the effects of the loss of LDP control over Diet committees when it was forced to incorporate tax reductions into its 1977 budget. At the same time regulatory powers acquired by some bureaucratic agencies not previously taken very seriously in government decision-making were introducing greater pluralism into government. These included the Environmental Agency, the Welfare Ministry and the Construction Ministry.[32]

On the other hand, by the time of the Fukuda Government, economic growth had begun to resume. Although it was not the ultra-high growth of the 1960s and early 1970s, it was rapidly becoming more than respectable in terms of international comparisons at 5 or 6 per cent per annum. Indeed, the strength of the economy from 1977 onwards caused continuing problems with other countries, particularly the United States. A record surplus in Japan's balance of payments for 1977 coincided with a huge balance of payments deficit in that country. In conditions of global economic recession the Carter administration put pressure on Japan to increase still further its growth rate and in particular to boost its imports. The two Governments went through a period of intensive negotiations without great practical result, but the situation stabilized to some extent following a massive rise in the value of the yen against the American dollar. Indeed the yen rose in October 1978 to a level, unprecedented since independence, of ¥175=$1·00, though it was later to fall back from this level.[33] Japan–US relations were also placed under strain by differences of policy over nuclear energy, the issue of withdrawal of American troops from Korea and other issues. In general, the Carter Government seem not to have been well respected in Tokyo, and the President's announcement of a planned withdrawal of troops from Korea was seen as all too reminiscent of President Nixon's shock announcements in 1971. In both cases a crucial factor in the Japanese unhappiness was the woeful inadequacy of consultation.

Two important steps were taken during 1978 towards better relations with China. In February a large-scale trade agreement was signed, and in August the Sino-Japanese Treaty of Peace and Friendship, long stalled over the issue of 'hegemony' (see chapter 12), was concluded. On the other hand, and partly no doubt in consequence of the development of closer relations with China, relations with the Soviet Union remained cool, with anti-Soviet feeling perceptibly gaining ground in Japan. Past policies of 'equidistance' between China and the Soviet Union were quietly forgotten by Government spokesmen. The Fukuda Government put considerable effort into improving Japan's image in Southeast Asia and watched the developing ties between the Soviet Union and Vietnam with concern.

In domestic politics, while the LDP faced problems, so did the parties in Opposition. In 1977 a running battle between moderates and leftists resulted in defections by some right-leaning members of the JSP, who formed yet another small (in this case minuscule) centrist party, which became the Social Democratic League (SDL) in March 1978. The presumptive leader of this movement, Eda Saburō, died shortly after its formation, robbing it of its best-known personality. After long delays the JSP elected Asukata Ichio, formerly mayor of Yokohama, as its new Chairman at the end of 1977, and to some extent regained its equilibrium. Meanwhile the image of respectability so carefully fostered by the JCP in the 1970s was shaken by publicity given in 1976 to a spy-lynching case of the 1930s, in which the Party's current Chairman and architect of its recent electoral advances was allegedly involved. This may partly explain the JCP setback in the 1976 elections. The Kōmeitō was also not free of trouble, being shaken by the sudden resignation in 1979 of Ikeda Daisaku, the Chairman of its parent sect the Sōka Gakkai, for reasons which were the subject of intense investigations and speculation by the mass media. Radicalism of the extreme left had greatly declined since the late 1960s, but a combination of radical student activism and objections by local farmers and residents groups delayed the opening of Tokyo's new international airport at Narita until May 1978, after it had been completed but unused for most of a decade. Two months before the opening a group of radicals broke into the control tower and smashed much of the computer equipment.

By 1977 there were signs that the electorate was no longer swinging to the left as it had been in the early and middle 1970s. The LDP held its precarious majority in the 1977 House of Councillors elections. In April 1978 an LDP candidate was elected Governor of Kyōto prefecture, ending 28 years of left-wing administration. Similar results were achieved by conservatives in Tokyo and Ōsaka in April 1979. In part the swing in local elections may simply have represented a reaction against existing administrations, and since a string of leftist governors and mayors were elected in the late 1960s and early 1970s, it was they who suffered electorally from this reaction.

The position of the Prime Minister was not rendered more secure by a conservative mood in the electorate. A new method of electing the LDP president, initiated by Miki when he was Prime Minister, provided for a primary election by all party members (not just Diet members and prefectural representatives as in the past) prior to the main election. Although heralded as a method of 'modernizing' or 'democratizing' party procedures, it had the effect of extending factional divisions down to the rank and file membership. Factions competed to recruit new members, and when the first primaries were held in November 1978, the combined organizational strength of the Ōhira and Tanaka factions proved too much for Fukuda. In a four-cornered contest Ōhira beat Fukuda and the other two candidates by a wide margin, and Fukuda decided not to contest the second-stage run-off election.

Further OPEC oil price rises prompted the second 'oil shock' for Japan in 1979, and the Ōhira Cabinet devoted extraordinary efforts to devising an energy policy which would conserve oil, increase oil stockpiles and accelerate the development of alternative sources of energy. The economy, however, had now achieved the capacity to withstand an 'oil shock' more effectively than in 1973–4. Economic growth rates were scarcely affected, although for a while the yen weakened against the dollar.

Even so, life for a Japanese prime minister was not, it seems, meant to be easy, and when Ōhira decided to go to the people prematurely in October 1979, the LDP did marginally worse than it had in 1976, though it still just managed to hang on to its parliamentary majority. The reasons for this unexpectedly poor showing despite what most commentators regarded as a conservative mood in the electorate is uncertain, but two possible factors may have affected the result. One was the extremely bad weather on polling day, which resulted in an exceptionally low turnout of voters, especially in the Tokyo area. Another was Ōhira's announcement before the election of planned tax increases. Although he retracted his statement in the face of widespread expressions of dismay, it seems that the electoral damage had been done. Following the elections Ōhira's tenure came under challenge from within the LDP, and a 'forty-day crisis' ensued, which was only resolved when the Party put forward two candidates, Ōhira and Fukuda, in the Diet election to determine the choice of prime minister. It was the first time in its history that the LDP had been unable to decide on a prime ministerial candidate and had had to entrust the selection, in a real not a formal sense, to a vote in the Diet.

The second Ōhira Government, which because of the crisis did not take office until November, soon faced a worsening international environment following the Soviet invasion of Afghanistan at the end of December. Japan now came under renewed American pressure to increase military spending. Ōhira appointed the renowned economist, Dr Ōkita Saburō, to be Foreign Minister in his new administration. The appointment, a rare example of a non-Diet member attaining Cabinet office, led to renewed interest by the Government in exploring schemes of regional economic co-operation among the nations of the Pacific basin. Dr Ōkita's long-standing interest in regional co-operation was clearly well known to the Prime Minister when he appointed him to Cabinet. The general foreign policy line remained, as before, one of alignment with the United States and other non-Communist nations. The Ōhira Government was generally responsive to American calls for co-operation from its allies in its policies towards the Soviet Union. Japan did not, for instance, send a team to the Moscow Olympics, and although the decision was made by the Japan Olympic Federation it was in line with the wishes of the Government.

For all its good intentions the Ōhira Government continued to be plagued by the political circumstances that had led to the forty-day crisis of October–November 1979. On 16 May 1980 the JSP presented to the Diet a non-confidence motion citing corruption, proposed defence spending increases and rises in public utility charges as reasons for the House of Representatives to withdraw its endorsement of the Government. Quite unexpectedly 69 LDP Diet members, from the Fukuda, Miki and recently formed Nakagawa factions, abstained from voting on the motion. The Government was soundly defeated (243 votes to 187), and resigned. For the first time a simultaneous double election was called for both Houses.

Although at the time of the non-confidence motion the LDP seemed to many observers to be headed for disintegration, the shock of the Government's resignation created the impetus for closing of ranks. The desire to unite was further strengthened when on 12 June Ōhira died from a heart condition. Itō Masayoshi, the Chief Cabinet Secretary of the Ōhira Government, became caretaker Prime Minister, and the LDP went to the people on 22 June carrying black-edged posters of its dead leader. In an extraordinary reversal of its fortunes the Party won a clear victory in both Houses, and in the House of Representatives secured its safest majority since 1969. The Opposition parties as a whole did not lose votes, but a 6·5 per cent increase in the turnout of voters compared with the 1979 House of Representatives elections was accompanied by an increase in votes for the LDP.

The ruling Party was once more in control of all Diet committees, and therefore had regained its former power over legislation. After intensive intra-Party negotiations Suzuki Zenkō, who had inherited the leadership of the Ōhira faction, became party President and thus Prime Minister.

The emergence of a new conservative Government enjoying a comfortable majority in both Houses of the Diet opened up the possibility of a more forceful policy-making style than had prevailed in the recent past. By early 1981 it was too early to say with certainty whether the Suzuki Government would pioneer new policy directions amounting to a fundamental change of direction. At the time of writing much of its policy appeared to be essentially an extension of the approach undertaken by its predecessor. In economic policy it was signalling a determination to tackle the problem of budgetary deficit, by increasing taxation if necessary. Statements by some Cabinet ministers critical of the Constitution and some outspoken remarks by the retiring Chief of Staff of the Self-Defence Forces in February 1981 prompted an outcry from the JSP and other Opposition groups. Defence spending was increased in the 1981 budget, but not to the extent suggested by the Suzuki Government soon after it took office. The JSP was right to point out that the Constitution had hardly been an issue at all during the *hakuchū* period. On the other hand, statements by the Prime Minister that the Government had no intention of revising the Constitution suggested that from his essentially moderate standpoint he preferred not to let the issue get out of hand. In any case the state of Government finances was such that defence was competing with a range of other powerful interests for a share of a financial cake whose size was being strictly controlled. This situation seemed unlikely to change until and unless the domestic defence industry became powerful enough to compete on equal terms with the other major institutional interest groups.

As the new decade began to unfold the main potential threat to the Prime Minister was likely to come, as for his predecessors, from rival combinations of factions within his own party. The political situation as a whole, however, was markedly more pluralistic than it had been a decade earlier, and the large size of the LDP majority merely served to make less evident for the time being the plethora of pressures and counter-pressures active throughout the political scene.

6 The National Diet and Parliamentary Elections

Although Japan has had what could strictly be called a parliamentary system of government only since the Occupation, she has had a Parliament since 1890, and the traditional nature of the institution has no doubt contributed to its ready acceptance in the postwar period. As should be clear however from previous chapters, parliamentary government in Japan is a somewhat idiosyncratic blend of various influences. The prewar Constitution was strongly German in its inspiration, and German models and examples still abound in the writings of at least the older generation of postwar constitutional lawyers. The fundamental relationships between emperor, prime minister, Cabinet, Parliament and the bureaucracy are highly reminiscent of British arrangements, while the Diet committee system and certain other features are American-inspired. Finally, habits of working which reflect Japanese social norms, and a hegemonic party system, have put their stamp on the functioning of these institutions in practice.

The key position which the National Diet was expected to occupy in the whole system of government was squarely presented in article 41 of the 1947 Constitution, where it was given the title of 'highest organ of state power', and 'sole law-making authority of the State'. There are two Houses, the House of Representatives or Lower House and the House of Councillors or Upper House.[1] Both Houses are elected (whereas the prewar Upper House, the House of Peers, had an appointed membership), and 'representative of all the people',[2] a phrase which can be interpreted to mean 'elected by universal suffrage'. The term of the Lower House is four years, although it can be ended prematurely by dissolution,[3] and its membership has risen from 464 at the time of the 1946 election to 511 at the time of the election of 1980. The term in office of members of the Upper House is six years, with half the membership being elected every three years.[4] Its membership remained at 250 throughout the postwar period, but rose to 252 with the return of Okinawa prefecture to Japanese sovereignty in May 1972. Nobody can be a member of both Houses simultaneously.[5]

Relations between the two Houses are complex, and reflect the fact that the initial (GHQ) draft of the Constitution envisaged a unicameral legislature, so that the addition of a second chamber was one of the few really significant changes which the Japanese Government of the day was able to effect in the course of its discussions with SCAP on the drafting of a new Constitution. Nevertheless, the constitutional position of the House of Councillors is inferior to that of the House of Representatives. It is widely felt in Japan that this inferiority has not been compensated for either by speciality of function[6] or by significant difference in the quality or background of its members.[7]

On a number of matters the two Houses have identical powers.[8] Each independently judges disputes about the qualifications of its members,[9] keeps and publishes records of its proceedings,[10] selects its president (speaker) and other officials,[11] establishes its own rules and punishes its own members,[12] receives petitions[13] and conducts 'investigations in relation to government'[14] (a power which is the basis of the committee system of each House). The members of each House enjoy freedom from arrest (except in cases provided by law) while the Diet is in session,[15] and freedom from liability outside the House for speeches, debates or votes cast inside the House.[16] There is also no difference in the rights of the two Houses concerning revision of the Constitution.[17]

On the other hand, only the House of Representatives has the power to force a Cabinet resignation by passing a non-confidence resolution (or rejecting a confidence resolution).[18] Also, dissolution of the House of Representatives means that the House of Councillors must be closed as well,[19] whereas the latter operates on the basis of fixed terms and cannot be dissolved prematurely.

The House of Councillors possesses one attribute which is peculiar to it, namely that it may be convoked by Cabinet in emergency session in a time of national emergency. The Lower

House, however, has to agree to measures taken by such a session within ten days after the opening of the next Diet session, or they become null and void.[20]

The constitutional inferiority of the House of Councillors is manifest in the restricted nature of its power to reject or delay the passage of legislation originating in the House of Representatives. In the case of ordinary bills, where the Upper House differs from the Lower House (in other words, when it rejects or amends the proposed legislation), the bill nevertheless becomes law if passed a second time by the Lower House by a two-thirds majority of the members present.[21]

On the other hand, in such a case another road is open to the House of Representatives, namely to call for a joint committee of both Houses to resolve the issue.[22] In order to avoid the possibility of indefinite delay by the House of Councillors, a bill on which that House fails to take action within sixty days of its receipt from the Lower House (time in recess excepted) may be regarded by the Lower House as having been rejected by the Upper.[23]

Since 1955 (but excepting to some extent the latter half of the 1970s), these provisions have been largely academic, because the Liberal Democratic Party has controlled both Houses and has maintained tight party discipline, at least so far as Diet voting is concerned. If, however, the LDP were to lose control of the House of Councillors, the possibility of frequent clashes between the two Houses would become considerable. The provisions of article 59 of the Constitution would be activated (as they were at times in the immediate postwar years), and the Opposition would have found a new channel through which to check (or obstruct) government legislation.

In the case of matters regarded as of outstanding importance, namely the budget, treaties and the designation of a new prime minister, the supremacy of the House of Representatives is more marked than with ordinary bills. The relationship between the two Houses is also much simpler. The annual budget, unlike other bills, must first be submitted to the House of Representatives.[24] In the case of a disagreement between the two Houses, reference of the budget to a joint committee is mandatory (not voluntary, as is the case with ordinary bills); but if the House of Councillors has taken no action within thirty days the decision of the House of Representatives is considered the decision of the Diet.[25] Hitherto, the budget has never been referred to a joint committee, although in 1954 the Upper House failed to take action and the budget automatically came into force after thirty days.[26]

Treaties fall under the same provisions as the budget, except that a treaty may be submitted first to the Upper House (although this is very unusual).[27] It will be recalled that in the case of the revised Mutual Security Treaty in 1960 the Opposition was able to delay passage of the Treaty in the Upper House until it automatically received Diet ratification thirty days after being forced through the Lower House on 19 May.[28]

The rules are similar for the designation of a prime minister, except that the decision of the House of Representatives becomes the decision of the Diet if there is no agreement between the two Houses or if the House of Councillors fails to make designation within a mere ten days of action by the House of Representatives.[29] There was one instance, in February 1948, where the composition of the two Houses was sufficiently different to produce different candidates from each. After a joint committee had failed to agree and ten days had elapsed, the candidate of the Lower House, Ashida, prevailed over the candidate of the Upper House, Yoshida, and became Prime Minister.

While the House of Councillors is potentially a forum which the Opposition could use to good effect in checking legislation with which it disagrees, hitherto one of the most powerful weapons at the disposal of the Opposition has been the rigidity of the Diet timetable. The 1960 crisis is only one of many instances in which the Government has been gravely embarrassed by Opposition filibustering, premised upon the Government's lack of control over the timetable of the Diet.

Provision is made for three types of Diet session (apart from the emergency session of the House of Councillors mentioned above). The first is the ordinary or regular session, which is held once every year.[30] This session is normally convoked in mid-December, and lasts for 150 days.[31] Since the revision of the Diet Law in 1955 it may be extended once only, although previously an indefinite number of extensions was permitted.[32] The second is the extraordinary session, which may be called by the Cabinet, or must be held when a quarter or more of the total members of either House makes the demand.[33] The third is the special session, called in fulfilment of the constitutional provision that after a Lower House dissolution, a Lower House general election must be held within forty days, and the Diet must be convoked within thirty days of the date of the election.[34] Both extraordinary and special sessions may now be extended up to twice;[35] and with all three types of session, if there is disagreement between the two Houses on, say, the length of extension, the House of Representatives prevails.[36]

The importance of the length of session is considerable because of the principle in the Diet Law that: 'Any matter not decided during a session shall not be carried over to the following session', except that in certain circumstances Diet committees can continue their deliberations into the adjournment, and matters entrusted to them can then be carried on into the next session.[37] For the most part, however, the Government is under strong pressure to complete its legislative programme by the end of the session (extensions included), and this task is not made any easier for it by the fact that the order in which legislation is to be discussed is in the hands of the Steering Committee of each House. Although in present circumstances the Liberal Democrats control the chairmanship and a majority of the membership of the Steering Committee, it provides another forum in which delaying tactics can be applied.

Indeed, the Opposition parties have a variety of means at their disposal to delay the passage of legislation,[38] so that the length of a particular session tends to assume magnified importance. If, when the end of a session is approaching, the Opposition is attempting to talk out, or otherwise delay, some contentious piece of legislation, the Government may decide to modify it in a direction favourable to the Opposition. If, on the other hand, the Government assumes an 'intransigent' position, the Opposition parties may decide to boycott the remainder of the session. The Government is then faced with a choice between bargaining with the parties in an effort to get them to resume their seats in the Diet, or brazening it out and pushing the legislation through unilaterally. Experience on a number of occasions has shown that the latter course carries with it the danger of precipitating a serious political crisis, with the Government standing accused of having 'broken consensus', or of having exercised the 'tyranny of the majority'. It is uncertain whether this kind of accusation represents primarily a genuine cultural norm, or primarily an Opposition strategy, but it can present the Government, despite its unchallenged majority, with a serious and embarrassing threat. On the other hand, in recent years the Government has rarely had to abandon a major piece of legislation, as happened with Kishi's Police Bill in 1958. Tanaka's abandonment of his electoral legislation in May 1973 was in this sense an unusual and stunning reverse.

One indication of the extent to which Cabinet has established its supremacy over the Diet is the fact that, since the establishment of the LDP in 1955, a variant of the British pattern has emerged in the sponsoring of bills. Whereas a bill may be sponsored by private members in either House, most bills are now proposed by Cabinet. While private members' bills are not uncommon, they frequently originate in a government ministry, which has been successful in finding a Diet member prepared to pilot a piece of legislation through the House.

In contrast, the most 'American' feature of the operation of the national Diet is its system of standing and special committees. Based on the constitutional right of each House to 'conduct investigations in relation to government',[39] the system replaces the prewar practice of taking bills through three successive readings on the floor of the House. Bills initiated by individual Diet members, by Cabinet or referred from the other House are normally sent straight to the appropriate committee. The committee has the power of 'killing' any bill referred to it (with the exception of bills transmitted from the other House), but it is a comparatively simple matter to pull a bill out of committee. If, within seven days of a decision by the committee not to submit a bill to the plenary session, its release is demanded by twenty or more members of the House, then it must be submitted to the plenary session.[40] In this respect, at least, the power of Japanese Diet committees is much less than that of their American counterparts, the committees of Congress.

Initially, there were as many as twenty standing committees of each House. In 1955 however the number was reduced to sixteen, which is the present number. All Diet members are obliged to belong to at least one standing committee. Before the

1955 revision of the Diet Law, Diet members were not allowed to belong to more than two standing committees, and if they belonged to two, the second had to be chosen from a restricted list. Since 1955 however this restriction has not applied, and the speaker, deputy speaker, prime minister, ministers and other Cabinet officials are no longer obliged to belong to any committees.[41] Membership of standing committees and special committees is allocated in proportion to party strengths in the House, with the Steering Committee being the arbiter.[42] Chairmen of standing committees are formally elected from the committee membership by a vote of the plenary session,[43] but in practice they are selected by the speaker according to the distribution of party strengths in each committee.[44] Chairmen of special committees, on the other hand, are elected by the committees themselves from among their members, not necessarily according to relative strengths.[45]

The following is a list of the standing committees of each House, with the number of members in each (as of January 1980):[46]

Table 1
Standing Committees of the House of Representatives

Name of Committee	*Lower House Committee*	*Upper House Committee*
Cabinet Committee	30	20
Local Administration Committee	30	20
Judicial Affairs Committee	30	20
Foreign Affairs Committee	30	20
Finance Committee	40	25
Education Committee	30	20
Social and Labour Committee	40	21
Agriculture, Forestry and Fisheries Committee	40	25
Commerce and Industry Committee	40	21
Transport Committee	30	20
Communications Committee	30	20
Construction Committee	30	20
Budget Committee	50	45
Audit Committee	25	30
House Management (Steering) Committee	25	25
Discipline Committee	20	10

Until the elections of 1974 for the Upper House and 1976 for the Lower House, the LDP provided the chairman and a majority of the members of each committee. Following those elections, however, it faced a less favourable situation. Since membership of committees was allocated to each party on the principle of proportionality to its House membership, the LDP lost undisputed control of many committees. In January 1980, for example, the LDP provided 261 members, and the Opposition parties 257 members, of the standing committees of the House of Representatives (there were also 2 vacancies). Of the 16 standing committees, the LDP held a majority in 4, the LDP and Opposition parties had equal numbers in 10, and the Opposition parties were in a majority in 2. A committee chairman, however, could not vote, and since the LDP continued to provide a majority of committee chairmanships (though it no longer monopolized them), effective committee control in the above example was distributed in the following way: LDP: 6; equal numbers: 2; Opposition: 8. The committees over which LDP control was lost included the key Cabinet, foreign affairs and budget committees. A similar calculation for the House of Councillors in January 1980 yields the following figures: LDP: 6; equal numbers: 6; Opposition: 4. In practice, of course the LDP could often exploit differences in the Opposition ranks to make its view prevail, but when the Opposition was united it possessed a powerful weapon against the LDP. After the double elections of June 1980 the LDP regained control of all standing committees of both Houses.

In 1980 the special committees of the House of Representatives covered the following areas: disaster policy (46 members); revision of the public election law (25 members); science and technology (25 members); coal policy (25 members); environmental pollution policy (25 members); prices policy and related problems (25 members); road safety policy (25 members); Okinawa and northern territories policy (25 members); aircraft import investigation (30 members). The House of Councillors had special committees on the same topics except that instead of a coal policy committee there was a committee on energy, and instead of pollution and road safety committees there was a single committee on pollution and traffic. Taking the special committees of both Houses together, the LDP in January 1980 held six chairmanships and controlled 11 committees, while the Opposition parties taken together held 11 chairmanships and controlled 3 committees, leaving 3 with equal numbers.[47]

The committees of each House are much the most important forum for parliamentary debate. This is particularly true of the Lower House standing committees on the budget and on foreign affairs, where debates of major national importance take place. As with Congress committees in the United States, the Japanese Diet committees are empowered to hold public hearings 'in order to hear the views of interested parties or persons of learning and experience'.[48] Whereas in the United States, however, government officials have no right to speak on the floor of Congress, but appear before Congress committees in a more privileged capacity than expert and interested witnesses, in Japan, with a fusion-of-powers system, ministers of state have a right to speak both in plenary session and in committee. They also appear frequently at the request of a particular committee, in order to answer interpellations on particular bills for which they are responsible. This activity may take up a good deal of a minister's time.[49] It would be difficult for a Japanese Cabinet minister to emulate some members of President Nixon's Cabinet and White House staff during his first term, who refused to appear before certain Congressional committees.

In this respect, the major standing committees in particular constitute a valuable forum for the Opposition to attack and embarrass the Government, and incidentally to gain wide publicity for so doing.[50] During the period when some committees were not controlled by the LDP, they were used by the Opposition to block legislation. The Government was forced into complex bargains and deals with the Opposition in order to salvage what it could of its legislative programme. At the same time, the majority of the committees, and particularly the more specialist ones, spend much of their time engaged in the more mundane activities of detailed legislative investigation. Sometimes, indeed, a committee view comes to overlay party political differences which divide the members.

They are also frequently targets of pressure group activity having relatively little to do with party politics as such. Moreover, a considerable number of former government bureaucrats who are Liberal Democratic Diet members gravitate towards the Diet committee most relevant to their former ministry, and maintain liaison with their former colleagues. In so doing they may be instrumental in facilitating the passage through their committee of legislation which, having originated in their former ministry, has been referred to the Diet committee by Cabinet. In this respect, therefore, some Diet committees may tend to reinforce the influence of the bureaucracy as the most important centre of successful policy initiation.[51]

What stands out most clearly in this discussion of the National Diet is that, after the emergence in the 1950s of a strong 'party of government', able to retain a majority in both Houses, Cabinet generally kept a tight hold over the Diet. The Opposition exploited a number of techniques whereby it could embarrass the Government, and with some exceptions the Government was prudent enough not to provoke the Opposition too far. The elections of the mid-1970s, however, created a different and more pluralistic politics because of the Opposition's new-found power within the committee system. Nevertheless, the Opposition parties were badly fragmented and their capacity to take advantage of the opportunities offered to them by this situation was limited. In any case the period of divided committee control came to an end in June 1980. The style of politics that would emerge if the Liberal Democrats were ever to lose their majority in the House of Representatives (or even in the House of Councillors, though this would be more serious for them) would differ markedly from any experienced hitherto, and parts of the Constitution which have become virtual dead letters might have to be reactivated. The only precedents are to be found in the early postwar years, when Japanese politics were fluid and unsettled for a variety of reasons, some of which however need not necessarily recur.

Any estimate of the future pattern of parliamentary politics must take account of the electoral system, and the patterns of electoral behaviour which have emerged in the postwar period. The electoral system has a number of defects which are extremely hard to remove, and electoral behaviour has shown a degree of stability for which it is difficult to find parallels in other advanced countries. The Liberal Democrats have greatly benefited from this electoral stability, but they have also taken shrewd advantage of the gross over-weighting of rural electorates.

National elections have been held regularly in Japan since July 1890, but it was not until after the Second World War that universal suffrage for men and women over twenty years of age was introduced. The size of the electorate grew from less than half a million in 1890 to over fourteen million in the late 1930s, jumped to nearly thirty-seven million in 1946, and was over eighty million in 1980.

The electoral law which governs elections for both Houses of the National Diet, as well as for governors and assemblies of prefectures, mayors and assemblies of cities, towns and villages, is the Public Offices Election Law.[52] The purpose of the law given in article 1 is 'to establish an electoral system . . . based on the spirit of the Japanese Constitution, to ensure that these elections are conducted fairly and properly according to the freely expressed will of the electors, and thus to aim at the healthy growth of democratic politics'. In many ways, there is in Japan today a reasonable approximation to this ideal, but as we shall see, some intractable problems have arisen.

Any citizen[53] having reached the age of twenty may vote after three months' residence in the constituency (there are some exemptions from this limitation), provided that he or she is not an 'incompetent' or serving a prison sentence. Twenty-five is the minimum age for candidacy to all the offices covered by the Election Law, except for membership of the House of Councillors and prefectural governorships, where it is thirty.[54] Voting is not compulsory.

The system of election for the 511 seats of the House of Representatives is an unusual one, where each voter casts a single, non-transferable vote in a multi-member constituency.[55] Of the 129 constituencies throughout the country, 47 elect 3 members, 41 elect 4 members, 41 elect 5 members and 1 (the Amami Islands) elects only 1 member. Since each voter has one single vote, it is not a preferential voting system as in Australia; nor is it, strictly speaking, a form of proportional representation, although it is more favourable to small parties than the British system of voting.

The procedure is that the voter has to write the name of the candidate of his choice on the voting paper, and this puts the onus on the voter to find out beforehand who the candidates are. The three- to five-member constituency system is known as the 'medium' constituency system, to distinguish it from the 'large' constituency system which operated for a period before 1925 and in the general election of 1946. Because of problems with the 'medium' system, there has been a considerable support for a 'small' (i.e. single-member) constituency system on the British model, but this is opposed by the smaller parties (which would be virtually wiped out) and by many Liberal Democrats who would expect to lose their present seats.

The Election System Deliberation Commission (Senkyo Seido Shingikai), which has met regularly over several years, has proposed various combinations of 'small' constituencies and constituencies operating on the principle of proportional representation.

In April 1973 Tanaka proposed a radical revision of the electoral system for the House of Representatives, substituting single-member constituencies for the multi-member constituencies, with a proportion of candidates also to be elected by proportional representation. Most commentators agreed that the reform would have increased the representation of the LDP against the four Opposition parties, and might well have provided it with the two-thirds majority necessary to override rejection of its bills by the House of Councillors. The bill caused major disruption in the Diet, and against an intransigent and foronce united Opposition, the Government decided to let it drop.

The problems to which the 'medium' system gives rise for political parties may be illustrated by the example of Shizuoka no. 2 constituency for the three successive elections of 1976, 1979 and 1980. The results were as shown in tables 2, 3 and 4. From these tables it can be seen that for the smaller parties the system was uncomplicated: either they enjoyed enough support in the constituency or they did not. The Communists persisted in putting forward a candidate at each election in what for them was a hopeless constituency as part of a national policy of developing party organization throughout the country. For the Kōmeitō the constituency was marginal in that its candidate was successful in one election out of the three. The votes it obtained in 1979 would not have been enough to have its candidate elected in 1980. The Democratic Socialists had sufficient votes to return their candidate comfortably at each election, even though his order of placement varied from first to fifth.

Table 2
House of Representatives Election 1976: Shizuoka no. 2 Constituency

(Elected)	WATANABE, R.	Democratic Socialist	97,968
(Elected)	KURIHARA, Y.	Liberal Democrat	86,612
(Elected)	SAITŌ, S.	Liberal Democrat	80,133
(Elected)	WATANABE, Y.	Socialist	74,761
(Elected)	KOJIMA, S.	Liberal Democrat	72,390
(Not Elected)	TAKAHASHI, S.	Kōmeitō	70,569
(Not Elected)	KIBE, Y.	Liberal Democrat	69,106
(Not Elected)	KATSUMATA, S.	Socialist	59,368
(Not Elected)	YAMADA, Y.	Communist	22,339

Table 3
House of Representatives Election 1979: Shizuoka no. 2 Constituency

(Elected)	SAITŌ, S.	Liberal Democrat	100,381
(Elected)	KATSUMATA, S.	Socialist	90,268
(Elected)	WATANABE, R.	Democratic Socialist	78,229
(Elected)	TAKAHASHI, S.	Kōmeitō	77,787
(Elected)	KURIHARA, Y.	Liberal Democrat	72,490
(Not Elected)	KIBE, Y.	Liberal Democrat	68,296
(Not Elected)	KOJIMA, S.	Liberal Democrat	67,032
(Not Elected)	WATANABE, Y.	Socialist	49,339
(Not Elected)	TSURUTANI, T.	Communist	14,118

Table 4
House of Representatives Election 1980: Shizuoka no. 2 Constituency

(Elected)	KATSUMATA, S.	Socialist	103,152
(Elected)	SAITŌ, S.	Liberal Democrat	95,195
(Elected)	KURIHARA, Y.	Liberal Democrat	93,985
(Elected)	KIBE, Y.	Liberal Democrat	89,838
(Elected)	WATANABE, R.	Democratic Socialist	84,218
(Not Elected)	TAKAHASHI, S.	Kōmeitō	75,829
(Not Elected)	KOJIMA, S.	Independent	75,391
(Not Elected)	TSURUTANI, T.	Communist	18,316

The situation facing the Japan Socialist Party was more tricky. When it put forward only one candidate, as in 1980, he was elected with many more votes than were required, but when it attempted to elect two candidates, as it did in 1976 and 1979, its votes proved insufficient. Even if both candidates had managed to divide the votes about equally between them (which was not the case in either election), there would not have been enough to have both elected. An interesting feature of this particular example is that the two Socialists were plainly competing with each other as much as with candidates of other parties, and indeed each relied on substantially separate organizational support. After a poor showing in 1976, Katsumata, a former national Chairman of the Party, made a successful bid in 1979 to regain the seat he had lost in the previous election to Watanabe Yoshio, who had the backing of the national public servants' union, of which he was local branch Chairman. When Watanabe failed to stand for election in 1980, it seems from the figures that only a small proportion of his support flowed to Katsumata.

The Liberal Democrats could normally expect to elect three of the five members in this constituency. They were able to do so in 1976 (though Kojima's margin was less than comfortable), but in 1979 two of their four candidates failed to be elected. The reason, however, lies not so much in their failure to win enough votes, since their proportion of the total vote was actually higher than in 1976. In 1979 too many Liberal Democratic votes were wasted on the party's most popular candidate, Saitō; and its fourth-ranking candidate, Kojima, while losing his seat, nevertheless polled well enough to spoil the chances of the third Liberal Democrat, Kibe. As a result, Kojima was refused endorsement by the LDP for the 1980 elections, in order that a fourth candidate should not split the vote. Despite this, he stood as an Independent, and showed that he commanded enough personal support to win more votes than in 1979, although he was not elected. Votes for the three remaining Liberal Democrats were more evenly distributed than in 1979, and all were returned. Ironically, an exactly even distribution of the vote in 1980 between Saitō, Kurihara, Kibe and Kojima would have elected all of them. (This would not have been the case in 1979.)

Thus, despite these complexities, the only actual change in

the distribution of the seats between the parties over the three elections was that in 1979 the Kōmeitō candidate replaced one of the Liberal Democrats, to be replaced in his turn by a Liberal Democrat in 1980 (see table 5). The internal struggle, however, between Kibe and Kojima in the LDP for the third LDP seat, and between Katsumata and Watanabe for the only seat the JSP could win, were crucial features of the politics of the constituency. As can be seen from table 6, in terms of seat distribution between conservatives and progressives, electoral justice was done within very broad limits, though the LDP arguably won a seat more than it deserved in 1976.

Table 5
House of Representatives Elections 1976, 1979 and 1980: Votes per Party and Number of Seats, Shizuoka no. 2 Constituency

Party	*Votes per Party* 1976	1979	1980	*Seats per Party* 1976	1979	1980
Liberal Democrats	308,241	308,199	279,018	3	2	3
Socialists	134,129	139,607	103,152	1	1	1
Democratic Socialists	97,968	78,229	84,218	1	1	1
Kōmeitō	70,569	77,787	75,829	0	1	0
Communists	22,339	14,118	18,316	0	0	0
Independents	—	—	75,391	—	—	0
Total vote	633,246	617,940	635,924			

Table 6
House of Representatives Elections 1976, 1979 and 1980: Votes per Party Grouping and Number of Seats, Shizuoka no. 2 Constituency

Party Grouping	*Votes per Party Grouping* 1976	1979	1980	*Seats* 1976	1979	1980
Conservatives (LDP plus Independents)	308,241	308,199	354,409	3	2	3
Progressives (All other parties)	325,005	309,741	281,515	2	3	2

A crucial effect of the system of election for the House of Representatives is that it reinforces factional conflict within the LDP (and to a lesser extent within the JSP; the other parties rarely put up more than one candidate per constituency). For electoral purposes it is the *kōenkai* (personal support groups) of individual candidates, and more generally their networks of personal connections, which drum up support for those candidates, especially outside the big city areas.[56] The voting pull of individual candidates remains a most important (if not *the* most important) factor in bringing out the vote. This makes it difficult, however, for the central party organization or local branches to exercise adequate control over candidates, and less than optimal strategies can and do occur.

The House of Councillors is elected on a different system. Of its 252 members, 100 are elected from a 'national' constituency (the whole nation considered as one constituency) and 152 (150 before the reversion of Okinawa) from 'large' multi-member constituencies which are coincident with the prefectures. As we have seen, the term of Councillors is six years, but elections are staggered, with half the seats (50 from the national constituency and 76 from the prefectural constituencies) being contested every three years. The voter, just as when he is voting in House of Representatives elections, has a non-transferable vote, but because there are two constituencies involved (the national and the prefectural), he in fact has two votes, and must vote for different candidates in each. As of early 1981 the Suzuki Government was actively considering the introduction of proportional representation for the national constituency.

The original purpose of this somewhat cumbersome arrangement was to attract to the House of Councillors 'men [and women] of talent', not necessarily connected with party machines, who would be able to bring a different approach to political deliberation. In recent Upper House elections, however, the term 'talent candidates' has come to mean national celebrities, such as television personalities, Olympic sportsmen and the like, some of whom by virtue of their popular appeal are able to obtain the massive vote throughout the country necessary for election in the national constituency. The national constituency also favours those with large national organizations, such as trade unions and religious groups, behind them. Such backing is often used to supplement party affiliation.[57]

One of the most criticized aspects of Japanese electoral procedure is the extent and nature of restrictions imposed upon pre-election campaigning. The intention of these restrictions was largely to prevent the corruption and bribery that had characterized some prewar elections, but the present restrictions are so stringent as to be self-defeating.

Door-to-door canvassing is not permitted.[58] This is a curious and unusual provision, which nevertheless does not prevent established politicians paying visits to their supporters in their homes, or trade unions, religious groups and so on doing overt door-to-door canvassing. There must be no signature drives.[59] Publication of pre-election polls is forbidden.[60] Newspapers, nevertheless, do in fact sample public opinion and publish the results. They are usually fairly accurate in election forecasts. This is largely a reflection of the stability of voting behaviour, but it may be noted that the public opinion poll industry is highly developed, and a variety of political topics are covered assiduously.

Food and drink must not be distributed, with the exception of tea and biscuits (and lunch boxes for party workers in campaign offices);[61] nor may monetary or material handouts be made to supporters.[62] There is a whole set of regulations about donations to political parties and candidates.[63] Only one motor vehicle (alternatively one boat) and one set of loudspeakers is permitted per candidate, although candidates for the national constituency of the House of Councillors enjoy the luxury of three with which to campaign throughout Japan.[64] Campaign posters are strictly limited in number, size and location,[65] and there are quite stringent regulations about campaign speech meetings.[66] On the other hand, official bulletins giving the names, parties and personal histories of the candidates, as well as a brief statement of their views by the candidates themselves, are issued and distributed to the electors at public expense.[67] Electioneering is permitted only during the official campaign period, and the limit on campaign expenditure in a House of Representatives constituency is calculated according to the following formula:

$$\frac{\text{number of registered voters}}{\text{number of seats}} \times ¥27 + ¥9{,}700{,}000$$

For the House of Councillors national constituency there is a flat rate of ¥38,000,000 and for the prefectural constituencies of the House of Councillors a rate which varies according to size of population. In 1981 the rate for Tokyo was ¥30,000,000.

It seems that many of these regulations are honoured mainly in the breach, simply because they forbid practices that are generally accepted. Food and drink prohibitions, for instance, are very widely ignored, and the limits on campaign expenditure are usually regarded as being so low as to ensure the defeat of any candidate who is so cautious as to observe them. The police, who are placed under considerable strain by being required to enforce unrealistic regulations, do nevertheless charge several thousand politicians and their supporters at each election with breaches of the regulations, often involving alleged bribery.[68]

One quite serious effect of the restrictions is that they make it difficult for a new candidate to enter politics. The established member has his *kōenkai* and network of personal connections which operate more or less continuously between elections despite all the official restrictions. A new man, on the other hand, has to create new supporters in the constituency, something which is much more difficult to do legally than to service old ones.[69] This is the principal factor creating such a low turnover of candidates at each election. This can be seen from table 7 where it is shown that in the 1980 House of Representatives election (which may be regarded as typical) sitting members had an overwhelming advantage over both previous members trying to make a comeback and new (or previously unsuccessful) candidates. The NLC was the only exception because it tripled its small representation since the previous election.

Even more seriously, it appears that the regulations on balance inhibit the development of programmatic appeals by candidates. A barrier is placed between the voter and the candidate, whose overt electioneering activities are frequently almost confined to touring the constituency in (or on) a loudspeaker van repeating his name and asking people to vote for him. More covertly, however, he will be cultivating a personal political machine (not of course without party ramifications) in a way that may break the law but will be far harder to check than the more open forms of electioneering which are also subject to severe restrictions.

Table 7
1980 Election – House of Representatives: Number of Candidates and Number Elected

	Sitting Members		*Previous Members*		*New Candidates*		*Total*		*1979*
	Candidates	Elected	Candidates	Elected	Candidates	Elected	Candidates	Elected	Election
LDP	252	240	29	26	29	18	310	284	248
JSP	106	87	22	13	21	7	149	107	107
Kōmeitō	57	32	3	1	4	0	64	33	57
DSP	35	32	2	0	13	0	50	32	35
JCP	39	27	3	0	87	2	129	29	39
NLC	4	4	6	4	15	4	25	12	4
SDL	2	2	0	0	3	1	5	3	2
Others	0	0	1	0	41	0	42	0	0
Independent	9	6	5	2	47	3	61	11	19
Total	504	430	71	46	260	35	835	511	511

Note: Of 28 women candidates, 9 were elected, 7 for the JCP and 2 for the JSP. Of 11 candidates elected as Independents, 5 subsequently joined the LDP, 1 joined the Kōmeitō, 1 joined the DSP, and 4 Liberal Democrats (including Tanaka Kakuei), on trial on corruption charges, remained Independent.

Source: *Asahi Nenkan*, 1981, p. 232.

Table 8 (below) shows that there are now less than twice as many candidates who stand as are elected. In the case of the LDP, votes for successful candidates were nearly 85 per cent of total votes (see table 9). A candidate's deposit is now ¥1,000,000 (¥2,000,000 in the House of Councillors national constituency). This is much higher than in other countries (e.g. Australia), but it is not the main barrier to greater electoral competition. If 'fringe' candidates are left out of account, the number of serious but unsuccessful candidates is remarkably low, and this is probably in large part a result of the innate electoral advantage possessed by the sitting member, as well as his easier access to electoral funds.

Table 8
House of Representatives Elections 1947–80. Number of Candidates and Voting Turnout

Date	*Number of Seats*	*Total Number of Candidates*	*Turnout (%)*	*Men*	*Women*
25/ 4/47	466	1,590	67·95	74·87	61·60
23/ 1/49	466	1,364	74·04	80·74	67·95
1/10/52	466	1,242	76·43	80·46	72·76
19/ 4/53	466	1,027	74·22	78·35	70·44
27/ 2/55	467	1,017	75·84	79·95	72·06
22/ 5/58	467	951	76·99	79·79	74·42
20/11/60	467	940	73·51	76·00	71·22
21/11/63	467	917	71·14	72·36	70·02
29/ 1/67	486	917	73·99	74·75	73·28
27/12/69	486	945	68·51	67·85	69·12
10/12/72	491	895	71·76	71·01	72·46
5/12/76	511	899	73·45	72·81	74·05
7/10/79	511	891	68·01	67·42	68·56
22/ 6/80	511	835	74·57	73·72	75·36

Sources: *Asahi Nenkan*, 1980, p. 267.
Asahi Shimbun, 9 October 1979.
Ibid., 25 June 1980.
Asahi Nenkan, 1981, p. 232.

Table 8 also shows that since the 1969 election the voting turnout among women has been slightly higher than that of men. Women, however, are rarely successful as candidates. Only 28 women stood as candidates for the Lower House in the 1980 elections, and of these 9 were elected (7 Communists and

2 Socialists). The JCP is the only Party to put forward numbers of women in winnable seats, so that the number of women in the Lower House has tended to fluctuate with the changing fortunes of that Party. They do a little better in the Upper House national constituency, where national fame can be translated into votes. In the 1980 House of Councillors elections the veteran human rights and anti-corruption campaigner Miss Ichikawa Fusae topped the poll with 2,784,998 votes, and 4 women were among the 7 highest vote-getters. Had their votes been more evenly distributed among women candidates as a whole, there could have been more women in the Upper House than the 9 actually elected (6 for the national constituency, and 3 for prefectural constituencies).

Table 9
House of Representatives Election 1980: Relation of Votes to Seats, and Vote Wastage

Party	*A*	*B* (%)	*C* (%)	*D*	*E* (%)
LDP	28,262,441	47·9	56·0	284	94·9
JSP	11,400,747	19·3	20·9	107	76·1
Kōmeitō	5,329,942	9·0	6·5	33	56·5
DSP	3,896,728	6·6	6·3	32	73·7
JCP	5,803,613	9·8	5·7	29	45·9
NLC	1,766,296	3·0	2·3	12	75·4
SDL	402,832	0·7	0·2	3	90·7
Others	109,168	0·2	0·0	0	0·0
Independent	2,056,967	3·5	2·2	11	48·4
Total	59,028,834	100·0	100·0	511	79·2

Key
A – Total vote
B – Percentage of total vote
C – Percentage of total seats
D – Number of seats
E – Votes for successful candidates as percentage of total votes

Perhaps the most serious defect of the Election Law is its lack of provisions for the regular redrawing of electoral boundaries. From table 10 (column *A*) it can be seen that the value of a vote in the most populous constituency at the time of the 1979 Lower House general election was 3·9 times less than that in the least populous constituency. (There is a similar inequality in the value of votes in the House of Councillors prefectural constituencies.)

This is largely accounted for by the movement of population from the countryside into the cities which has taken place since the end of the war. The present constituencies were drawn up at a time when the urban population was unusually depleted by wartime destruction, and since then a major shift in population has taken place, both into the cities themselves and into new suburbs in their formerly rural environs. Despite the efforts of the Election System Deliberation Commission, it has proved extremely difficult for political reasons to rectify the resultant gerrymander, except that nineteen new seats were added in urban and suburban areas before the 1967 Lower House general elections and a further twenty in time for the elections conducted in 1976. In December 1980 a judge of the Tokyo High Court held that when the discrepancy in the value of a vote in different constituencies substantially exceeded a two-to-one ratio, the regulations were in breach of article 14 of the Constitution, which is concerned with equality before the law. He nevertheless dismissed the case before him, which had cited the discrepancy between Chiba no. 4 and ten other urban constituencies on the one hand, and Hyōgo no. 5 on the other, in a judgment based on the circumstances of the case.[70]

In table 10 the number of valid votes per seat has also been tabulated (column *B*), together with percentage voter turnout (column *C*). From this it can readily be seen that there is a smaller spread, when valid votes per seat are counted, than when one considers the number of electors per seat. In 1979 the discrepancy between Hokkaidō no. 1 (largely the city of Sapporo), where the highest number of votes per seat was cast, and Hyōgo no. 5 (a depopulated rural area in Kansai), where the smallest number was cast, was only 2·6 times, as against a 3·9 times discrepancy recorded in column *A*. (Both figures represent an improvement on the figures for the 1969 elections, which were, respectively, 3·1 and 4·3, but uncorrected imbalance of population is still much greater than that permitted by the electoral laws of most parliamentary democracies.) The table shows that there is, very roughly, an inverse relationship between the size of population of a constituency and the turnout of voters at the polls. Since the addition of a further twenty seats before the 1976 elections, some of the congested urban constituencies in Tokyo, Ōsaka, Kanagawa (which includes the

Kawasaki–Yokohama industrial belt), Aichi (which includes the Nagoya conurbation), and so on have slipped a little further down the scale. Those which now fall within the top ten include a number which take in rapidly growing outer surburban areas of the largest cities. A good example is Tokyo no. 11, which includes the fast-developing outer western commuter belt of Hachiōji, Fuchū, Hino and Chōfu. Those at the bottom end of the scale are nearly all rural constituencies in the more remote and sometimes depopulated northern, southwestern and Japan Sea coastal parts of the country.

Whereas in crowded urban constituencies the voting turnout runs at only 50 or 60 per cent (though it went higher than this in the 1980 double elections), in sparsely inhabited rural areas it is mostly in the 70 or 80 per cent range. This does not indicate greater individual political awareness in the countryside, but rather the persistence of traditional inter-personal and group ties which can be utilized for political purposes. The act of voting is still widely regarded as an expression of local group solidarity rather than as an individual act of choice. This is not, of course, to say that it is irrational in terms of the interests of the individual who is a member of the local community. Perhaps the main reason why elections are so expensive for candidates is that local communities tend to regard local Diet members as sources of material benefaction for local interests. A candidate who is not prepared to spend lavishly in his electorate is unlikely to be regarded with favour by his electors. More broadly, however, choice of party is also generally governed by a pragmatic sense of local – as well as class and occupational – interest.

Conversely the lower urban voter turnout appears to represent not so much a less finely tuned political awareness as a substantial breakdown of traditional ties of group solidarity in an urban or suburban setting. But whereas the old motivations and pressures which brought people to the polling booth on election day have weakened with the move to the cities, the parties and their candidates have not succeeded in generating motivations among electors that would bring them to the polls in the numbers that are usual in rural electorates. Comparisons, however, with voting turnout rates in advanced Western countries suggest that it is Japan's high rural rates that are exceptional

Table 10
House of Representatives Elections October 1979: Constituencies in Descending Order of Electors on Roll per Seat (first 10 and last 10 only)

Constituency	*A*	*B*	*C* (%)	*D*	*E*
Chiba 4	314,004	164,643	52·43	A	c
Kanagawa 3	295,878	171,817	58·07	A	c
Saitama 2	284,041	171,610	60·42	B	b
Tokyo 11	274,927	154,176	56·08	A	b
Hokkaidō 1	269,752	180,897	67·06	A	b
Chiba 1	268,071	141,751	52·88	A	b
Ōsaka 3	265,971	162,951	61·27	A	b
Kanagawa 4	264,372	143,453	54·26	A	b
Saitama 4	261,447	172,013	65·79	C	e
Ōsaka 5	259,254	161,151	62·16	A	b
Miyazaki 2	100,848	79,957	79·29	E	f
Yamagata 2	100,271	81,184	80·96	E	f
Nagano 3	99,509	86,484	86·91	C	e
Niigata 4	98,509	85,185	86·47	D	f
Niigata 2	98,499	80,563	81·79	D	f
Akita 2	94,612	76,946	81·33	E	f
Ehime 3	91,400	77,584	84·88	E	f
Ishikawa 2	88,062	70,967	80·59	C	e
Kagoshima 3	84,869	71,021	83·68	E	f
Hyōgo 5	81,096	70,448	86·87	D	f

Key

A – Number of electors on roll per one seat (calculated by dividing number of electors on roll in each constituency by that constituency's number of seats)

B – Number of valid votes cast per one seat (calculated by dividing number of valid votes cast in each constituency by that constituency's number of seats)

C – Voter turnout (*B* as a percentage of *A*)

D – A five-point measure of the proportion of the population engaged in primary industry:
A (urban): 0–9%
B (semi-urban): 10–19%
C (medium): 20–29%
D (semi-rural): 30–39%
E (rural): 40–59%

E – A six-point measure of population concentration:
a: 90–100%
b: 70–89%
c: 50–69%
d: 40–49%
e: 30–39%
f: 0–29%

Sources: Columns *A*, *B*, *C*, given or calculated from data in *Asahi Shimbun*, 9 October 1979. Columns *D* and *E* are from data on constituency type kindly supplied to the writer by Professor Nishihira Shigeki.

Table 11
House of Representatives Election Results, 1946–80

Election	*PP*			*LP*			*JSP*			*LFP*
10/4/46*	94 (20·3) 10,351 (18·7)			140 (30·2) 13,506 (24·4)			92 (19·8) 9,858 (17·8)			
25/4/47	*DP* 121 (26·0) 6,840 (25·0)			131 (28·1) 7,356 (26·9)			143 (30·7) 7,176 (26·2)			
23/1/49	69 (14·8) 4,798 (15·7)			*DLP* 264 (56·7) 13,420 (43·9)			48 (10·3) 4,130 (13·5)			7 (1·5) 607 (2·0)
1/10/52	*RP* 85 (18·2) 6,429 (18·2)			*LP* 240 (51·5) 16,939 (47·9)		*LSP* 54 (11·6) 3,399 (9·6)		*RSP* 57 (12·2) 4,108 (11·6)		4 (0·9) 261 (0·7)
19/4/53	76 (16·3) 6,186 (17·9)		*HLP* 35 (7·5) 3,055 (8·8)		*YLP* 199 (42·7) 13,476 (39·0)	72 (15·4) 4,517 (13·1)		66 (14·2) 4,678 (11·6)		5 (1·1) 359 (1·0)
27/2/55		*DP* 185 (39·6) 13,536 (36·6)			*LP* 112 (24·0) 9,849 (26·6)	89 (19·1) 5,683 (15·3)		67 (14·3) 5,130 (13·9)		4 (0·9) 358 (1·0)
22/5/58			*LDP* 287 (61·5) 22,977 (57·8)				*JSP* 166 (35·5) 13,094 (32·9)			
20/11/60			296 (63·4) 22,740 (57·6)			*JSP* 145 (31·0) 10,887 (27·6)			*DSP* 17 (3·7) 3,464 (8·8)	
21/11/63			283 (60·7) 22,424 (54·7)			144 (30·8) 11,907 (29·0)			23 (4·9) 3,023 (7·4)	
29/1/67			277 (57·0) 22,448 (48·8)			140 (28·8) 12,826 (27·9)			30 (6·2) 3,404 (7·4)	
27/12/69			288 (59·2) 22,382 (47·6)			90 (18·5) 10,074 (21·4)			31 (6·4) 3,637 (7·7)	
10/12/72			271 (55·2) 24,563 (46·8)			118 (24·0) 11,479 (21·9)			19 (3·9) 3,661 (7·0)	
5/12/76			249 (48·7) 23,654 (41·8)			123 (24·1) 11,713 (20·7)			29 (5·7) 3,554 (6·3)	
7/10/79			248 (48·6) 24,084 (44·6)			107 (20·9) 10,643 (19·7)			35 (6·3) 3,664 (6·8)	
22/6/80			284 (55·6) 28,262 (47·9)			107 (20·9) 11,401 (19·3)			32 (6·3) 3,897 (6·6)	

* The election system at the 1946 election differed from that of all later elections.

For each entry: number of seats (% of total seats)
number of votes, in thousands (% of total votes).

Party name abbreviations
CP: Co-operation Party (Kyōdōtō)
DP: Democratic Party (Minshutō)
DLP: Democratic Liberal Party (Minshujiyūtō, Minjitō)
DSP: Democratic Socialist Party (Minshatō)
HLP: Hatoyama Liberal Party (Jiyūtō (Hatoyama-ha))
JCP: Japan Communist Party (Nihon Kyōsantō)
JSP: Japan Socialist Party (Nihon Shakaitō)
KP: Kōmei Party (Kōmeitō)
LDP: Liberal Democratic Party (Jiyūminshutō, Jimintō)
LFP: Labour Farmer Party (Rōdōshanōminto, Rōnōtō)
LP: Liberal Party (Jiyūtō)

	JCP	*CP*		*Others*	*Indep.*	*Total*
	5 (1·1) 2,136 (3·8)	14 (3·0) 1,800 (3·2)		38 (8·2) 6,473 (11·7)	81 (17·4) 11,325 (20·4)	464 55,449
		PCP				
	4 (0·8) 1,003 (3·7)	29 (6·2) 1,916 (7·0)		25 (5·4) 1,490 (5·4)	13 (2·8) 1,581 (5·8)	466 27,362
	35 (7·5) 2,985 (9·7)	14 (3·0) 1,042 (3·4)		17 (3·6) 1,602 (5·2)	12 (2·6) 2,008 (6·6)	466 30,593
	0 (0) 897 (2·6)			7 (1·5) 949 (2·7)	19 (4·1) 2,355 (6·7)	466 35,337
	1 (0·2) 656 (1·9)			1 (0·2) 152 (0·4)	11 (2·4) 1,524 (4·4)	466 34,602
	2 (0·4) 733 (2·0)			2 (0·4) 497 (1·3)	6 (1·3) 1,229 (3·3)	467 37,015
	1 (0·2) 1,012 (2·6)			1 (0·2) 288 (0·7)	12 (2·6) 2,381 (6·0)	467 39,752
	3 (0·6) 1,157 (2·9)			1 (0·2) 142 (0·3)	9 (1·9) 2,554 (5·5)	467 41,017
	5 (1·1) 1,646 (4·0)			0 (0) 60 (0·1)	12 (2·6) 1,956 (4·8)	467 41,017
KP						
25 (5·1) 2,472 (5·4)	5 (1·0) 2,191 (4·8)			0 (0) 101 (0·2)	9 (1·9) 2,554 (5·5)	486 45,997
47 (9·7) 5,125 (10·9)	14 (2·9) 3,199 (6·8)			0 (0) 81 (0·2)	16 (3·3) 2,493 (5·3)	486 46,990
29 (5·9) 4,437 (8·5)	38 (7·7) 5,479 (10·5)			2 (0·4) 143 (0·3)	14 (2·9) 2,646 (5·0)	491 52,425
		NLC				
55 (10·8) 6,177 (10·9)	17 (3·3) 5,878 (10·4)	17 (3·3) 2,364 (4·2)		0 (0) 45 (0·1)	21 (4·1) 3,227 (5·7)	511 56,613
			SDL			
57 (11·2) 5,283 (9·8)	39 (7·6) 5,626 (10·4)	4 (0·7) 1,632 (3·0)	2 (0·4) 368 (0·7)	0 (0) 69 (0·1)	19 (3·7) 2,641 (4·9)	511 54,522
33 (6·5) 5,330 (9·0)	29 (5·7) 5,804 (9·8)	12 (2·3) 1,766 (3·0)	3 (0·5) 402 (0·7)	0 (0) 109 (0·2)	11 (2·1) 2,057 (3·5)	511 59,029

SP: Left Socialist Party (Nihon Shakaitō (Saha))
'LC: New Liberal Club (Shin Jiyū Club)
CP: People's Co-operation Party (Kokumin Kyōdōtō)
P: Progressive Party (Shimpotō)
P: Reformist Party (Kaishintō)
SP: Right Socialist Party (Nihon Shakaitō (Uha))
DL: Social Democratic League (Shakaiminshurengō, Shaminren)
LP: Yoshida Liberal Party (Jiyūtō (Yoshida-ha))

ources: *Asahi Nenkan*, 1977, p. 323; *Asahi Shimbun*, 9 October 1979; *Asahi Nenkan*, 1981, pp. 232–3.

rather than her low urban rates. Also the unusually high city turnout generated by the 1980 double elections indicates that electoral behaviour in cities and their suburbs is now quite complex and difficult to predict.

7 The Liberal Democratic Party

The formation of the Liberal Democratic Party in 1955 was a political achievement the long-term effects of which can hardly be exaggerated. The most obvious and widely welcomed effect has been the establishment of political stability over a long period: Japan has enjoyed continuous rule by a single political Party which has commanded a majority of seats in both Houses of the national Diet, though since the 1960s with a minority of the total vote. When this is contrasted with the high turnover of Cabinets and constant party manœuvring that took place in the 1920s and 1930s, or even with the rather unstable situation between 1945 and 1955, the benefits appear obvious.

On the other hand, it is widely argued that two quite unfortunate effects have resulted from the LDP monopoly of power. One is the long-term demoralization of the Opposition parties, reflected in their fragmentation and failure to win a parliamentary majority. One writer argues that it was its remoteness from power that fostered ideological extremism on the part of the Japan Socialist Party, rather than the other way round.[1] Before 1955 there was always a real possibility that the Socialists might participate in a coalition government, whereas after 1955 the only way they could hope to come to power by legal means was to defeat the LDP at the polls – a far tougher proposition given the conservative hold on the countryside. In other words, the temptation to engage in irresponsible attack rather than constructive criticism of government performance can be seen as one of the less happy results of the Opposition's long exclusion from power.

The other argument is that the Liberal Democrats have become so entrenched as the effective centre of the national power structure that they have grown self-satisfied and too much beholden to a particular set of outside interests. Here again, it is argued, the result is widespread frustration, revealed in disillusionment with the political system as such, and by a tendency towards both apathy and extremism, especially in the cities. The close liaison between the LDP, the government bureaucracy and big business, especially in the period of high economic growth from the late 1950s until 1973, was accompanied by large-scale industrial pollution, spiralling land prices and unchecked urban sprawl. These problems, however, caused such a popular outcry that the Government modified its priorities, and in any case lower economic growth rates followed the oil crisis of 1973–4. The earlier view that the Party only listens to big business also needs modifying in the light of the proven political effectiveness of many other interests, both local and national, though the linkages between the LDP and big business remain close. The problem of political corruption is one that has plagued the Party since its inception and continues to do so.

Certainly it is true that the Liberal Democratic Party has become the hub of the political system. No party could have aspired to such a role before the war. The electoral basis for this position has been remarkably free from fluctuation, although a secular decline in support for the LDP was in evidence from the 1950s until the late 1970s, when the trend was stemmed and then impressively reversed in the double elections of 1980. This may be seen from the left-hand column of table 11.

It will be observed from this table that the absolute number of votes cast for the LDP in successive elections was extraordinarily even, although since the electorate was steadily increasing in number, this represented a declining share in the total vote until 1979. In the 1976 and 1979 Lower House elections the number of seats won by the LDP actually fell below an absolute majority, but the Party attained a majority when a small number of Diet members elected as Independents subsequently joined its ranks. Thus, as was noted earlier, the LDP is able to maintain a majority of seats with a minority of the total vote, largely because of the over-weighting of rural electorates and the Party's success in minimizing vote wastage (see tables 9 and 10). Negatively, it also represents a relative failure to optimize the effectiveness of their vote by the fragmented Opposition parties.

Taking these factors into account, it is easy to understand why earlier forecasts of an inexorable decline of the LDP, leading to an eventual loss of its Lower House majority, have so far not been realized.[2] In the early 1970s it was sometimes argued that the imbalance between votes and seats across the country might begin to work against the LDP instead of for it.[3] In the elections of the 1960s and early 1970s the LDP progressively lost votes and seats in the big cities, whereas its performance in rural areas remained fairly stable at a high level. If, however, the erosion of LDP support in metropolitan areas were to be repeated in the countryside, the Party would indeed be facing a serious situation.

To lose ground in the big cities is no doubt disturbing to the Liberal Democratic leaders, as well as to those Diet members who have lost their seats, but in terms of parliamentary representation it is far less serious than a similar loss of votes in the under-populated and over-weighted rural constituencies would be. Indeed table 12 indicates that rural support for the LDP has actually been increasing both absolutely and relative to the vote in city constituencies, when one compares the three most recent Lower House elections. The table takes the elections of 1976, 1979 and 1980 (all held since the addition of 20 extra metropolitan seats), and compares the number and percentage of seats held by the LDP and Independents[4] in different types of constituency. Categories A to E are in ascending order of the proportion of the population engaged in primary industry. Categories a to f are in descending order of population concentration. A most interesting pattern emerges when the constituencies are grouped according to these two different measures. When primary industry is taken as the criterion, there is seen to be little change in any category between the 1976 and 1979 elections, while the increase in LDP seats between the 1979 and 1980 elections occurs fairly evenly as between the five categories. When, however, we take the measure of population concentration, the picture is rather different. In those constituencies with the heaviest concentration of population (exclusively the metropolitan areas of Tokyo, Yokohama, Nagoya, Kyōto and Ōsaka), the LDP and associated Independents made hardly any headway over the three elections. In those constituencies, on the other hand, with the lowest population density, conservative

Table 12

Number and Percentage of Seats Held by LDP in 1976, 1979 and 1980 House of Representatives Elections, According to Type of Constituency

	Total No. of Seats	1976				1979				1980			
		LDP Share	LDP (%)	LDP and Indep. Share	LDP and Indep. (%)	LDP Share	LDP (%)	LDP and Indep. Share	LDP and Indep. (%)	LDP Share	LDP (%)	LDP and Indep. Share	LDP and Indep. (%)
A	138	40	29·0	46	33·3	38	27·6	39	28·3	48	34·8	50	36·2
B	86	44	51·2	45	52·3	43	50·0	44	51·2	47	54·7	49	57·0
C	135	75	55·6	76	56·3	75	55·6	80	59·3	85	61·5	87	64·4
D	101	60	60·4	67	66·3	59	58·4	66	65·3	65	64·4	67	66·3
E	51	30	58·8	36	70·6	33	64·7	37	72·5	39	76·5	39	76·5
a	73	22	30·1	27	37·0	19	26·0	20	27·4	22	30·1	23	31·5
b	44	12	27·3	13	29·6	11	25·0	11	25·0	12	27·3	13	29·6
c	64	27	42·2	27	42·2	27	42·2	28	43·7	32	50·0	33	51·6
d	55	31	56·4	31	56·4	30	54·6	31	56·4	32	58·2	35	63·6
e	135	72	53·3	78	57·8	73	54·1	81	60·0	87	64·4	92	68·1
f	140	85	60·7	94	67·1	88	62·9	96	68·6	99	70·7	99	70·7

Key

A–E: A five-point measure of the proportion of the population engaged in primary industry.
a–f: A six-point measure of population concentration.
For details of these measures see table 10.

Sources: Calculated from data in *Asahi Nenkan*, 1977, 1980, 1981. Data on constituency type was kindly supplied to the writer by Professor Nishihira Shigeki.

gains were substantial, and can be observed not only between the 1979 and 1980 elections but even between the 1976 and 1979 elections as well. These figures, of course, are seats, not votes, but in the ultimate analysis the Party's ability to stay in power depends upon its capacity to retain seats. It will be observed that the number of constituencies in categories a and b are fewer than those in categories A and B. The former are metropolitan or big city areas, whereas the latter include areas which, while no longer agricultural, do not suffer from the extremes of urban congestion found most markedly in constituencies of category a. We suggest, therefore, that the elections of the late 1970s and early 1980s have revealed a swing to conservatism across the country except in those big city areas where problems of pollution, congested living and cost of housing produced a swing against the LDP in the 1960s. These remain the core areas of disillusion with LDP rule.[5]

The continuing heavy rural bias in LDP representation shows that the national gerrymander is still important for its survival. Although the number of seats with heavy concentrations of people was increased by 19 before the 1967 elections and by a further 20 before the elections of 1976,[6] they remain substantially fewer than those in any of the other categories (see tables 10 and 12). As table 10 demonstrates, this represents neither electoral justice nor the reality of the situation today. There is little sign of the LDP being prepared to make a radical reform of the electoral system in ways that would reduce the weighting of rural and small town electorates, and it is reasonable to expect that the present rural bias will continue.

A significant effect of this rural over-weighting is that the importance of agricultural interests within the Party remains disproportionate. The total agricultural population declined from about 45 per cent at the end of the war to around 10 per cent in the late 1970s, though the number of people having some identification with agriculture was perhaps twice this amount. The Party clearly cannot afford to ignore the interests of agriculture, which constitutes the electoral base of so many of its Diet members.[7]

It is generally agreed that Liberal Democratic Diet members form the active core of the Party. It is they who dominate party organization at the central level, and both cultivate and are

Table 13

LDP* *Members of the House of Representatives, 1980 Election*

Electorates	*Total Number*	*Average Age (Years)*	*Sitting Members*		*Previous Members*		*New Members*		*Average No. of Times Elected*	*Graduated University*		*Did not Graduate University*		*Graduated Tokyo University*	
			No.	%	*No.*	%	*No.*	%		*No.*	%	*No.*	%	*No.*	%
A	49	54·6	36	73·5	8	16·3	5	10·2	4·6	44	89·8	5	10·2	16	32·6
B	48	57·3	38	79·2	6	12·5	4	8·3	6·1	40	83·3	8	16·7	16	33·3
C	85	56·0	73	85·9	3	3·5	9	10·6	5·2	69	81·1	16	18·8	28	32·9
D	66	57·9	58	87·9	7	10·6	1	1·5	6·3	51	77·3	15	22·7	15	22·7
E	39	56·7	34	87·2	3	7·7	2	5·1	6·3	29	74·3	10	25·6	11	28·2
Total	287	56·5	239	83·3	27	9·4	21	7·3	5·6	233	81·8	54	18·8	86	30·0

* Includes Independents who joined the LDP following their election.

Source: *Kokkai Binran*, 61st edition (August 1980), pp. 85–131. Data on constituency type was kindly supplied by Professor Nishihira Shigeki. For details, see table 10.

cultivated by outside interest groups. They also dominated party presidential elections until the introduction of a primary election system in the late 1970s, which served to enhance the role of individual party members in the constituencies. LDP Diet members alone are in practice eligible for Cabinet positions (though from time to time a person who is not a member of a party has been given Cabinet office), and the intra-Party factions derive their major purpose from the desire of Diet members to have electoral funds and positions of influence.[8]

As can be seen from table 13 they also have a high level of formal education, about four-fifths of those elected to the House of Representatives in June 1980 having graduated from university. Of those who failed to graduate the average age was 61·1 years, or 4·5 years older than that of LDP Lower House Diet members as a whole. Moreover, of the non-graduates, no more than three individuals were younger than 51. In other words, practically all of those with a postwar education whom the Party elects to the House of Representatives have a university education of some sort. Moreover about 30 per cent graduated from the élite but meritocratic Tokyo University, and many more from other famous institutions of quality. At the same time local roots clearly remain an important criterion for election. An overwhelming majority of LDP Diet members are born in the prefecture to which their constituency belongs (not shown in table 13), and unlike the situation in many countries, in Japan it is extremely rare for a candidate to move from one constituency to another, especially when that constituency is in another part of the country.

A high proportion of LDP Diet members elected in 1980 had served in Parliament for a long time. The average member had been elected 5·7 times, or in other words had already served for about 12 years. 92·7 per cent had been elected at least once before, and 83·3 per cent were sitting members. Their average age was also quite high at 56·6 years. It is interesting to compare table 13 with a similar table drawn up for the 1972 elections. From this it can be seen that the characteristics of LDP Diet members have changed extraordinarily little over a 7½-year period.[9]

As has already been remarked in chapter 6, an important reason for the low turnover of Diet members (especially those affiliated with LDP) is the crucial role played by the network of supporters and supporting organizations, which any candidate must cultivate in order to be elected. A general term used to denote such a network of supporters is *jiban*, a word whose primary meaning is 'constituency' but which is also used in a more specific sense to indicate the personal 'bailiwick' of an individual candidate.[10] A rather formal manifestation of this, which has come into prominence in recent years, is the *kōenkai*, or personal support group, which is organized by candidates as an association having regular meetings and engaging in activities of various kinds, not all of them directly connected with politics.

Curtis argues that the *kōenkai* may represent a transitional stage between rural and urban patterns of electioneering.[11] Thus in particularly remote or backward rural areas, the association of the candidate (and probably also his family) with the local scene over a long period will give him the personal connections necessary to be elected. At the other extreme, in crowded big-city suburban constituencies, much of the population is new and mobile, and therefore more susceptible to programmatic, party-based appeals than to traditional campaigning through personal connections. In the bulk of constituencies, however, the existence of a specific organization, or *kōenkai*, which can act as a focus for the candidate's campaign, appears to fit in well with contemporary social norms.

Kōenkai themselves, however, are not unvarying in their mode of organization. Thayer identifies both 'vertical' and 'horizontal' *kōenkai* within the same constituency.[12] A candidate has a 'vertical' *kōenkai* where the bulk of his support is concentrated in a single town or area of the constituency, usually his birthplace and place of long-term residence. A 'horizontal' *kōenkai* is one whose membership is spread more widely, and is recruited from several or most areas of the constituency. The presumption is that the second pattern represents a rather more urban set of norms, whereas the former is associated with habitual rural ways of thinking.

The Party itself has local branches at constituency as well as at prefectural level. The effectiveness of the role which the local branches are able to play is however limited by the strong tendency of candidates to rely upon their own personal connections and support groups, rather than upon an backing which the Party as such may be able to give them. Where they do play a significant role however is in the granting of official party endorsement to candidates. Because of the exigencies of the multi-member constituency system, a party can be seriously handicapped at election time if it has endorsed too many candidates. Considering, therefore, the powerful and independent nature of candidates as vote-getters, the LDP local branches appear to have been remarkably successful in refusing to be pressured into endorsing too many candidates. It is true that a certain number of would-be LDP candidates who are refused endorsement are subsequently elected as Independents (and then join the Party), but their success rate is far lower than that of endorsed candidates (see table 9, column *E*, p. 108).

The degree of discipline over candidates that the party branches are thus able to achieve is probably in large part a result of the controlling influence which the central party machine is able to exercise over prefectural and other local branches. Diet members, who are overwhelmingly strong in the central machine, also predominate to an extreme degree as presidents of prefectural branches.[13] The system is thus very much weighted in favour of candidates who are already well entrenched as Diet members in the constituencies. It can readily be imagined that a branch dominated by local Diet members or their supporters will be reluctant to endorse new candidates whose candidacy might place the safety of their own seats in danger.

In one sense, therefore, the local branches may be regarded as a kind of closed shop, working in the interests of the current body of LDP Diet members. For many years the impression of a rigid party hierarchy was reinforced by the character of party membership. At successive national congresses of the LDP the aim of increasing the individual party membership was always proclaimed. In fact, however, the figures officially produced were often inflated, and repeated membership drives organized from Tokyo merely resulted in large numbers of *kōenkai* members being swept, temporarily, into the party net. Their primary loyalty was retained by their Diet member rather than by the Party as such.[14] The introduction, however, of a primary voting system in the election of the party president (see below, p. 128) served both to enhance the importance of individual members of the Party at the local level and to increase their number severalfold. The system was widely and justifiably criticized for extending factionalism down to the grass roots, but there is also evidence that it served to consolidate the Party's local influence by introducing the principle of mass membership.[15] At the time of writing, however, it is highly uncertain whether the system of primary elections will be retained in any real sense, and it remains difficult to regard local party organization as an independent and countervailing force capable of checking the power of the central party organs which are largely dominated by Diet members.

There is however another factor of great importance, which introduces a contrasting pluralistic element into the picture. Despite the fact that local party branches can boast an impressive record of controlling the number of candidates endorsed for election, the relationship between those candidates that are endorsed is frequently antipathetic. Moreover, it is extremely difficult for a local branch to give impartial and wholehearted backing for a number of endorsed candidates. For the most part, this is neither expected by the candidates nor attempted by the branch. Most branches are close to a particular candidate, and the others are more or less left to fend for themselves.

Into this vacuum step the factions, which are such a crucial part of the informal organization of the LDP. Something of the nature of Japanese political factions (*habatsu*) has already been noted in chapter 3. As was then suggested, they are an integral part of the Japanese social environment, and are to be found in many walks of life. Factions within the LDP, however, are adapted to the needs of a particular political environment, and play a specific set of roles within the environment.

It is generally agreed that a key reason why factions have been so vital a part of the LDP since its foundation is the multi-member constituency system, combined with the considerable expense required to run an election campaign. Since very few, if any, parliamentary candidates have the personal resources to run the kind of personal electoral campaign required by the system, they have to seek electoral funds from faction leaders. Because in any constituency where the LDP is putting up more than one candidate, those candidates are fighting each other as well as candidates from other parties, support from the party machine is generally regarded as insufficient. In these circumstances, candidates have very little choice but to join a faction, and it is unusual to find members of the same faction as candidates in the same constituency.

Much has been written, both in Japanese and English, about factionalism in Japanese political parties, and especially about the factions within the LDP since its formation.[16] Some of the questions which have been asked about them have a strongly normative content, and indeed it is rather difficult to escape evaluative considerations when discussing them. For many observers (including sections of the Japanese press) factions are seen as having a bearing on the 'health' of Japanese politics. Do they not, for instance, result in the over-emphasis of narrow and selfish personal interests within the Party? Are they not associated with a considerable degree of corruption? Do they not make achievement of Cabinet and party office excessively dependent on an inter-factional bargaining process which takes insufficient account of merit or suitability for office? Do they not produce instability and policy paralysis?

On the other hand it is sometimes argued that factionalism is a pluralistic element within the LDP, and makes it more difficult for a prime minister to act in an autocratic manner. It has also been held that factions perform worthwhile 'functions' both for their members and for the 'system' as a whole.[17] Bargaining between LDP factions for political office has also been likened to bargaining between parties in multi-party coalition governments such as those in Fourth Republic France, postwar Italy or the Weimar Republic,[18] although Japanese party politics has been much more stable than in any of these examples.

How factionalism works, however, is a question logically prior to any of these. We have seen that a principal reason why Liberal Democratic Diet members join factions is to obtain electoral funds. Despite the fact that the Party has partially succeeded in centralizing the provision of party funds through the Kokumin Kyōkai (People's Association),[19] set up in 1961, and its successor, the Kokumin Seiji Kyōkai (People's Political Association, established in 1975 following the financial scandals of the previous year, the competitive spirit fostered by the multi-member constituency system leads candidates to rely heavily on funds provided by faction leaders.

If the election system were changed, however, it seems doubtful whether factionalism would be wiped out for that reason alone. Factionalism depends for its viability and persistence upon two other factors of great practical importance.

One is that for Liberal Democratic Diet members the road to Cabinet and party office lies almost exclusively through membership of a faction. When the prime minister is forming his Cabinet, he is faced with a slate of claims for specific offices from each of the factions in the Party, and the eventual composition of his Cabinet will reflect in large measure a complex bargaining process with the factions over their competing claims. Following the deaths of three major faction leaders in the mid-1960s, there were as many as twelve factions, of very unequal weight, within the LDP, and it was in these circumstances that Satō Eisaku was able to exercise wide discretion in constructing his Cabinets, and could remain Prime Minister for far longer than either his predecessors or his successors. From 1972 to 1980 five major factions, those led by Fukuda, Miki, Nakasone, Ōhira and Tanaka, dominated the Party, though a few much smaller groups existed from time to time. Cabinets became much more difficult to build and maintain, and prime ministerial tenure became a mere two years on average. With the formation of the Suzuki Cabinet in July 1980, the factional scene was once more entering a fluid stage, with several potential faction leaders busy cultivating embryo factions.

The factions themselves for the most part operate a seniority system in determining who of their members shall be put forward to the prime minister as a candidate for office. Faction leaders have frequently been Cabinet ministers, but just as frequently more junior members of a faction attain Cabinet office. This seems to reflect the predilections (and perhaps abilities) of the faction leaders themselves, since some have held a succession of Party and Cabinet posts, while others have not. On the other hand, some Cabinets have included a number of faction leaders, and are often referred to as 'strong-man Cabinets', while others have had very few. This appears to depend on the kind of Cabinet a prime minister feels he can best handle at any particular time.

The other factor which tends to perpetuate factionalism as a major element within LDP politics is the procedure for electing a party president. Since, so long as the Liberal Democrats retain their parliamentary majority, the title of Liberal Democratic Party president carries with it the post of prime minister, the contest for the party presidency is perhaps the most keenly fought contest of the Japanese political scene. Between November 1955 and the mid-1970s LDP presidential elections were held regularly every two years (for a period in the early 1970s every three years), by a vote of all LDP Diet members from both Houses and one representative from each prefectural branch. If a party president stepped down in mid-term, the practice was for his successor to be chosen following intra-Party discussions, as when Miki succeeded Tanaka in 1974. Although over that period no president who stood for re-election was ever actually defeated, survival was by no means assured. (Indeed, Ikeda came close to defeat when he stood for his third term in July 1964.) The tone of presidential elections was set in December 1956, when a contest based on factional alliances and involving a large expenditure of funds was fought between three candidates, Kishi, Ishibashi and Ishii.[20]

The pattern established over successive biennial party presidential elections was for each election to be followed, once the result was known, by a division of factions into two rival coalitions, the 'mainstream', consisting of those factions whose members had supported the successful candidate, and an 'anti-mainstream', whose members had supported an unsuccessful candidate.[21] Cabinet formation by the prime minister between presidential elections was based to a considerable extent on calculations either of how to reward the various factions in such a way as to keep the existing mainstream alliance intact or, failing that, of how to reconstruct a new mainstream alliance in time for the next elections which would be capable of winning a majority. Thus, although the bulk of the available offices would be distributed to factions within the mainstream alliance, some would also go to the anti-mainstream in order to 'buy goodwill' for the future.[22] From the prime minister's point of view, it was also desirable to reinsure himself with the anti-mainstream within his own Party in order to secure their co-operation, or at least to avoid their active hostility, towards the implementation of his policies.

A new and radical element was introduced into the situation

in the mid-1970s, when the Miki Government pioneered, and the Fukuda Government implemented, a two-stage method of electing the party president. The first stage, or primary election, for the first time placed in the hands of the party membership at large the right to influence directly the choice of party president, and thus prime minister. Those individuals fulfilling the criteria of party member (and a much smaller category designated 'party friends') could now vote in a primary election which would determine which two of the various candidates were to contest a run-off election for which the electorate was confined to LDP Diet members. For the primary, each prefecture was allotted a number of points proportionate to the number of members and 'friends' in the prefecture. Following the election, points were then distributed to the two leading candidates according to the proportion of the vote they had polled in the prefecture. This can be illustrated by the results in Tokyo prefecture at the November 1978 primary:[23]

Electors: 101,034 (members: 78,180; 'friends': 21,962)
Total points: 102

Results:	Ōhira:	26,032 votes;	42 points
	Fukuda:	37,283 votes;	60 points
	Nakasone:	16,570 votes;	
	Kōmoto:	5,316 votes;	

The 1978 primary is so far the only time the system has been tested, and even then it was not tested fully, since Fukuda, unexpectedly defeated in the primary, decided not to contest the run-off election. The experience of the 1978 primary attracted much criticism, mainly on the grounds that the efforts of the factions, normally confined within the Diet and to some extent among the officials of local branches, had been allowed to spread among the membership as a whole. Indeed, during the period leading up to the primary, LDP membership (including 'friends') increased from about a quarter of a million to almost a million and a half. Certainly competitive efforts by factions backing particular candidates were responsible for recruiting many new members (many of them, of course, already associated with the *kōenkai* of particular Diet members), and the 'money politics' of the Tanaka faction recruiting Ōhira supporters was widely blamed for Fukuda's defeat. Allegations were heard that membership lists had been 'padded' with the names of individuals who did not even regard themselves as members.[24]

The results of the 1978 primary were as follows:[25]

Electors: 1,499,265 (members: 1,328,696; 'friends': 167,646)
Total points: 1,525

Results:	Ōhira:	550,891 votes;	748 points
	Fukuda:	472,503 votes;	638 points
	Nakasone:	197,957 votes;	93 points
	Kōmoto:	88,917 votes;	46 points

The future of the system is now uncertain, and it seems unlikely that it will be retained in anything like its original form.[26]

From the standpoint of the established intra-Party factions the uncertainties produced by the primary system (graphically illustrated by the result of the primary in 1978) were sufficient reason for emasculating it, if not for abolishing it altogether. On the other hand those who continued to support it did so in the name of 'party modernization', which had especial appeal among younger Diet members.[27]

'Party modernization' is a notion which has a respectable history within the LDP. Broadly speaking, it means two things which parallel ideas of modernization in Japanese politics generally. One is the idea that factionalism within the Party should be either abolished or made less important. The other is that the workings of the Party be made more representative of its membership. The two are closely connected. As we have seen, the Party's difficulties in fostering a broad membership primarily identified with the Party as such is not unrelated to the prevalence of personal support groups (*kōenkai*) at the local constituency level. To finance their *kōenkai*, local members and candidates need support from intra-Party factions with headquarters in Tokyo. The Party's organization has to compete with faction organization at every level, including that of membership.

At fairly regular intervals since the Party was founded, party leaders (including prime ministers on several occasions) have called upon the factions to disband. The purpose, however, seems to have been for the most part declamatory rather than substantive, even though a prime minister on occasion has formally dissolved his own faction in order to induce others to follow his example.[28]

Much the most effective attack on factionalism has come in the form of attempts to centralize the channels of finance flowing into the LDP from outside pressure groups, notably business firms. Some of the moves in this direction have come from business groups themselves. Thus in 1955 various business groups banded together to form the Keizai Saiken Kondankai (Economic Reconstruction Council), whose principal purpose was to co-ordinate the provision of funds for political purposes. Although it was quite successful in channelling funds into the LDP, the Kondankai did not manage to eliminate financial contributions from businessmen to faction leaders, and moreover it attracted a great deal of adverse comment from the mass media.[29] In February 1961 it was dissolved.

Shortly afterwards, however, a new body, the Kokumin Kyōkai (People's Association), was formed, essentially for the same purpose as the Kondankai, but with the trappings of citizen participation.[30] After its formation the Kokumin Kyōkai gradually developed into the main supplier of political funds for the Party itself, and a very significant competitor with funds solicited by the factions. In April 1975 it was reorganized under a new name, as the Kokumin Seiji Kyōkai (People's Political Association), following the adverse publicity given to 'money politics' during the 1974 House of Councillors election campaign and its aftermath.[31] Despite the existence of this body, it still remains the practice for major business firms to make political donations, not only through the Kokumin Seiji Kyōkai, but also to a number of faction leaders. The links established between leading businessmen and LDP faction leaders in this fashion (also sometimes confusingly referred to as *kōenkai* or personal support groups) are an important part of a pattern of connections which tie the business and political worlds closely together.

A misconception sometimes held by foreign observers about LDP factions is that they are primarily bodies serving to promote a particular set of policies of a distinct ideological approach.

While this is true to an extent of factions in the Japan Socialist Party, the relationship between LDP factions and policy is more tenuous. As previously stated, the principal *raison d'être* of the factions consists in the channelling of electoral funds, the achievement of high office for their members and control of votes in party presidential elections. These three purposes involve Diet members in an essentially transactional set of relations with the factions to which they belong, and there is little pressure on them to conform to a common pattern in respect of policy. Indeed, when policy differences are seen to exist between factions, they mostly turn out to be differences between faction leaders, in which the rank and file faction membership is only peripherally involved.

Nevertheless, broad differences in the character and approach of some at least of the factions can be distinguished. For a long time the separate traditions of the Liberal and Progressive (Democratic) Parties before the 1955 amalgamation continued to set their successor factions apart from each other. Rivalries of more recent origin continue to affect current attitudes, although pragmatic considerations bring old rivals together when the power balance changes. Thus Satō and Ikeda, both originally protégés of Yoshida in the old Liberal Party, became rivals for the prime ministership in the early 1960s. The faction led by Ikeda's immediate successor, Maeo, found it difficult to co-operate with the Satō faction during Satō's prime ministership. On the other hand, Tanaka and Ōhira, the successors of Satō and Maeo respectively, joined forces as part of a 'mainstream' alliance once Tanaka succeeded to the prime ministership. Between 1972 and 1980 the rivalry between Fukuda (whom Tanaka had defeated) and a fairly stable combination of Tanaka and Ōhira became the most salient factor in the factional scene, with the Miki faction (ideologically somewhat to the left) and the Nakasone faction (rather to the right) seeking their own advantage by changing alliances from time to time. While Fukuda could be regarded as an orthodox conservative and Ōhira as more liberal, the bitterness of their rivalry between 1978 and 1980 seems to have had far more to do with the struggle for power than with differences over policy. Following Ōhira's death in June 1980 Suzuki Zenkō, who inherited both the Ōhira faction and the prime ministership, soon found himself co-operating with the Fukuda faction in his drive to forge a new mainstream alliance. Kōmoto Toshio, who in the same year took over leadership of the Miki faction, differed radically from Miki in his political standpoint. Where Miki had been a left-of-centre liberal, concerned with a range of progressive policy issues, Kōmoto tended to reflect closely the views of big business interests.

Another factor by which factions are said to be distinguishable from each other is the proportion of former government bureaucrats among their members. Thus the press sometimes distinguishes 'bureaucratic' factions from 'party man' factions. The influence of former civil servants within the Party is very considerable indeed, but it is doubtful whether their predominance in any particular faction is currently as important as it was.[32] For the most part it is the career origin of the faction leader which is being confused with the career origins of the members as a whole.

Although factions are not primarily policy-oriented bodies, it is certainly possible to detect a spectrum of opinion, from conservative to progressive, among LDP Diet members, and to some extent at least the factions can be ranged along such a spectrum. On certain contentious issues there are policy groups representing a particular point of view, and these groups are separate from factions. (Fukui calls them 'intra-party interest groups'.)[33] The best known example of two rival policy groups on the same issue were the Asian Affairs Study Group and the Asian–African Affairs Study Group, representing right-wing and left-wing positions respectively on the China issue between 1965 and 1972. Policy groups representing particular sets of views on defence, the Constitution, education and other sensitive issues are also often active within the Party. Perhaps the most famous was the Seirankai, an overtly nationalist body with extreme right-wing views, founded in 1973.

In a sense, however, groups such as these are unusual within the LDP. Much more numerous are economic interest groups of various kinds, representing doctors, farmers and so forth. Moreover, it is noticeable that the groups putting forward a strong and consistent point of view on matters having ideological overtones (such as constitutional revision or defence) tend to inhabit the political periphery within the Party rather than the political centre. Political leaders realistically aspiring to party leadership have tended to dissociate themselves from policy positions that could prove ideologically divisive, preferring to rely upon a general consensus so far as possible. The prime ministership of Miki, however, was a notable exception to this rule, though he came to office in unusual circumstances and the effect of his leadership upon the Party was disturbing. Suzuki Zenkō as Prime Minister has studiously avoided extreme positions, but the safe majority which the Party won in 1980 makes him somewhat vulnerable to pressure from those who want to assert conservative policy positions decisively.

The party organization has come to reflect, in a rather subtle and complex way, the various forces at work within the Party. Nominally, the highest legislative organ of the LDP is the party Congress, which is held once a year and consists of all LDP Diet members from both Houses of the National Diet, four representatives from each prefectural branch, including one from each prefectural party youth group and one from each prefectural party women's group. Extraordinary congresses may be held on the resolution of LDP Diet members of both Houses or following a request from one-third of the prefectural branches, and must be held within a month of the receipt of a request.[34]

When there are 'important or emergency matters to discuss', a General Meeting of Both Houses (Ryō Giin Sōkai) may be summoned, and consists of the LDP Diet members from both Houses of the Diet. A two-thirds quorum is required for any resolution contrary to a resolution of a party congress, and such a resolution must gain acceptance from the following congress, or it loses effect.[35]

In practice, however, both the party Congress and the General Meeting of Both Houses are little more than bodies which rubber-stamp decisions made elsewhere. Of the formal organs of the Party, the most important in actual fact is the Executive Council (Sōmukai). Functioning as a body which 'discusses and decides important matters of Party management and Diet activities', it currently consists of thirty members. Of these, fifteen are elected from the members of the House of Representatives, seven from among members of the House of Councillors and eight are appointed by the party president. There is a chairman and up to four vice-chairmen.[36]

What may be regarded as the Party's chief legislative organ is the Policy Affairs Research Council (Seimu Chōsakai). According to the party rules, the purpose of the PARC is to conduct 'investigations and research into policy and into the drafting of legislation', and all proposed legislation must be referred to it. The PARC is divided into numerous divisions (*bukai*) and special research committees (*tokubetsu chōsa iinkai*) which correspond to particular policy areas. Membership is open to all LDP Diet members and to 'people of learning and experience selected by the Party President'. The PARC has a chairman and not more than six vice-chairmen. Since such a large and fragmented body needs central co-ordination, a crucial role is played by an Inquiry Commission (Shingikai), headed by the PARC chairman and including a vice-chairman and up to twenty members. Policy recommendations made by PARC divisions or special research committees have to be processed by the Inquiry Commission before being sent on to the Executive Council.[37]

The Executive Council exercises considerable influence through its power of appointment to the PARC. Thus the chairman of the PARC is chosen by the party president with the agreement of the Executive Council, while the PARC vice-chairman and the members of the Inquiry Commission, as well as the chairmen and vice-chairmen of the various divisions, also have to be agreed to by the Executive Council, although they are formally appointed by the PARC chairman.[38]

In practice, questions of appointment and decision-making within the Party are determined through compromises between a number of principles. These include most notably the accommodation of external interest groups, the balancing of factional interests and the dominance of the current mainstream factional alliance headed by the party president.[39] The numerous divisions and special research committees of the PARC are commonly used as channels by interest groups (including government ministries seeking to give their views a hearing within the Party). Whereas the PARC Inquiry Commission used to reflect the principle of factional balance, that no longer seems to be the case, and instead each faction provides at least one deputy secretary-general (of which no more than ten may be appointed).[40] The secretary-general (Kanjichō),[41] chairman of the Executive Council (Sōmukaichō) and chairman of the PARC (Seimuchōsakaichō) are the key central officials of the Party, and together with the party president (prime minister) constitute an informal ruling group which is able to have its own way on many issues.

Although the formal and especially the informal organization of the LDP has undergone considerable fluctuation since the Party was founded, it now has a great deal of experience to fall back on in handling the problems with which it is most frequently faced. The greatest instability in party organization occurred in the early years of the Party's existence, whereas the 1960s saw the gradual evolution of more stable patterns. Satō's long tenure of the party presidency, helped by the deaths in the mid-sixties of three major faction leaders, was instrumental in creating such a consolidation. At the same time the general consensus which had evolved on the priority to be given to economic growth meant that the major policy clashes that had rent the LDP during the late 1950s while Kishi was Prime Minister were no longer so much in evidence. The 1970s saw a return to a more unstable situation, as the Party found itself coping with a resurgence of factional strife, a drastic reduction in its parliamentary majority, a difficult economic environment and persistent controversy about 'money politics'. The achievement of a stable majority in the 1980 elections made the Party once more easier to control, though how long this relatively peaceful atmosphere would continue remained an open question. The broad range of political opinion, external interests and factional aspirations which the LDP managed to contain within a single organization ensured that party management would always be a delicate and sensitive operation. For most of its history the Party had shown a preference for low-key leadership based on the principles of internal compromise. The frequency with which the LDP changed its leaders suggested an inbuilt suspicion of any leader likely to be excessively strong or self-willed.

8 The Structure and Process of Central Goverment

The impressive performance of the Japanese economy at a time when other economies of the advanced industrial world have been performing comparatively poorly has focused the interest of outside observers upon the structure and process of central government and the role of government in economic policy. Few observers would question the view that relative to many other advanced economies the Japanese economy is quite closely supervised, and in many of its aspects controlled, by government. The question of how far the astonishingly high levels of productivity in many key Japanese industries have resulted from government action or government involvement is beyond the scope of this book. At the very least it would be necessary to analyse in detail aspects of industrial practice in individual firms, such as management recruitment and training, manpower policy, investment and planning (both short- and long-term), research and development, and quality control, in order to determine the breakdown of responsibility in these areas between government and the firms themselves.[1]

Nevertheless, in creating an economic climate which facilitates productivity and rapid adaptation to changing circumstances, the role of government has been crucial. The achievement of productivity increases and the fostering of new industries at the frontier of technology has been a consistent policy aim since the high-growth period of the 1950s and 1960s, as has been the expansion of foreign markets and sources of supply. More recently government has been heavily involved in the area of pollution control, and especially in the conservation of energy, where the results have been impressive indeed. The measures used have included taxation policy; control over interest rates (the market remains 'managed' rather than free);

the issuing of government bonds; the granting or withholding of subsidies, contracts, licences and so on to favoured industries and firms; a much-publicized process of indicative economic planning (which while it binds nobody absolutely is regarded with interest by industry as showing the way things are likely to move); decisive control over legislation in relevant fields; and what is termed 'administrative guidance'.[2]

This last term is used to describe a practice whereby public servants affect the actions of industrialists through a process of direct contact and discussion, utilizing specific weapons of persuasion (such as the threat to withhold contracts), but also making use of an atmosphere of common interest in a mutually satisfactory outcome. The most famous exponent of administrative guidance has been the Ministry of International Trade and Industry, which has exercised it to good effect in pursuit of a range of policy goals.[3]

Intelligent discussion of the role of central government in Japan has been plagued by the use and popularity of some unsophisticated ways of describing it, and particularly by the use of the term 'Japan Incorporated' (Nippon KK) in journalistic and even academic discussion. The comparison of the Japanese politico-economic system with a huge industrial firm, government being the top executive responsible for basic policy decisions while the individual firms ('branches') have a degree of commercial independence within defined limits, and a process of constant discussion and interaction ensures that the 'branches' carry out the grand design of the 'executive', is a dramatic metaphor. As a serious argument, however, it suffers from the following defects.

First, it strongly suggests a pejorative connotation: that 'Japan, Inc.' in effect constitutes a conspiracy to maximize Japanese exports and minimize foreign penetration of the Japanese market. Though the Japanese market has not been easy to enter, the failure of foreign firms to prosper in the Japanese environment speaks as much about their lack of interest and adaptability as of a conspiracy to keep them out. Secondly, it ignores the dynamics of the government–business relationship. Whereas in the 1950s and 1960s MITI, for instance, had at its disposal a battery of legislative and administrative controls which it used to ensure that its priorities were followed by industry, many (though not quite all) of these have now been dismantled. As a result, moreover, of the liberalizing and internationalizing of the economy, most of the larger firms are in a far stronger and more independent financial position than they were in the earlier period.[4] Relations between the bureaucracy and industry have materially changed as a result, even though a great deal of mutually satisfactory discussion and interaction still takes place. Thirdly, by focusing exclusively on the consensual elements in the situation, the model fails to admit the importance of conflict in the system as a whole. Jurisdictional disputes, for instance, between different ministries, or between a ministry and financial institutions, are often intense and chronic. Fourthly, it defines too narrowly the range of significant actors in the system. As Pempel and Tsunekawa point out, it is not only the industrial giants that interact corporatively with the bureaucracy and the LDP, but increasingly agriculture and small business.[5] Indeed, it is arguable that a principal motivation for corporatist patterns of government is protection of the weak. In Japan, as the major firms have become increasingly strong, internationalized and free of government control, so corporatist protection has been extended to those areas of the economy that still remain relatively weak and vulnerable. Finally, it ignores some notably immobilist areas of decision-making, notably in foreign policy, defence, administrative reform, constitutional interpretation and educational policy.

We therefore reject the theory of 'Japan Incorporated', but support a more limited view which regards the corporate aspect as a salient characteristic of the system, while not ignoring continuing change, institutional conflict, basic incompatibility of interests and areas of policy immobilism.

To produce a complete and satisfactory explanation of why the government bureaucracy has been able to exercise such a central role in the Japanese case is beyond the scope of this book. The response to international economic weakness from the Meiji period onwards, and the requirements of a war economy in the late 1930s and early 1940s (see chapter 2), were certainly factors of great importance.[6] A crucial part of Japan's pre-1945 political legacy was a tradition of dominance by élite government officials and, as we saw in chapter 4, the American occupying authorities failed to make much impact on a government bureaucracy which, perforce, they had to work through to implement their reforms in other areas. Even so, things might well have turned out differently had not the conservatives managed to consolidate their political position in the mid-1950s. The relative harmony of interests that existed, particularly during the high-growth period of the 1960s, between the LDP, the public service (or at least, key ministries in it) and dominant business interests, enabled the bureaucracy (or certain sections of it) to exercise unusual influence over key aspects of economic policy.

Conversely, the failure of the Opposition parties (especially the JSP) to realize their political potential over the same period, as well as the weakness and division of the interests (notably those of organized labour) which they represented, produced a peculiarly one-sided power structure in which the influence of public servants was given extraordinary scope. Pempel and Tsunekawa have called this 'corporatism without labour', and one result was that both the level of wages and the level of public welfare provision lagged well behind the rate of economic growth.

Some features of the system as it emerged from the 1950s were rather reminiscent of C. Wright Mills' 'power élite' concept which he attempted to apply to American politics and government of the 1950s.[7] In particular, the patterns of close communication between similarly educated élite officials of three separate but interlocking hierarchies (in Japan's case the LDP, big business and the public service), together with the relative absence of effective countervailing power, especially from labour unions, suggests that the 'power élite' model fitted Japan of the late 1950s and 1960s rather better than it ever fitted the United States.

This impression is strengthened by the presence of some particular features of the Japanese political system, especially at that period. Although in a formal sense Cabinet is the central decision-making organ of government, Cabinet ministers typically do not set out actively to reshape the policies of their ministries, though there have been some significant exceptions. The frequency of Cabinet reshuffles, the pressure on prime ministers to place factional appointees in Cabinet posts, and a tradition of decision-making within the bureaucracy rather than within Cabinet or the Diet have tended to reduce the role of Cabinet as an effective centre of power. Another unusual feature is the strategic position occupied by former senior public servants as LDP Diet members and in many cases as Cabinet ministers. This is one aspect of a broader phenomenon known as *amakudari* (descent from heaven), which will be discussed later in the chapter. It is reasonable to suppose that the influence of a ministry in Cabinet will be enhanced when one of its former senior officials is a member of that Cabinet, or even if he is an influential member of the Diet. Also, ministries commonly not only draft, but even initiate bills which are then formally presented to the Diet by Cabinet, or less often by a private member. This is totally unlike the American pattern of legislative process, but it even carries the principle of executive dominance typical of the British or Australian political systems to extreme. It hardly needs to be added that Japanese senior public servants in the most important ministries are a carefully selected group of highly trained men, with a well-developed consciousness of their élite status, and a network of contacts with leaders of similar background and status in other walks of life, notably business and politics.

This, however, as we have already suggested, is not the whole picture. Some features which we have described also have the effect of entrenching conflict and making decisions in particular areas of policy especially hard to manage. Moreover, with elements of pluralism increasing in the system as a whole, political cohesiveness may well prove more of a problem in the future than in the past. For instance, whereas political factionalism serves to weaken the authority of the prime minister and Cabinet and thus enhance that of the public service, it on the other hand leaves the LDP open to all sorts of pressure from interests of various kinds. This involves not only the much-publicized problem of corrupt connections, but also the weakening of central authority. Moreover, the public service is itself subject to the practice of '*nawabari*', whereby individual ministries 'rope off' their own spheres of jurisdiction and jealously guard them against outside encroachment.[8] Indeed the 'sectionalism' of individual ministries (and even of individual bureaux within ministries), the pressure from 'client' interest groups

groups upon particular sections of the government bureaucracy, public apathy and lack of leadership from Cabinet are often blamed for the slow progress of administrative reform.[9]

Generalization in these areas is difficult because of the sheer complexity of the administrative process. In the most crucial areas of economic policy there is an enviable record of adaptive response to changing circumstances, far-sighted planning and rapid implementation. This is where the close connections, similar background and thorough administrative training of the élite in the bureaucracy, politics, industry and finance come into play. Even here, of course, conflict is much in evidence, but the quality and commitment of senior personnel in such key ministries as MITI and the Ministry of Finance tend to ensure an intelligent outcome in areas of high national priority. Where the national priority is less, the personnel are of lower quality and political pressures are more diverse, the result may be bureaucratic and immobilist.

The present structure of the government bureaucracy bears comparison with the system set up in the late nineteenth century. When a Cabinet was first instituted in 1885, its ministers respectively held the portfolios (each corresponding to a ministry) of foreign affairs, home affairs, finance, army, navy, justice, education, agriculture and commerce, and communications. When the new Constitution came into effect in 1947, the following ministries existed: Foreign Affairs, Home Affairs, Finance, Justice, Education, Welfare, Agriculture and Forestry, Commerce and Industry, Transport and Communications. Today the Ministries of Foreign Affairs, Finance, Justice, Education and Transport still remain, but in addition there is a Ministry of Labour and a Ministry of Construction. The Ministry of Commerce and Industry has been replaced by the Ministry of International Trade and Industry, often referred to as 'MITI'. The former Ministry of Communications is now the Ministry of Posts and Telecommunications (though the Japanese title has not changed), the Ministry of Welfare is the Ministry of Health and Welfare (again, no change in Japanese), and the Ministry of Agriculture and Forestry has had 'Fisheries' tacked onto its title, to make it the Ministry of Agriculture, Forestry and Fisheries. The former Ministry of Home Affairs was replaced during the Occupation by the Local Autonomy Agency, a branch of the Prime Minister's Office, but in 1960 it became the Ministry of Local Autonomy, and now uses 'Ministry of Home Affairs' as the English translation of Jichishō (Ministry of Local Autonomy), thereby seeking to make an important point about its status.

It has proved very difficult in practice since the Occupation to increase the number of ministries or basically change their structure. In addition to the twelve ministries (*shō*), however, a variety of commissions (*iinkai*) and agencies (*chō*) are grouped under the Prime Minister's Office (Sōrifu), which now has a formal status equivalent to that of a ministry. These include the Fair Trade Commission, the National Public Safety Commission, the Environmental Disputes Co-ordination Commission, the Imperial Household Agency, the Administrative Management Agency, the Hokkaidō Development Agency, the Defence Agency, the Economic Planning Agency, the Science and Technology Agency, the Environment Agency, the Okinawa Development Agency and the National Land Agency (see the chart, pp. 144–5).

The Constitution, in article 66, defines Cabinet membership as consisting of the prime minister and the other ministers of state. Article 2 of the Cabinet Law places an upper limit of twenty ministers of state, plus the prime minister, within the Cabinet. No provision is made for an inner Cabinet. All ministers are members of Cabinet, and nobody apart from a minister can be a Cabinet member. Since, however, a Cabinet restricted to thirteen members (the number of ministries plus the Prime Minister's Office) would be too small for the breadth of government responsibilities, advantage is taken of article 3 of the Cabinet Law, which permits ministers without portfolio. Several of the more important commissions and agencies of the Prime Minister's Office have therefore been designated as requiring a minister of state to head them, thus giving them full representation at Cabinet level. The chief Cabinet secretary, the director-general of the Prime Minister's Office, and the director-general of the Cabinet Legislative Bureau have also been elevated to Cabinet membership status in this way. Formally speaking, the ministers of state concerned remain ministers without portfolio, despite the fact that their departmental responsibilities may be as great as those of some ministers heading actual ministries.[10] This explains why, for instance, the director-general of the Defence Agency (Bōeichō Chōkan) is a minister of state with full entitlement to sit in Cabinet, despite the fact that efforts to raise the status of the Agency to that of the ministry have so far failed. Cabinets have generally had twenty-one or twenty-two members, so that some ministers have to take on more than one portfolio.

In its task of co-ordinating the functions of central government, the Cabinet has the assistance of the Cabinet Secretariat (Naikaku Kambō), the Cabinet Legislation Bureau (Naikaku Hōseikyoku), the National Defence Council (Kokubō Kaigi) and the National Personnel Authority (Jinjiin).

The role of the Cabinet Secretariat overlaps somewhat with the functions of the Secretariat of the Prime Minister's Office. The chief secretary, however, is always a most powerful figure within the Government, and a close confidant of the prime minister, acting as Cabinet spokesman on many issues, and as a channel of communication with both Government and Opposition parties.[11] The Cabinet Secretariat itself is principally concerned with the preparation of matters for Cabinet discussions, policy research and co-ordination between different ministries.

The Cabinet Legislative Bureau was abolished on American insistence during the Occupation but was revived later. Its main task is to investigate and oversee legislative technicalities, including drafting of legislation, throughout the civil service.[12]

The National Defence Council is more like a Cabinet committee than an advisory bureau of Cabinet. It consists of the prime minister, the foreign minister, the finance minister, the director-general of the Defence Agency and the director-general of the Economic Planning Agency. It was originally set up by the Defence Agency Establishment Law (Bōeichō Setchi Hō) of 1954 as a safeguard for civilian control over the Self-Defence Forces, and the prime minister is supposed to refer to it important matters of defence policy, including draft defence plans.[13] Charges that it had been bypassed by Cabinet, and that items for the Fourth Defence Plan had been included in the national budget before the Plan had been ratified by the Diet, led to a major political row in February 1972.

The National Personnel Authority was established during

The Central Administrative Structure

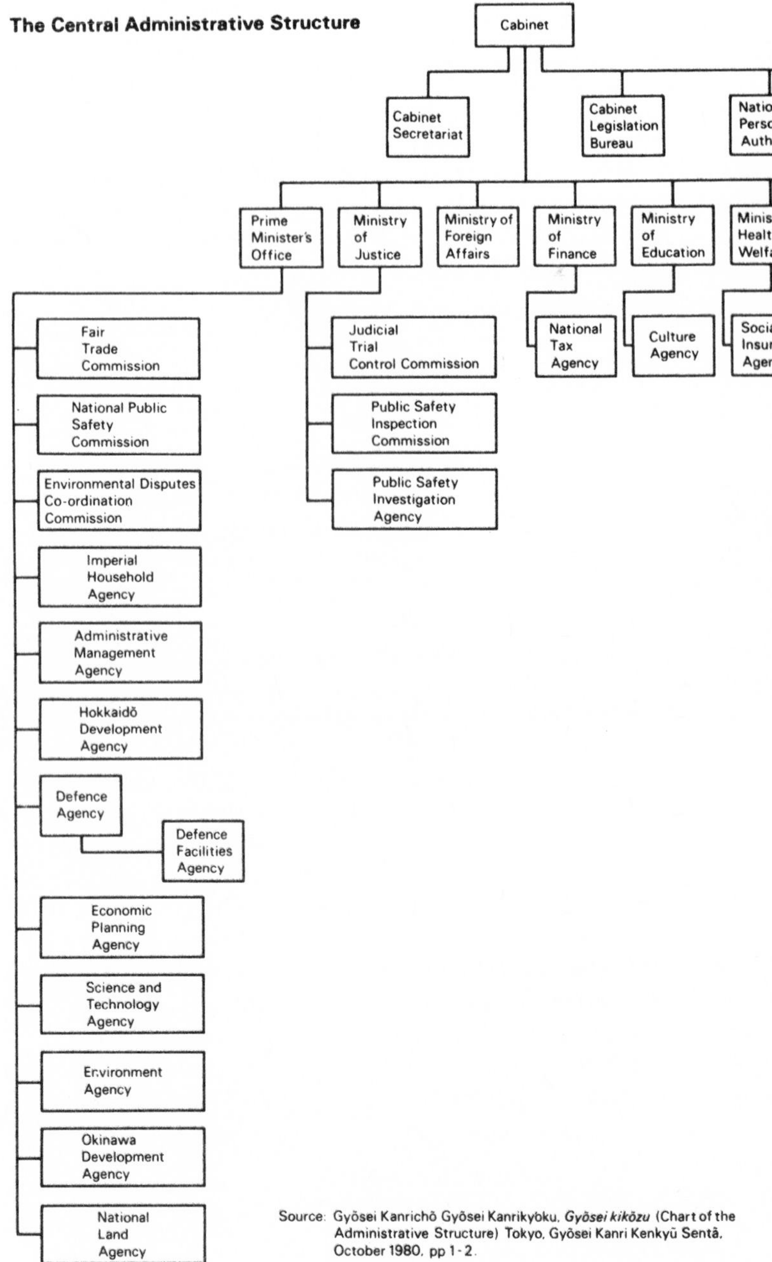

Source: Gyōsei Kanrichō Gyōsei Kanrikyoku, *Gyōsei kikōzu* (Chart of the Administrative Structure) Tokyo, Gyōsei Kanri Kenkyū Sentā, October 1980, pp 1-2.

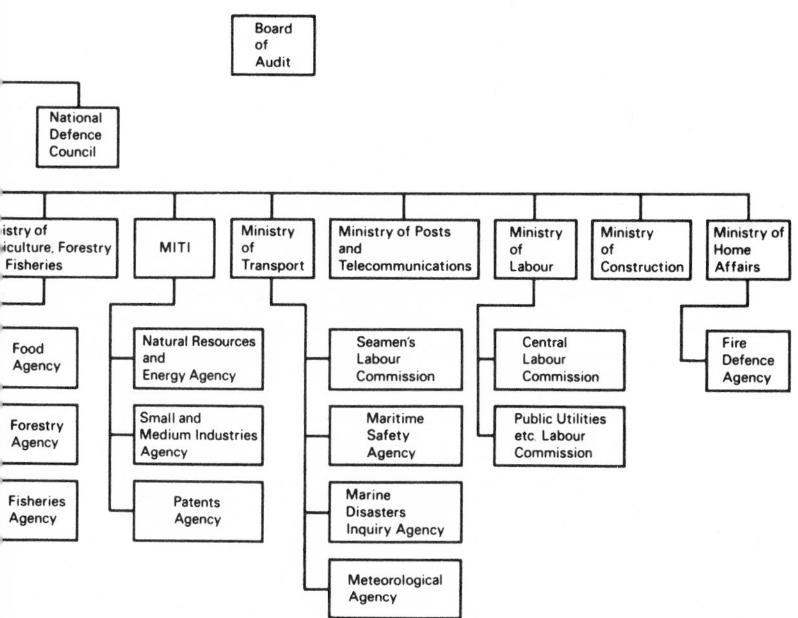

the Occupation in an attempt to rationalize the recruitment and conditions of civil service personnel, and bring them under some sort of centralized control, thus reducing bureaucratic 'sectionalism'. It was deliberately given the status of an independent advisory bureau of Cabinet, so that it could exercise authority in personnel matters over the civil service as a whole. The influence of the National Personnel Authority was much resented by the established ministries, who were used to controlling their own affairs in questions of personnel, so that various attempts were made to emasculate it once the Occupation had ended. Nevertheless it has survived, and continues to make recommendations to Cabinet on matters affecting civil servants. It touches upon some issues which are highly sensitive politically, such as the bargaining rights of civil service personnel, and especially of school teachers (see chapter 11). In recent years it has been particularly concerned to see that civil servant salaries should not fall too far behind the rapidly rising salaries in private industry.

In October 1980 the National Personnel Authority initiated a comprehensive investigation of salaries, conditions and duties of public servants, the first time that this had been attempted in any thorough fashion since 1957. The Authority was also particularly concerned with the implications for public service employment of Japan's 'ageing society', and planned to raise the age of retirement to 60 by 1985.[14] The practice of higher civil servants moving into private industry following their retirement (of which more will be said later) has required the Authority's approval since 1963.[15]

Significantly enough, a major role in the task of co-ordinating submissions to Cabinet from the various ministries and other civil service organs is played by a body consisting of senior civil servants. This is the Conference of Permanent Vice-Ministers (Jimu Jikan Kaigi), which, although it has no status in law, meets regularly under the chairmanship of the chief Cabinet secretary. A permanent vice-minister is the highest career position in the civil service, and the Conference represents an attempt by the ministries themselves to smooth over their differences and reach a high degree of consensus before submissions are made to Cabinet. On certain items, notably the draft budget and high personnel appointments, it is normal to bypass the Conference of Permanent Vice-Ministers, while issues so controversial that no administrative compromise is likely to emerge may also go straight to Cabinet for a political decision.[16] There is also a regular Conference of Parliamentary Vice-Ministers (Seimu Jikan Kaigi), but this appears to be rather less important. The parliamentary vice-ministers are political appointees, required to resign if the Cabinet is replaced, and there are one or two of them to assist the minister in each ministry.

Of the ministries themselves, those most closely associated with national economic policy-making have tended to carry most weight politically and in terms of status. To some extent this is a question of tradition. Thus a career in the Ministry of Finance continues to be regarded as difficult to match for its prestige and influence.[17] On the other hand, the Ministry of International Trade and Industry (MITI) is now seen as one of Japan's best known and powerful ministries largely as a result of the central role it has had in formulating industrial and trade policies during the period of spectacular economic growth.[18] The Ministry of Agriculture, Forestry and Fisheries has also had an important role, but much of this is because of the continued importance of the farm vote for the LDP.[19] The status of other ministries reflects changing national priorities. Thus the Ministry of Foreign Affairs was not highly regarded during the postwar period, but has slowly been rising to a position of greater prominence with the emergence of Japan into a somewhat more active role in international affairs.[20] Other ministries, notably the Ministry of Education, the Ministry of Justice and the Ministry of Labour, have been involved in areas of ideological controversy, and this to some extent has affected their respective images. The other ministries have operated in more specifically technical areas.

One important civil service reform carried out during the Occupation was the abolition of the powerful Ministry of Home Affairs, which had had pervasive power over local administration and most significantly over the police. In the prewar system officials belonging to the Ministry of Home Affairs had ranked alongside those from the Ministry of Foreign Affairs and Finance as the most prestigious within the bureaucracy, while Home Affairs was the background for many successful political careers. With the dismantling of a considerable portion of the Occupation reforms in the area of local government during the 1950s, some part of the former position of the Ministry of Home Affairs has been restored to its eventual successor, the Ministry of Local Autonomy, but despite the earnest efforts of former home ministry members, something much less than the old position of supremacy over local government and status within the bureaucracy has had to be settled for.

Finally, it should not be forgotten that the powerful Ministries of the Army and the Navy completely disappeared as a result of the Occupation, thus excising what had been a crucial instrument of bureaucratic control. Although they were eventually replaced by the Defence Agency, within the Prime Minister's Office, this has so far remained a pale shadow of the former military bureaucracy, in terms of its status, independence and effectiveness.

There is a considerable contrast between the civil service today and its prewar counterpart. Before the war, governments had been less concerned to impose checks upon the abuse of administrative power by officials than to ensure that government control extended to the remotest corner of the land. As servants of the emperor, government officials for the most part did not hesitate to use their power. The notion of bureaucratic arrogance is summed up in an oft-quoted phrase, *kanson mimpi* ('reverence for the Government and disdain for the people'), which seems to have been an apt description of the prevailing ethos over much of the prewar period.[21]

The Occupation made an attempt to bring democratic principles to bear upon the status and behaviour of the bureaucracy. The term 'government official' was changed to 'public servant' (*Kōmuin*), and new legislation was brought in to regulate their status and conditions.[22] Article 15 of the 1947 Constitution states, in a complete break with the former tradition of subservience to the emperor, that 'the people have the inalienable right to choose their public officials and to dismiss them. All public officials are servants of the whole community and not of any special group.' This did not mean, of course, that all civil service positions were to be subject to popular election, but that the civil service was to be subject to popular control through the National Diet, to which the Cabinet was responsible. Moreover, article 73 of the Constitution stated that: '[t]he Cabinet ... shall ... [a]dminister the civil service, in accordance with standards established by law.'

Nevertheless, it is widely agreed that the impact of the Occupation upon the civil service was considerably less than it was in other areas. Part of the reason for this was that the Americans were forced to utilize the existing bureaucratic structures in order to administer the country and put their reformist programmes into effect. Typically, a wide-ranging programme of social, political and economic reform requires extensive administrative resources to make it a reality, and such resources existed in abundance in the old government bureaucracy. The task of reforming the bureaucracy, and cutting it down to size, therefore had to take second place in the scale of American priorities. Since the Occupation has been followed by an extraordinary period of economic development, the bureaucracy has continued to have ample opportunity to exercise influence because of the sheer scope and rapidity of the changes which have been taking place.

Another factor cited by one writer to explain the resilience of the government bureaucracy in the 1950s is popular faith in the neutrality and impartiality of civil servants as contrasted with the venality and self-centredness of party politicians.[23] This was indeed one of the reasons why the recentralization of local government during the 1950s met comparatively little local resistance, since the 'independent' local authorities that had been set up proved remarkable more for their parochialism than for their progressiveness. At the same time problems of urban overcrowding, poor municipal amenities, polluted air and rivers and inflated land prices provoked widespread disillusionment with bureaucratic dominance in the late 1960s and early 1970s. This became evident in anti-Government voting trends in urban and metropolitan areas, and in an upsurge of activity by 'unstructured' citizens' groups such as consumer associations, groups to fight environmental pollution and so on.

It would however be difficult to interpret this as a clear preference for party politicians over government bureaucrats. The two are so closely interlocked with each other, both in fact and in the popular consciousness, that the Liberal Democratic Party is commonly regarded as largely an extension of the civil service.

Japan is not the only country about which it has been argued that the civil service exercises dominant influence over parties in power, but it is one of the few in which senior civil servants actually enter politics in considerable numbers after retirement, and form a kind of core élite within the ruling party. This, in fact, is part of a wider phenomenon, since most public corporations and private firms can also point to influential former civil servants on their boards of management. The practice of early retirement, followed by a second career in either business or politics, by civil servants is known in Japan as 'descent from Heaven' (*amakudari*), and is only lightly controlled by the National Personnel Authority.[24]

Of retiring higher civil servants, much the highest proportion enter employment with public corporations and with private industry. A careful and exhaustive study of data from the 1950s concluded that at that time about 30 per cent of higher civil servants joined public corporations, a similar proportion joined private industry, while about 6 per cent became Diet members. The proportion not entering any form of employment was almost negligible, and very few failed to step into high-ranking positions in their new employment. The Ministry of International Trade and Industry was, as might be expected, particularly heavily represented among those higher civil servants who on retirement made second careers in private industry, while the Ministry of Finance was well ahead of any other section of the bureaucracy in proportion of its senior officers who joined public corporations on retirement.[25] In the late 1970s and early 1980s, those ministries whose senior civil servants were most likely to 'descend from Heaven' were the Ministries of Finance (much the most numerous), Transport, Agriculture, Forestry and Fisheries, Construction, and International Trade and Industry. The pattern had changed remarkably little over the years, and the ministries most easily able to find their senior officials important jobs on retirement were those which had the most to do with industrial and other enterprises in the course of their day-to-day affairs.[26]

One study argues that there are three main patterns of career transfer for senior civil servants. The first, which is the least common, is where a private firm deliberately seeks out a civil servant with expertise relevant to its operations. The second, which is the most likely to involve corruption, is where a civil servant in the course of his career has accumulated obligations from businessmen, and on retirement is able to 'cash them in' for a position in private business. The third is where a ministry actively seeks out posts for its retiring civil servants in firms with which it has connections.[27] Here again we have evidence of the continued importance of 'connections' in Japanese politics, and the relatively permissive attitude of officialdom to practices that in some Western countries would be regarded as bordering on the corrupt.

The number of former civil servants who stand for Parliament and become Diet members is much smaller than the number who go into public corporations or private business. Nevertheless, it is generally established that their political importance is very considerable. Practically all of them, for instance, enter the ruling Liberal Democratic Party, the only party in present circumstances to offer prospects of effective power. A high percentage of them ultimately achieve Cabinet office. Moreover, they contribute a steady and substantial proportion (perhaps a quarter) of LDP Lower House members and an even higher proportion of the party's Upper House members. LDP Diet members of bureaucratic origin have occupied a more than proportional share of Cabinet and party positions since 1955, and as the three prime ministers between 1957 and 1972 (Kishi, Ikeda and Satō) were similarly recruits from the bureaucracy, it was common to speak of a bureaucratic ascendancy within the Party. The pattern is now more varied, with Fukuda and Ōhira having attained the prime ministership following careers which started in prestige ministries, but Tanaka, Miki and Suzuki having followed other paths.

A retired civil servant standing for election to the Diet under the LDP label appears to have an excellent chance of success. This may have something to do with a popular respect for civil servants, as suggested above, but in many cases the man's former organization will do much, through its contacts, to promote his campaign. An example is given of a former senior official of the Japan Monopolies Corporation (Nihon Senbai Kōsha), which controls the sale of government monopolies such as tobacco, who stood for election in the national constituency of the House of Councillors in 1965. Every tobacco kiosk in the land was mobilized in his support, and although he was standing for the first time he was elected by a handsome margin.[28]

The significance of the 'descent from Heaven' by senior civil servants into business and politics is enhanced when one considers the élitist character of recruitment into the government bureaucracy. Japan has long boasted a system of recruitment to the bureaucracy based upon open examinations, and indeed anybody who is motivated enough and bright enough to pass the civil service examinations can make a brilliant career for himself whatever his socio-economic background or whatever part of the country he comes from. Nevertheless, the civil service is heavily dominated by recruits from Tokyo University, even though a few other major universities now provide rather more élite civil servants than was previously the case. No other advanced country takes its top administrators so exclusively from one single tertiary institution.

The reasons for this lie partly in civil service tradition, and partly in the character of the educational system in contemporary Japan. When the government bureaucracy was in its formative stage in the Meiji period, Tokyo Imperial University (as it was then called) was practically the only university which could provide recruits of sufficient standard, and the tradition created at that time has persisted. In the postwar period, despite the American attempts to democratize tertiary education, such has been the pressure upon available places by aspirants towards high status occupations that the competition to obtain entry to those universities (especially Tokyo University) which had traditionally nurtured the national élite has become unbelievably fierce. What in Japan is usually referred to as the 'examination Hell' leads thousands of ambitious teenagers every year to spend one or more years, at their parents' expense, in 'cram schools' (*yobikō*) between graduating from high school and attempting the entrance examination into Tokyo University or other prestige universities.

The entrance examinations to the national universities such as Tokyo University test all-round academic ability. It would be inconceivable for anyone to gain entrance to Tokyo University through the national university entrance examinations if he or she were weak in any one major discipline, whether it were mathematics, natural science, history, literature or foreign languages. The examinations also require the candidate to reproduce an enormous amount of information, rather than simply testing his or her potential ability. Such is the intensity of competition to obtain entrance to Tokyo University, and such is the versatility required to pass the examination, that the mere fact that somebody is a Tokyo University *student* has come to be widely regarded as a *de facto* guarantee of high-level competence across a range of disciplines.

The civil service, moreover, continues to prefer to recruit generalists rather than specialists into its core élite, and it practises a policy of moving its personnel regularly from one area or specialty to another in the course of their careers. A generalist, however, is not simply someone who has graduated from a university arts faculty, but a person who has more than a passing acquaintance with mathematics and the natural sciences, as well as a 'liberal' education at tertiary level. The main recruiting ground for the civil service in Tokyo University is not the Arts Faculty but the Law Faculty, which has dominated the élite of certain ministries in particular, notably the Foreign Ministry, as well as sections of private industry. Law faculties in Japan, however, have not been regarded as providing training primarily for those wanting to go into legal practices, while political science, as well as economics, has usually been part of the curriculum. One writer compares a Japanese law faculty to 'a combination of a political science department and a business administration school in an American university'.[29] In sum, therefore, a Tokyo University product (especially the product of the Law Faculty) remains far more attractive than any alternative when applicants for the civil service are being considered.

Clearly, the working of this system practically guarantees the constant rejuvenation of the civil service top echelons with ambitious and talented men in their forties, who are motivated to bring in innovations because of the relatively short tenure of their positions. It also produces a steady supply of older men, highly experienced in the ways of government, for industry and politics. The system has developed in this way as a kind of counterpoint to the very different state of affairs in the LDP and in Cabinet. As we have seen, the LDP is extraordinarily slow at rejuvenating its ranks, while its decision-making processes verge on immobilism as it works out a series of compromises between a variety of local and national interest groups. Moreover Cabinet ministers have typically been factional appointees, enjoying relatively brief tenure and relying overwhelmingly on the expertise of their permanent officials. With the LDP permanently in power, the tradition of bureaucratic dominance remains strong, and is maintained by the recruitment of former senior civil servants into the LDP. The need, therefore, for a rejuvenating mechanism to counteract bureaucratic stagnation is acute. Whether the system could be copied with advantage by other countries whose recent policy performance has been less impressive than Japan's needs to be considered with this whole picture in mind.

On balance the system produces dynamic and innovative government, while the aspect of 'immobilism' which we have spoken of could also more positively be regarded as 'stability'. Countries which have experienced frequent changes of government accompanied by drastic changes of policy might regard not only the innovative, but also some of the 'immobilist' features of Japanese politics as not wholly disadvantageous.

For the universities themselves, the narrow base of recruitment into the civil service is perpetuated not entirely without social cost. The dominant position of Tokyo University tends to have a dampening effect upon the morale of other universities, as well as upon their students, and this was certainly one factor in the student unrest of the late 1960s. The very general belief that since there is an informal 'pecking order' of universities it is only worth a bright student seeking to enter the very 'best', does not always accurately reflect the quality of instruction or facilities in particular disciplines in universities occupying different levels in this informal scale. Some private universities, such as Waseda and Keiō in Tokyo, are institutions of very high standing indeed, but their students find it far more difficult to enter the government bureaucracy than graduates of Tokyo University. Failure to enter the civil service on graduation practically excludes it as a career, since transfer at a later stage is infinitely more difficult. It is also the case that once a student has passed the entrance examination to an élite university, the intense pressure that was upon him until he gained entrance greatly relaxes, and he can afford to coast along at his own pace. For all these reasons there has been a great deal of criticism of the system from within Japan itself.[30]

In examining government involvement in the economy, it is important to distinguish a number of separate areas. Economic planning in the sense of the production of plans is regularly practised. The Economic Planning Agency (EPA) draws up estimates of future economic growth across the economy. These are not directly enforceable by government action, but they have an 'announcement effect' which probably has some influence on business confidence, but very little in practice on the direction or quantity of capital investment. These plans are now based on sophisticated econometric models, and their credibility is somewhat assisted by the general consistency of government policies, but their effect on business behaviour seems rather small. Nationalized industries are also rather unimportant as instruments of government planning or control. Apart from the deficit-ridden National Railways (which in any case have to compete with private lines on many commuter services), the salt and tobacco monopolies, post and telecommunications, the two national airlines and most importantly a number of banking and financial institutions, practically all of the economy is in private hands.

The Government has in recent years been able to make quite effective and sophisticated use of the credit structure operating within the economy in order to make its influence felt over the nature and direction of capital investment by industry and similar matters. A large proportion of capital investment by Japanese firms is financed by bank loans, and the banks themselves are prepared to extend credit to firms far beyond the level that would be acceptable to most Western banking systems. This is in part because, to a very considerable extent, the banking system replaces the securities market as a source of business capital. In the past the government, through the Bank of Japan, has been in a strong position to exercise influence through monetary policy upon the extent and nature of capital investment by major firms. This, however, was a feature of the situation of capital shortage which existed until the late 1960s. In the late 1970s and early 1980s the lower level of private investment and higher level of government debt (which has produced a capital surplus) have greatly reduced the government's capacity to use this method of control. Most major firms are now able to raise capital adequate to their needs on overseas capital markets, and are therefore much less susceptible to government influence through monetary policy. In any case, since the larger firms typically have a number of much smaller firms which are principally dependent upon them through subcontracting arrangements, they are able to shift any burden of the increased cost of credit onto their subcontractors, and this may have far-reaching effects throughout the economy. One of the more untoward results of this situation has been that in times of monetary squeeze many of the smaller firms will move into export markets, where they can expect to be paid promptly, since in the domestic market payment is likely to be greatly delayed.[31]

To understand the role of the government in the Japanese economy it is essential to appreciate the extent to which this has changed over time. In the Meiji period the Government laid the foundations of certain industries for which immediate profit opportunities were not apparent, and then when they were functioning properly, handed them over to private entrepreneurs. During the military period of the 1930s and early 1940s the autonomy of private industry was greatly reduced as it came to operate under close official supervision and control. Industry was also hedged around with all kinds of regulations during the Occupation period, and into the 1960s businesses needed government authorization for several purposes including the obtaining of foreign exchange. Despite promptings from the international economic community, the liberalization of foreign capital imports was late in coming, but by the mid-1970s official restrictions on the operation of foreign firms in Japan were about on a par with those in other comparable countries (agriculture being an exception, as in Europe and elsewhere).[32]

'Administrative guidance' (see above, p. 137), particularly by MITI, continued to be exercised for certain purposes, and as a very broad generalization it still achieved considerable success. During the high-growth period of the 1960s MITI used administrative guidance to promote the rationalization of the motor car and other industries (meaning a reduction in the number of firms). Following the oil shock of 1973–4 a quite different economic climate prevailed, in which job opportunities in new and growing high technology industries no longer absorbed sufficient labour from the older and less cost-effective industries to speed the decline of the latter. In these circumstances MITI exerted itself to promote the retrenchment of heavy industries such as aluminium and steel production. These industries, however, were able to exert considerable political leverage, and MITI had to provide various material incentives in order to make its views prevail and ease the process of decline.[33] MITI has also exercised pressure to increase the size and effectiveness of Japan's research and development programme in a number of industries and fields, while government involvement in pollution control and energy conservation has already been mentioned.

Up to the 1970s there was a strong sense in government and business alike that the economy was vulnerable to more highly capitalized enterprises based overseas, and especially in the United States. Capital liberalization was very much delayed and Japan came under intense foreign criticism on the grounds that she was not prepared to allow foreign firms to compete effectively in the Japanese market with local firms until Japanese industries had demonstrated beyond doubt their international effectiveness. Japan still remains the target of such criticism, even though the objective circumstances have radically changed and the extent of government control over the economy is far less. This is not to say government is no longer an important factor in the management of the economy, but that in the 1970s and 1980s the relationships between government and the industrial world have become much more complicated and subject to pressures and counter-pressures, than they were in the euphoric period of the 1960s.

Consultation between government and industrial organizations is continuous and occurs at many levels and in many ways. Connections forged between ministries and sections of industry (and ministries and the LDP) as a result of *amakudari* has already been noted (see p. 149). There is a proliferation of investigative committees (*shingikai*) reporting on matters of concern to a particular ministry, and these committees usually include significant representation from the business world, particularly where their frame of reference is some area of economic policy. Informal contacts of course abound, as they do in virtually any political system of the advanced world, but it would be a mistake to see the totality of these contacts as indicating a 'monolithic' structure of relations between business and government.[34] The provision of funds by business firms both to the factions of the LDP and to the Party's central organization through the People's Association was noted in chapter 7. The amount of money which flows into the Party in this fashion is thought to be very large indeed,[35] and lubricates the wheels of communication between the Party and industry. Two things, however, need to be noted about the role of such contributions. One is that when businessmen give money to faction leaders they normally spread their contributions among more than one faction leader. This practice no doubt stems from a realistic appraisal of the potential for change in any given factional balance in the LDP. Its effect however is to avoid the kind of situation that existed in the 1920s and 1930s, when some of the conservative political groups were seen to be almost wholly dependent financially upon one particular *zaibatsu* or business conglomerate. That kind of situation, which did much to discredit the political parties at that time, has at least been avoided in the recent period.

The second point is that, generally speaking, business is content to allow the LDP to function as it sees fit, without seeking to alter the system. Provided that a conservative government is securely in power under a reliable prime minister, business organizations have mostly been content to allow politicians and civil servants to formulate policy. Although the policy preferences of the business world are made clear, particularly on economic matters, there have been comparatively few concerted attempts to interfere openly with the political process. One exception was the ultimately successful campaign mounted by businessmen in 1955 to persuade the warring conservative parties of the time to amalgamate into one party. After some notoriously 'corrupt' LDP election campaigns in the mid-1970s, some business organizations and firms threatened to withhold funds from the Party. Nevertheless, the possibility of a government led by the JSP or including the JCP would be regarded as highly unpalatable by industry, both on the grounds that those parties are (in the view of many industrialists) hostile to free enterprise, and also because they are seen as both incompetent in matters of government and unduly beholden to labour unions.[36] Political interference of one kind or another in such circumstances could hardly be ruled out.

The business world has a variety of organized channels for making its views known on policy matters and for exercising influence. Each industry has its own independent organization, which among other things may be an important contributor of political finance. These include, for instance, the Japan Steel League (Nihon Tekkō Remmei), the Electrical Manufacturing Federation (Denki Jigyō Rengōkai) and the Automobile Industry Association (Jidōsha Kōgyo Kai). There are also associations based on geographical areas, such as Tokyo, Ōsaka or Nagoya. Some associations specialize in labour relations, and some in more general matters of economic policy affecting their members. Others are the meeting grounds for top leaders of a single *keiretsu*-type combine such as the Mitsui or Mitsubishi groups. There is the Central Association of National Medium and Small Industry Groups (Zenkoku Chūshō Kigyō Dantai Chūōkai) representing small and medium industry. There are others such as the Japan Productivity Centre (Nihon Seisansei Hombu), which include representatives of labour, consumers and the Government, as well as of business, and therefore cannot strictly be regarded as business pressure groups.[37]

The most important and influential associations representing Japanese industry as a whole (but chiefly the major firms and industries) are four 'peak associations'. These are the Federation of Economic Organizations (Keidanren), the Japan Federation of Employers' Associations (Nikkeiren), the Japan Chamber of Commerce and Industry (Nisshō) and the Japan Committee for Economic Development (Keizai Dōyūkai).

Undoubtedly the most important of these four groups is the Federation of Economic Organizations. Founded in August 1946 as a national centre to represent all kinds of economic enterprise, it initially included in its membership the Japan Chamber of Commerce and Industry, as well as organizations representing small and medium industry. These groups however defected about the time that Japan regained her independence in 1952, and since then the Federation of Economic Organizations has been the chief spokesman for large-scale enterprises, both in private industry and, curiously enough, also in the government sector. It maintains a considerable number of standing and special committees, covering aspects of domestic and foreign economic policy, and is in constant contact with government.

The Japan Federation of Employers' Associations has much the same membership as the Federation of Economic Organizations, but concentrates mainly on relations with labour. Consisting of both regional and industry-based groups, it has concerned itself with employment, wages and conditions, labour legislation and welfare matters, at times putting up an aggressive front against labour union demands. It also co-ordinates the policy of management towards the annual 'Spring Struggles' launched by the trade union federations.

The Japan Chamber of Commerce and Industry is the only one of the four groups which existed before the war, and indeed its history goes back to the Meiji period. It is based on more than four hundred local Chambers of Commerce, and acts as a spokesman for its members on a variety of economic matters.

Finally, the Japan Committee for Economic Development

(so named after the US Committee for Economic Development – its Japanese title, Keizai Dōyūkai, translates literally as 'Economic Friends' Association') was founded in April 1946 on the initiative of younger, progressive industrial managers and businessmen who wished to promote economic policies and practices in keeping with the new order being introduced by the Occupation. During the Occupation period, serious attempts were made by the Committee to build a basis of understanding between management and trade unions. Since the Occupation it has concentrated on issues such as productivity, balanced economic growth and social policies. It differs from the other three groups in being based on individual rather than corporate membership. Its leading members, originally seen as 'young turks' in the immediate postwar period, now occupy positions of the highest responsibility in industry, commerce and banking, and to all intents and purposes this organization does not differ from the Federation of Economic Organizations, except to some extent in function.

Although these four groups are distinguishable from each other in the ways mentioned, they have overlapping membership and a considerable similarity of interest. It would be inaccurate to regard them as representing separate sections of industry with conflicting interests. For the most part, conflicts of interest and of view which appear between different personalities, firms or industries are expressed and, when possible, reconciled within the collective forum which the groups provide. In this sense, and in the sense that 'big business' as a whole has in effect had privileged access to policy-making, the major firms and bodies representing their views may be regarded as Japan's most powerful interest, having considerable internal cohesion on matters of general economic policy, though naturally divided over the detail of many issues. During the high economic growth period representatives of small and medium industry had by contrast very little impact on government policy.

With much slower growth rates from the mid-1970s there has been a perceptible diversification of the sources of influence. When industries at the frontier of technology were rapidly absorbing labour from declining industries, rearguard action by those industries was muted, but in circumstances where jobs are threatened and new jobs are much harder to obtain, the path of political action is taken more frequently. Since not only the Opposition parties, but also many LDP Diet members depend on the votes of those in firms and industries which are in difficulties, the pressure on government to modify its policies now comes from a variety of sources. Meanwhile agriculture, despite the fact that its share of total output and of total population has declined (though the rate of decline slowed in the 1970s), has developed political organization of great effectiveness, through the Nōkyō (Agricultural Co-operative Associations). LDP Diet members, and to a much lesser extent those of the JSP and DSP, simply cannot afford to neglect the interests of the farmers, and it is no coincidence that successive LDP governments have maintained policies of high agricultural protection.[38]

Apart from the representatives of industry and agriculture, some associational interest groups (the Japan Medical Association is an example)[39] have good access to government on matters within their interest and competence. With struggles for control of local authorities coming into prominence in the 1970s, pressure on government to provide better services of interest to local communities has increased substantially, and for the most part the government has responded to such pressure by seeking to institutionalize such channels of influence. Citizens' groups, on the other hand, because of their generally low level and permanency of organization, have proved harder to incorporate in this way. Resort to the courts by many local groups, particularly over questions of environmental pollution, has tended to enhance the judicial role in the political system, thus injecting a further element of pluralism.

Decision-making within the central power structure is generally efficient, though as we argued earlier (p. 146), the administrative capacity of the core ministries (Finance, MITI and so on) is much higher than that of ministries on the periphery of key economic decision-making. The habit of making wide-ranging consultations is well entrenched, and though often time-consuming, tends to produce effective implementation because of the commitment to the decision taken by those who have been consulted. A further point worth making is that Japanese bureaucracies, both public and private, show a concern with detail that surprises many foreign observers. While this at times results in excessively burdensome procedures, it also arguably improves quality of service and minimizes mistakes.

Thus in discussing the structure and process of central government in Japan it is important to distinguish the characteristics of the period of rapid economic growth before the 1973–4 oil crisis from those of the subsequent period. Before the oil crisis the effective participants in the political process were an unusually narrow set, and internal conflict was relatively muted among those with real access to decision-making. In retrospect this may be seen as the product of a particular set of circumstances, in which the necessity for hard choices was minimized by the very speed at which the economy was growing. Even in that period, however, there were certain policy areas in which immobilism prevailed. During the 1970s and early 1980s, the system has become notably more pluralist and complex. Policy choices have more of a zero-sum character, and the vigour with which interests that feel their interests threatened exert political influence in defence of those interests has markedly increased. The response of government to these changes has been consciously to seek to incorporate a more diverse set of interests into a structure of consultation and decision-making of an orderly kind. But there is little doubt that the system is more difficult to manage than it was in the 1960s.

9 The Politics of Opposition

It is easy to dismiss the forces of Opposition in postwar Japanese politics as a political irrelevance. They have failed to win a majority of seats in any election, though they were close to doing so in the Lower House between 1976 and 1980, and in the Upper House between 1974 and 1980. The JSP had one spell in office as part of a coalition Government during the confused and difficult years 1947 and 1948, but the Party in government achieved little, and discredited itself in the eyes of the voters. Internal cohesion has been a constant problem: the JSP split five times between 1947 and 1960, another splinter group broke away in 1977, and since the 1960s it has come under effective challenge from other parties contesting the anti-LDP vote. The high point of success for the JSP came in the 1958 Lower House election, when it obtained 166 out of 467 seats. Apart from one seat which went to the Communists, the anti-Government vote was represented entirely by the JSP.

Between the 1958 and 1972 elections the Opposition parties as a whole became stronger, but the share of the JSP in that success diminished. Although during the 1970s the JSP performance stabilized to some extent, there was little evidence of a coming revival of its fortunes. What is particularly striking is that in metropolitan and urban constituencies, which in the 1960s saw the most spectacular advances by the Opposition, the JSP fell behind very badly indeed. A situation of Opposition strength but JSP weakness in the big cities has persisted through the 1970s and into the 1980s. Compared with the 1950s, therefore, the balance of JSP representation has shifted drastically towards the small town and country constituencies (see tables 19 and 20). Considering that the JSP is still closely reliant upon trade unions for its organizational support, the extent of defections from it in the cities is particularly striking.[1]

The fragmentation of the Opposition began in 1960 with the

defection of right-wing factions from the JSP and the formation of the Democratic Socialist Party (DSP). Despite its moderate appeal, the DSP has never succeeded in making a major political impact, though it occupies a strategic position between the LDP and other Opposition parties (see table 22). Perhaps the most important effect of its emergence was to upset the balance of forces in the JSP in favour of ideological extremists and narrowly sectional trade union officials. Thus the defection of the DSP ultimately damaged the prospects of the JSP, without much contributing to the cause of moderate democratic socialism.

The troubles of the Socialist parties during the 1960s left the field open for new political forces to emerge. The first of these was the Kōmeitō, the political arm of the neo-Buddhist sect the Sōka Gakkai. Having earlier tested its strength in Upper House elections, the Kōmeitō first contested a House of Representatives election in 1967, when 25 of its 32 candidates were elected. Its support subsequently fluctuated between a low of 29 Lower House seats in 1972 and a high of 57 seats in 1979, though in 1980 it fell back again to 33 seats. Its supporters are concentrated in big city areas (see table 21). In 1969 it further increased its Lower House strength to 47, but by the elections of 1972 had passed its peak and dropped back again to 29 seats, with a substantially reduced vote. The second new force was the Japan Communist Party (JCP), which, although it had had a brief success in the immediate postwar period, had been negligible in electoral terms through the 1950s. By the late 1960s its support was rapidly increasing, and in the 1972 elections it jumped ahead of both the Kōmeitō and the DSP to become the second Opposition party, with 38 seats in the Lower House. This advance, however, failed to be sustained, and in the early 1980s it was one of the smaller Opposition parties (see table 23). If the 1960s had seen the emergence of quite substantial new forces within the Opposition, the late 1970s produced the phenomenon of the 'mini-party'. In 1976 a splinter broke from the LDP and formed the New Liberal Club, while in 1977 an even smaller group of disillusioned JSP members formed the Social Democratic League (originally Socialist Citizens League). The former drew most of its strength from the Tokyo area (see table 24).

It can be seen from tables 19 to 24 (see pp. 193–5) that the appeal of the 'new' parties was largely concentrated among big city voters, who were now dividing their votes among a range of parties. The ability of these parties to carve out a sphere of electoral influence in big city electorates was the obverse of a decline by 'established parties' in the same areas, though the LDP made something of a comeback in the 1980 elections. Both the Liberal Democrats and the Socialists were regarded as rather unappealing by city electorates attracted by the organizing ability and progressive orientation of the newer parties. By the early 1980s, however, some of these parties themselves were coming to look distinctly stale.

The effect of these trends upon the Opposition as a whole was highly confusing. The grossly over-weighted rural and semi-rural electorates remained solidly conservative, and the LDP was rather unlikely to lose its majority of seats under the existing system. The JSP also, however, could not be eliminated or reduced to minor party status by inroads into its support in the cities alone. Moreover, it was not one but five minor parties that were contesting the hegemony over the Opposition possessed hitherto by the JSP. None of the current Opposition parties appeared poised to make the kind of advance that had transformed Opposition politics in the 1960s, so that moves towards the merger of some existing parties was being actively canvassed.

The view that the Opposition is politically irrelevant or generally ineffectual stems from the long tenure of office by the Liberal Democrats. A fragmented Opposition, more or less permanently out of power, heavily dependent for organizational support upon labour unions, whose influence upon Government is limited, is a weak counterpart to a central government machine of the kind we have described in chapter 8.

On the other hand the picture needs to be kept in perspective. With factionalism endemic in politics generally, and fragmentation therefore a constant danger for every party, the failure of the Opposition to gain power has been premised upon the ability of the LDP, sometimes against considerable odds, to hold together. When the LDP was formed in 1955 many people did not expect it to survive intact for very long. Curiously enough, one of the factors which seems to have accentuated the divisive tendencies within the Opposition was this unexpected ability of the LDP to close ranks and avoid defections. Until 1955 there was always a real possibility that the Socialists might once more be in a position to participate in a coalition government with moderate conservatives, as in 1947–8. Once this possibility was foreclosed the only way to defeat the LDP was to gain a clear majority of seats in the House of Representatives. To do this however would have entailed broadening the base of the JSP far beyond the ranks of organized labour, which in Japan was a much newer and narrower power base than it was in, say, Great Britain or Australia.

Attempts by the right wing of the Party to form a 'mass party' rather than a 'class party' (to use the jargon of the time) ended in frustration since the left wing, with its radical labour union support, was always numerically superior. The frustration of the right-wing Socialists (which led, among other things, to the formation of the DSP in 1960) made the left wing of the Party even more complacent in its reliance upon narrowly sectional support from left-wing labour unions and radical activists, and in its indulgence in extremist polemics far removed from the concern of the average voter. The JSP in the 1960s was therefore caught in a vicious spiral of frustration, faction-fighting and ideological extremism which led inexorably to electoral decline. It failed to attract new members of outstanding talent, and new political forces stepped into the vacuum that was being created. If, however, the prospect of participation in power had come nearer to reality, the JSP might well have become a far different party from what it is today. Between 1976 and 1980 the near parity with the LDP held by the Opposition parties taken together caused them to be taken more seriously by government and by some interest groups, and this in turn produced a certain revivifying effect.

Votes for the Opposition parties increased steadily if slowly between the early postwar years and the mid-1970s, reflecting principally the massive shift of population into the cities during the period of rapid economic growth. By 1976 they commanded an absolute majority of the popular vote, while from 1955 they had always had enough seats in the Lower House to block constitutional revision. Failure to redraw the electoral boundaries effectively, coupled with lack of unity among the parties themselves, greatly reduced the effectiveness of that vote. Nevertheless, there was a major qualitative change in the configuration of party support when compared with the prewar period or the immediate postwar years. The rapid urbanization of Japan tended to replace rural patterns of community solidarity and mutual support networks with more individualistic and critical urban attitudes. The process has undoubtedly been slowed by the tenacity of small group consciousness even at the urban level, and also by the uninspiring performance of the Opposition parties when considered as an alternative government. Nevertheless, in a period of unprecedented and sustained growth of individual prosperity, the Opposition did not do badly, as might appear at first sight.

It is also not so easy as it might appear to determine whether the Opposition has any significant influence upon government decision-making. Certainly the Opposition does not initiate or carry through major policy decisions. On the other hand between 1976 and 1980 its majority position on some Lower House committees placed it in a strategic position to affect legislation, and many compromises had to be hammered out taking Opposition party views into account. This situation, however, ended with the 1980 elections. For the most part, the LDP has maintained strict voting discipline on the floor of the House and in committee, though there were occasions during the *hakuchū* period when this was not the case. Pressure groups close to the Opposition parties are generally much less effective than those close to the LDP. Also, as can be seen from tables 13 to 18, the educational level of Opposition party Diet members is generally lower than that of those affiliated with the LDP. Parties permanently out of power are obviously a less attractive career prospect for the politically ambitious than a party which has long monopolized power.

On the other hand the Opposition parties do affect decisions in certain ways by their very presence, although their influence is largely a negative one. In the postwar period they evolved techniques of filibustering, boycotting the Diet or its committees, and engaging in large-scale demonstrations against objectionable legislation or acts of Government. These have sometimes been portrayed as expressions of frustration with a political process over which they are unable to gain control, but they do have a more specific and rational purpose. When anti-Government Diet members decide to boycott a Diet session because the Government is pushing ahead with a bill to which they object, the principal aim is to embarrass the LDP both by upsetting its legislative timetable and by placing it in a bad light as a dictatorial, undemocratic party, unwilling to take into account the legitimate views of the Opposition. The mass media are, in effect, participants in this process, because of the generally critical attitude they take to Government 'high-handedness' in forcing through legislation despite an Opposition Diet boycott. Although the Government will usually get its way on the substance of the legislation (it may have to make minor concessions as the price of bringing the Opposition back into the Diet), both its programme and its image will suffer.[2]

Much the most important base of support for the Opposition parties (except for the Kōmeitō) has been the labour union movement, and it is difficult to understand the politics of the Opposition without some knowledge of the structure of Japanese trade unions. For practical purposes, the most significant unit of union organization in Japan is the enterprise union. This stems from the permanent employment system which became the norm in much of Japanese industry after the Second World War, having existed to some extent since about the 1920s. A firm will hire staff for the most part from school- or college-leavers in the expectation of retaining them permanently or semi-permanently. The individual hired by a well-known firm will tend to see himself as privileged in relationship to employees of less famous or less financially sound enterprises. Even though his starting salary may be quite low, it will rise steadily with age, and his privileged position can be quantified by the size of bonus payments and other fringe benefits that the firm can afford to pay him.

The system has a number of consequences. Being committed to a particular company on a more or less permanent basis, the individual will be expected to show loyalty towards it; and since his own prosperity is likely to depend upon the prosperity of the company, it will be in his interests to demonstrate such loyalty. Distinctions of rank within a given enterprise are taken most seriously, but the system tends to promote mobility within firms rather than mobility between them. The consequences of dismissal for any employee are grave, because he is unlikely to be taken on at anything like the same level by another employer; but conversely the employer will be reluctant to use the sanction of dismissal. The permanent employment system is easier to maintain in conditions of high than in conditions of low economic growth, because the costs to a firm of an ageing work force to which seniority payments must continue to be paid despite poor economic conditions may be excessive. In these circumstances the scope of permanent employment contracts tends to be progressively narrowed. In any case, many firms have a number of casual or temporary employees who do not share the privileges of the permanent staff, and may be dismissed at short notice, though many have a kind of *de facto* permanency. These are usually non-union labour.

It is easy to see why in these circumstances each company has its own union. From the point of view of the individual employee it is his firm which is of much more significance than his craft or the industry to which the firm belongs. Rather than being divided between members of several craft unions, the enterprise union will be able to present a united front to management. At the same time, the union may be torn between co-operating with management in order to hold down costs and thus ultimately improve the firm's ability to pay well, or confronting management in order to obtain immediate improvements in pay and conditions. In many cases the dividing line between management of the firm and leadership of the union is not entirely clear, whereas in other cases the union adopts a tough radical stand against management as a kind of protest against the system.[3] Disputes leading to strike action undertaken by a radical union leadership group sometimes led in the past to the formation of a 'second union', prepared to come to an understanding with management in the interests of preserving the viability of the firm and thus the jobs of the employees. There is no doubt that management has proved adept at exploiting such union differences in order to emasculate union power.

A number of union federations exist at the national level. The biggest and most radical of these, Sōhyō (General Council of Japanese Trade Unions), with some four and a half million members in affiliated unions, is composed predominantly of employees of the public service and government instrumentalities, who for various reasons tend to be more radically oriented than workers in private industry. Dōmei (Japan Confederation of Labour), with about 2,100,000 members, Chūritsu Rōren (Federation of Independent Unions), with less than a million and a half, and Shinsambetsu (National Federation of Industrial Unions), with less than a million, comprise almost entirely private industry unions and have been much more moderate politically. In addition the Kinzoku Rōkyō (International Metal Workers' Federation: Japan Chapter, or IMF:JC), which has a membership approaching two million in affiliated unions, has become a particularly active force influencing wages and conditions across a wide range of industries.

The enterprise unions still play a large role in the bargaining process between labour and management. But the annual Shuntō (Spring Struggle), begun in the 1950s as a means of promoting co-ordinated wage bargaining, has become the principal means of setting wage guidelines throughout industry generally.

In economic terms, labour more than held its own in the period of rapid economic growth of the 1960s (though it was seriously disadvantaged up to about 1960), but wage settlements achieved in the Shuntō, held annually since the mid-1970s, have steadily declined in size. The sense that labour is failing to maximize its overall bargaining potential has promoted moves towards the reunification of the labour federations which were separately formed in the turbulent conditions of the Occupation and its aftermath. This question has a political dimension, since whereas Chūritsu Rōren, Shinsambetsu and the IMF:JC generally stay aloof from party politics, Dōmei backs the small Democratic Socialist Party, and Sōhyō has given support mainly to the more radical Japan Socialist Party, although the Japan Communist Party also commands some support within the Sōhyō leadership. To what extent these political and organizational divisions can be overcome in the 1980s remains to be seen.

Despite its repeated setbacks, the JSP still remains the main Opposition party, and the only one to have significant Diet representation outside the major cities and towns. Three things stand out when one contemplates its complex and traumatic history. The first is the extent to which the record of the Party's past experience (including the experiences of its predecessors before the war) has lain heavy upon it, often to the point of inhibiting reasonable innovation. The second is the disruptive nature of the factionalism to which it – like most other political parties in Japan – has been subject. The third is its relationship with the labour union movement, and the long-term effects which its labour union connections have had upon the Party's flexibility.

Socialism in Japan has a history which can be traced back to the late nineteenth century, but it was not of any electoral significance until the franchise was extended in 1925 to include all adult males. In its early stages it was largely an intellectual movement, in which a bewildering variety of doctrines contended, including Christian socialism, syndicalism, anarchism and various strands of Marxism. Connections with the embryo labour union movement existed and were consolidated in the 1920s, but the more radical sections of the movement faced constant harassment from the police. This was one of the factors which made unity among Japanese socialists almost impossible, since the radicals (by the late 1920s largely Marxists) were forced underground and gradualists needed to dissociate themselves from the radicals in order to avoid the attentions of the police. Personal factionalism also played a large part in the extreme fragmentation which the socialist movement experienced between 1925 and 1932.[4]

In 1932 most of the existing left-wing parties joined forces to form the Socialist Masses Party (Shakai Taishūtō), which made some electoral progress during the 1930s.[5] The Party, however, had to contend with a climate of increasing militarism and nationalism, to which in considerable degree it accommodated itself.

When political parties were revived after the war the newly formed Japan Socialist Party was in effect a coalition of several factions with widely differing ideological antecedents.[6] The most important of these were a right-wing group associated with moderate, largely non-political, labour unionism, a left-wing group, strongly imbued with a kind of Marxism derived ultimately from Kautsky, and a group whose ideological position was somewhere between the two. Each of these three groups or factions traced its parentage to small independent parties which had existed at various times before the war, and their respective leadership groups were composed largely of the same people in the prewar as in the postwar periods.

During the earlier stages of the Occupation the running was made largely by the right-wing group, whose most significant figure, Nishio Suehiro, dominated (though he did not lead) the coalition Cabinets of 1947–8. The centre group was gravely weakened by the fact that much of its personnel were out of politics because of the purge edict, having been the dominant element in the Socialist Masses Party during its pro-militarist period. Following the fall of the coalition Cabinets, and the catastrophic electoral defeat of the JSP in the 1949 general elections, the centre of gravity within the Party shifted towards the left.

The ideological disputes which took place within the Party at this time were of crucial importance for its later development. Thus, in the Inamura–Morito dispute the JSP was divided between supporters of class as a basis for the Party's organization and those who thought that in order to gain power the Party would have to seek support not only from members of the 'proletariat', but also from the lower levels of the middle class (small shopkeepers and businessmen, and some salaried employees) and from the poorer farmers. There were also keen disputes about how sacred the parliamentary process was as a means of gaining power. The left, with its memories of police persecution before the war, frequently hinted at being prepared to take a semi-revolutionary road should the forces of 'monopoly capitalism' combine to frustrate a takeover of power by the Socialists. The right, on the other hand, with its more gradualist outlook held firm to the principles of parliamentarism.

Despite its predominantly Marxist heritage, and its tendency to think in terms of 'struggle' and 'confrontation' rather than 'normal process', the left wing of the JSP was seldom on good terms with the Communist Party. In part this was a question simply of political rivalry (for instance, when the Socialists were so badly beaten in the 1949 elections, the Communists picked up 35 seats), but also of long-standing ideological debate going back to the 1930s. The ramifications of the Rōnō–Kōza dispute in academic and political circles are too complex to go into here. In essence, however, it was an argument in Marxist terms about the stages of development of Japanese society, and the appropriate strategy of revolution. The Kōza ('Lectures') faction saw Japan as still dominated by 'feudal' elements and habits of mind (thus the Meiji Restoration had not been a true revolution in the Marxist sense), and thus requiring a two-stage revolution, first bourgeois–democratic and secondly proletarian–socialist. This view was close to the revolutionary strategy of the Communist Party in the 1950s and went along with a conspiratorial form of party organization and narrow élitist membership.

The Rōnō ('Labour–Farmer') faction, on the other hand, tended to regard feudal remnants in Japanese society as less important than the forces thrown up by capitalist development of the economy, so that it should be possible for the working class, having attained sufficient strength, to take over the reins of power without the intervening stage of a 'bourgeois–democratic' revolution. This view, first put forward in 1926 by a Marxist ideologue and former member of the then clandestine Communist Party, Yamakawa Hitoshi, remained highly influential among left-wing Socialists throughout the 1950s, and appears to have lingered on even into the 1970s.[7] In contrast to the Kōza position, the organizational principles of the Rōnō supporters have been more relaxed, so that internal discipline or even close co-ordination has seldom been a conspicuous feature of Socialist Party organization.

The differences between the Communists and the left-wing Socialists at this period were based on more than ideological differences within the framework of Marxism. Right through the Occupation era there was a struggle between them for control of the labour union movement, in which the Communists were ultimately unsuccessful. Since it was predominantly the left wing of the Socialist Party which made the running in this struggle, the prestige of the left Socialists was further enhanced in comparison with their right-wing colleagues.

Left-wing and right-wing Socialists had difficulty holding together from the time of the coalition Governments. Left-wing doctrines of 'social democracy' were set against right-wing doctrines of 'democratic socialism', the apparent subtlety of the ction being belied by the fervour with which the difference ›ursued by both sides. The question at issue was, of course, w...her the attainment of socialism was more important than the maintenance of democracy, or vice versa.

It was however the introduction of defence and foreign policy into the forefront of political debate in 1950 and 1951 that proved the final blow against Socialist unity. The outbreak of the Korean War in June 1950, the decision to form the paramilitary National Police Reserve, and the arguments between proponents of a 'Total Peace' (that is, a peace treaty with all the former Allied Powers) and a 'Partial Peace' (a peace treaty with the United States and her Cold War allies only) were more than the already fragile structure of Party unity could stand. In 1950–1 the left-wing factions within the JSP took up the slogan of 'four peace principles' – a 'Total Peace', no foreign troops to be stationed in Japan (this was an attack upon the proposed Japan–US security pact), permanent neutrality, and no rearmament. The right-wing factions attacked these four principles as expounded by the left, but were less clear about their own position. Thus when the JSP split into two separate parties in October 1951 over the San Francisco peace settlement, the left opposed the Peace Treaty, the Security Treaty and the existing and proposed build-up of paramilitary forces, while the right (strictly, the right and centre factions) supported the Peace Treaty as the best deal available in the circumstances, but was ambivalent about the Security Treaty and rearmament. This ambivalence reflected divisions between the right and centre factions, and it was therefore no accident that in a later party split (that of 1959–60) a substantial number of centre-faction members aligned themselves with the left, rather than following Nishio and the right-wing faction out of the Party to form the Democratic Socialist Party.

The 'Great Split' of 1951 was a most traumatic event for the Japanese Socialists, and accounts to a considerable extent for the preoccupation they have subsequently shown with matters of foreign policy, specifically the American alliance, relations with China and the Soviet Union and rearmament. These were not issues that concerned them greatly until about 1950, but the Socialist objection to the American policies which emerged during the later part of the Occupation certainly coloured their view of American relations with Japan after the Occupation was over.

The early 1950s was a period of difficult economic conditions for labour and of fairly rapid electoral gains for the two socialist parties, especially the Left Socialist Party. There was increasing identification between the Left Socialists and Sōhyō (formed in 1950 with Occupation support as an anti-Communist federation of labour), accompanying a rapid radicalization of the latter. At this time a radical left-wing appeal was attractive because of the economic situation in which wages were being held down, and the 'reverse course' policies of the post-Occupation Governments. The Left Socialists therefore stood on a platform of direct confrontation with the Government of the day, whereas the Right Socialists were still clearly hankering after the possibility of participating in a coalition Government together with elements from the conservative camp.[8]

The amalgamation of the two socialist parties, which took place in 1955 (shortly before the formation of a unified Liberal Democratic Party), was made possible by a number of factors, some of which were only temporary. One was that the international situation had become somewhat less tense following the death of Stalin, and Cold War confrontations were not so tense as they had been in 1951. (On the other hand, the Japan-US Security Pact had been considerably strengthened by the Mutual Security Assistance Agreement of 1954, in which the United States agreed to provide assistance to Japan in building up her newly formed Self Defence Forces.) Neutralism, newly fashionable in the third world at the time, was a convenient platform on which various sorts of socialists could unite, even though interpretations of what neutralism actually meant differed substantially between Right and Left Socialists.[9] Another condition for amalgamation was that both parties happened to be led, temporarily, by their moderate wings, which were reasonably close to each other in ideological outlook. Nevertheless, a unified platform was hammered out only after tenacious bargaining by each side. On fundamentally irreconcilable issues it was necessary to paper over the cracks with ambiguous or vague wording.[10]

The Socialist Party amalgamation of 1955 was accomplished among high hopes that the achievement of a parliamentary majority was only a matter of time. It was not long, however, before this euphoria began to dissolve, and the Party's hard-won unity was soon under considerable strain. There were a number of interconnected reasons for this. The most obvious manifestation of strain was that the central party leadership did not remain in the hands of moderates, but drifted progressively towards the left. Even a formerly middle-of-the-road leader such as Asanuma Inejirō (later assassinated in front of television cameras by an ultra-rightist fanatic) threw his lot in with the left, and made increasingly radical speeches. In part, this was a reaction against the prime ministership of Kishi Nobusuke and his provocative stance on a number of issues, notably the Police Duties Law Amendment Bill in 1958 and the negotiations to revise the Security Treaty.

Another factor was the increasing influence of Sōhyō over the JSP. This was expressed at the electoral level, where a high proportion of endorsed party candidates were former trade unionists from unions attached to the Federation, and derived much of their electoral organization and funds from their former unions rather than from the Party itself. This continued dependence upon trade unions both for its supply of electoral candidates and for much of the logistics of local organization remains the Achilles heel of the JSP, and has inhibited the growth of a broader and more independent organizational base. In the late 1950s, dependence upon the Sōhyō labour unions involved the JSP in a serious struggle within the labour union movement itself between radical, politically minded unionism and a unionism which put a high premium upon the cautious pursuit of limited economic improvements for unionists within the prevalent enterprise union structure. A confrontation between these two principles resulted in the formation of a number of 'second unions' at this period, in opposition to radical strike action by Sōhyō affiliates. This kind of issue had already resulted in the formation of the breakaway federation Zenrō (later Dōmei) in 1954, supported by moderate and conservative unions which found it impossible to coexist with the Sōhyō radicals. The lines of this division within the labour union movement paralleled very closely the emerging ideological divisions within the Socialist Party, culminating in the defection of the right wing and formation of the DSP in 1960.

A related concern within the socialist movement was the failure of the JSP to maintain the momentum of its electoral advances earlier in the decade. Having gained one-third of the seats in the House of Representatives (and thus being in a position to block attempts by the Government to revise the Constitution), the JSP seemed incapable of advancing any further. There was much discussion at the time of the Party's practically non-existent base of organization at the local level, and its excessive dependence upon radical trade unions for backing and support, thus allegedly preventing it from breaking through the 'one-third barrier'.[11] Few however seem to have suspected that the Party's electoral support would actually begin to decline from the early 1960s.

In the aftermath of the 1960 Security Treaty revision crisis and the defection of the DSP, the Socialist Party once more made an attempt to put its house in order. The emergence from 1960–1 of the programme of 'Structural Reform' was significant in a number of ways. It represented a series of realignments in the complex factional structure of the Party, a bid for power by a new generation of leaders, notably Eda Saburō and Narita Tomomi (JSP chairman from 1970 to 1977) and an ultimately unsuccessful attempt to form a power base within the Party upon other than factional lines. Ideologically, it sprang from a movement within the Italian Communist Party, but in the Japanese Socialist context it was largely an attempt to project a more pragmatic image to an electorate which was observed to be less amenable than before to radical Marxist appeals.

Ultimately the Structural Reform movement found itself mired in old-style factional disputes, largely because the activist clientele of the party consisted of labour unionists who found radical anti-system appeals most relevant to their circumstances and their way of looking at the world. Because of the absence of a mass base of party members owing allegiance to the Party as such (as distinct from factions and individuals within it), it proved impossible for reformist leaders such as Eda to mount a broad-based and moderate appeal. Those such as his left-wing rival Sasaki Kōzō (who attained the party chairmanship in 1965) were successful because they appealed to activists, who continued to be receptive to a radical Marxist approach.

The failure to cultivate a mass base independent of the Sōhyō labour unions seriously reduced the Party's electoral appeal in a period of increasing economic prosperity and left a political vacuum, in which the new image and considerable organizational abilities of the Kōmeitō and the JSP were able to make inroads into the traditional bases of Socialist support.

As the decade of the 1960s wore on these tendencies were accentuated. Factionalism within the JSP came to be embroiled with arguments about the Sino-Soviet dispute, and the new chairman, Sasaki, toyed with Maoist principles for a time. The Vietnam War was an important factor in pushing the Party to the left. By the end of the decade the factional problem appeared to have been semi-permanently resolved in favour of the left wing, but under a compromise chairman, Narita (formerly associated with the Structural Reform group), there was a retreat from some of the ideological extremism experienced earlier. Another factor, however, inhibited basic reappraisal of policies. The Party remained heavily dependent upon the Sōhyō labour unions, among which unions based on workers in the public service and public utilities such as the National Railways predominated. These unions were by and large both more radical and more politically oriented than unions in private industry. Suffering from various restrictions on their right to strike and to organize, and being in the employ of the Government or its instrumentalities, they provided the bulk of activists in a number of left-wing causes.

The narrowness of outlook thus engendered in the JSP brought its nemesis in the 1969 Lower House general election, when the Party lost fifty seats compared with the previous election, and found itself with more appeal in the countryside than in the cities. Following this disaster, the JSP made a partial electoral recovery in the early 1970s under the leadership of Narita as Chairman and Ishibashi Masashi as Secretary-General. This pair was elected in November 1970 and remained until 1977, surviving so long in part because neither had strong factional affiliation. At this period Socialist- and Communist-backed administrations were emerging in many of the larger cities, primarily as a result of the widespread environmental and quality-of-life problems which had resulted from unchecked economic growth. In attempting to develop its influence on the basis of these issues, however, the JSP faced vigorous competition from the better organized Japan Communist Party, and in 1974 the Kyōto branch of the JSP split on the issue of relations with the organizationally superior JCP uring the campaign for re-election of the Kyōto Governor.[12]

Changed economic circumstances following the oil crisis of 1973–4 ultimately checked the revival of the left in Japanese politics, whereas the forces of moderate opposition tended to do rather better. Eda Saburō, long opposed to the Marxist left within the JSP, maintained close links with the Democratic Socialist Party and the Kōmeitō at this period. Within the Party itself, however, the Shakaishugi Kyōkai, a Marxist–Leninist group with Rōnō-ha origins, was gaining strength in local branches, some related unions and at party congresses. This group had minimal representation among JSP Diet members, who were often more conservative than their rhetoric suggested, but a party rule enabling local branches to elect whom they pleased (not necessarily party Diet members) as delegates to the annual party Congress enabled it to exert a major influence on party decision-making. The relaxation of this rule in the late 1970s fairly quickly redressed the intra-Party balance of power in favour of party Diet members, but before this had taken place a factional realignment had occurred in which Eda and his old enemy Sasaki found themselves co-operating against the Shakaishugi Kyōkai in a factional group called the Atarashii Nagare no Kai (New Current Society). When, at the party Congress of February 1977, most of this group's candidates for executive positions were defeated by candidates backed by the Shakaishugi Kyōkai, Eda and a few of his supporters defected from the JSP and formed the Socialist Citizens' League. He died, however, shortly afterwards.

1977 was indeed a traumatic year for the JSP. Narita and Ishibashi wished to retire from party leadership, but the problem of finding new leaders to replace them caused further internal divisions. During lengthy negotiations over the leadership issue, three members of the Atarashii Nagare no Kai, led by Den Hideo, left the JSP and joined with the Socialist Citizens' League to found the Social Democratic League, now the smallest party with Diet representation. Finally, in December 1977, Asukata Ichio, the popular mayor of Yokohama, was persuaded to become Chairman of the JSP, and Tagaya Shinnen replaced Ishibashi as Secretary-General. Under the Asukata leadership internal conflict has subsided, but the Party fared poorly at the 1979 and 1980 elections.

Socialist Party organization has perforce been loose and relatively unco-ordinated. The absence of a mass base of individual members is even more evident than in the case of the Liberal Democrats. Party membership does not exceed 40,000 (compared with about 300,000 for the JCP) and appears to have declined since the 1950s. Active membership seems largely confined to organizers at the local level. Sympathetic labour unions act as a kind of substitute organization, but the Party as such has little control over their activities, and the sectional concerns of trade unions tend to dominate party policy-making. Factional structures, with their personal and ideological rivalries, are important at all levels. The Central Executive Committee is the top decision-making organ of the Party, which also has a range of committees on special policy areas.

In one respect, at least, policy formulation and matters of personnel are determined in a more 'democratic' fashion than in the case of the LDP. The National Congress of the JSP is a forum of real debate, in which personnel rivalries and policy clashes are exposed to public view. The Congress on occasion has a real influence on the contents of the Party's Action Policy, a document which is supposed to guide party leaders in their everyday decisions until the subsequent Congress. After 1962 the Party's Diet members had no *ex officio* right to be delegates at the Congress, though this right was reasserted in 1977, as a result of the extreme influence that the Shakaishugi Kyōkai has been able to assert through annual Congresses. The Party is therefore now better able to control internal conflict, but its chronic inability to broaden its base beyond the Sōhyō labour unions, and the fact that about half of its Diet members are former union leaders makes it difficult for the Party to improve either its image or its organization.[13] Nevertheless, it remains an important force in Japanese politics, and it continues to champion the peace Constitution and to resist moves towards a greater military role for Japan. Since sympathy with these positions is still quite strong in the electorate, and since the

Party's union base remains more or less intact, it is likely to stay a factor of significance in future political equations (see tables 14 and 20).

The Democratic Socialist Party (DSP), since its formation in 1960, has never been more than a minor party, but it has held a steady six to seven per cent of the popular vote, and this has given it enough seats to exercise significant influence within the Diet. It was founded with the aim of occupying the middle ground of politics, with moderate anti-LDP but also anti-Communist policies. Its most positive appeal has been to the idea of a welfare state, which has been put forward as a more sensible and pragmatic way of countering the 'politics of big business' than the Marxist rhetoric of the JSP.

The difficulty was however that the Party's organizational structure and base of support was inadequate to sustain the image of a go-ahead party. Most of the former JSP Diet members who defected in 1959–60 were labour unionists associated with the Zenrō (now Dōmei) federation, and the DSP thus came into existence with much the same kind of organizational structure as the JSP. Because the number of Diet members was fewer, the distribution of support for the DSP took on a regional character, reflecting the fact that the Party was essentially an alliance of individuals, each with his own power base, usually associated with a local union or unions. The DSP was strongest in the Nagoya and Ōsaka areas, but rather less strong around Tokyo. As can be seen from table 22, though more of its representation came from big city electorates than elsewhere, it was proportionately much less dependent upon the votes of big city voters than the Kōmeitō, JCP or NLC. Chains of motor service stations were important recruiting grounds for the Party, through its influence on Dōmei-affiliated workers in the motor car industry. These and similar linkages in other sections of industry tended to steer the Party towards conservative political positions, because of the close co-operative relationships existing between management and labour in most of the industries with which it was associated. Also the Party enjoyed a certain degree of support among small businessmen, and even in sections of agriculture, though this was not an important factor. Party support among munitions workers may or may not have been important in swinging the Party in the late 1970s towards quite hawkish attitudes on defence, although its traditional anti-Communism was also certainly a contributory factor.

The DSP has experienced some internal factionalism, largely based on clashes of personalities, but the Party has been small enough for factionalism to be much less of a problem than in the JSP. In the *hakuchū* period of the late 1970s the DSP seemed the most likely candidate for the role of junior partner in a coalition government with the LDP, but since the 1980 elections the Party has been more actively exploring once again the possibilities of forming a new party together with other moderate Opposition parties. It remains strongly opposed to any kind of alliance with the JCP (see tables 16 and 22).

The Kōmeitō rapidly rose to prominence in the 1960s, but its growth has not been sustained. It is based upon the Sōka Gakkai, the most successful of the many 'new religions' that have sprung up in response to social change and the disestablishment of state Shintō since the war. It originated in 1937 as a small study group devoted largely to educational reform, but it was not until the emergence of an organizational genius called Toda Josei after the war that the movement began to attract attention.[14] Toda built up the Sōka Gakkai from a membership of 5,000 households in 1950 to an estimated 750,000 households in 1958 at the time of his death. Using an aggressive form of proselytizing technique known as *shakubuku* (literally 'break and subdue'), he not only built up a huge membership of converts, but earned the suspicion and fear of many others who had come into contact with his organization. In 1960 Ikeda Daisaku succeeded to the presidency, and continued the work of proselytism so that by 1968 there was an estimated membership of 6,500,000 households. Ikeda's style was much smoother and less aggressive than that of Toda, and attempts were made to avoid alienating outsiders. In 1964 the Kōmeitō was founded as a political party, having the very closest links with the Sōka Gakkai, although the religion had been sponsoring candidates for various types of public election since the 1950s.

The Sōka Gakkai is a sect of Nichiren Buddhism, and claims to comprise the only true followers of Nichiren (a thirteenth-century monk). Unlike most Japanese religions, it is highly intolerant of all other religions and talks, on paper at least, of converting the whole world. Its social beliefs are vague in the extreme, but its central political belief appears to be that of the necessity of humanizing and cleaning up the political system. Through the Kōmeitō it has attacked political corruption, party factionalism and impersonal, bureaucratic government. For this it would substitute a populist insistence upon organized participation in politics by hitherto apathetic or apolitical citizens. The domestic policies of the Kōmeitō are much as one would expect from the socio-economic characteristics of its supporters, and include social welfare improvements and policies to help small and medium industry. Its representatives in local government have prided themselves on the care with which they investigate and attempt to rectify individual complaints about inadequate services or bureaucratic insensitivity.

One of the most interesting things about the Sōka Gakkai is its organizational structure, which appears to have been most carefully devised to have the maximum impact upon converts. The main unit of organization at the grass roots is the *kumi*, or group consisting of converter and converted. The essence of the *kumi* is that it is a face-to-face quasi-familial group, which splits when it becomes too big. There are also geographical area groups, common interest groups and peer groups, which supplement the basic structure founded on the *kumi*. In a highly group-conscious society, intensely affective face-to-face groupings are a most useful means of socialization for any organization seeking to build up a mass following. Great emphasis has been placed by the Sōka Gakkai on group therapy sessions, in which the personal problems of an individual can be discussed in a sympathetic group atmosphere. Desire for advancement in a status-conscious society is catered for by the provision of a hierarchy of ranks up which the individual can climb by passing successive examinations. Those who rise in that hierarchy would in many instances have little chance of advancement in the society at large because of rigidities in education and employment. The religion in practice has also stressed some of the practical aspects of worldly success, so that many of its members have been motivated and helped to improve themselves in their jobs and in their everyday lives.

Apprehensions frequently expressed during the growth period of the Sōka Gakkai that it was potentially or actually fascist seem to have been overstated. The membership composition is certainly rather similar to that associated with fascist or similar movements in Europe and elsewhere, but the Japanese social and cultural context is significantly different. The organizational structure of both the Sōka Gakkai and the Kōmeitō is geared towards unity and discipline (and factionalism appears to have been minimal), but it is somewhat looser in form and rather more consultative than organizational structures associated with either fascist or communist movements. There are indeed chauvinistic elements in its beliefs, but in practice these have been played down in the political arena.

In 1970–1, when the movement received much adverse publicity for allegedly attempting to suppress a publication which attacked it, the organization of the Kōmeitō was made officially separate from that of the Sōka Gakkai. In practice the two organizations remained closely linked, and voting for the party was always closely correlated with membership of the sect. During the 1970s the Kōmeitō had reached a plateau of support, and seemed unable to make further headway, either in its big city heartland or in small town and country areas where it had always been weak, so that in 1981 the idea of merger with other moderate parties was being carefully considered. In April 1979 Ikeda Daisaku, President of Sōka Gakkai, unexpectedly resigned amid a spate of rumours about his recent life and activities. By the early 1980s the reputation of the sect was affected by continuing adverse publicity. The Kōmeitō itself, under the extraordinarily durable leadership of Takeiri Yoshikatsu and Yano Junya, had changed little over the past decade, either in its policy positions (though on matters of foreign policy it had moved slightly to the right from its formerly centre-left position) or in the profile of its Diet membership (see table 15).[15] As a party it was still highly disciplined and structured, but found it hard to shake off the unpopularity of its parent sect, or further expand its following (see tables 15 and 21).

The Japan Communist Party was an insignificant factor in politics between the 'Cominform criticism' of 1950 and the mid-1960s. During the 1960s and early 1970s, however, it had striking success in building up its organization.[16]

In the 1950s the JCP was racked by factional discord, swayed by shifts of party line in Moscow and Peking, often ludicrously out of tune with the realities of Japanese politics and society, and hopelessly out-numbered and out-manœuvred by the Socialist Party. The early flowering of the postwar years appeared to have faded beyond hope of revival. In 1973, in contrast, the JCP was well organized, self-financing, apparently united and largely independent of any foreign communist party. It was already an important political force in the Diet with a substantial power base in the big cities. It was a serious rival of the JSP at the electoral level, in the labour unions and in left-wing movements in general.

To a large extent, this transformation of the Party's fortunes was attributed to intelligent leadership and organizational flair. The Party went through a series of leadership struggles in the 1950s and early 1960s, but by the mid-1960s was ably and shrewdly led by an apparently united group under the chairmanship of Miyamoto Kenji. In much the same way as the Sōka Gakkai, the JCP concentrated on producing mass organization and in carefully socializing its members. Attention to local issues and personal problems was also given priority, and an image of respectability and moderation was assiduously cultivated. The Party's publishing enterprises prospered, and the Sunday edition of the daily newspaper *Akahata* (*Red Flag*) – publishing material suitable for all members of the average family – sold well over two million copies of each issue. The financial independence which its publications brought was a crucial factor in enabling the JCP to establish a position as an autonomous communist party – a marked change from its situation in the 1950s.

The Party's youth group Minsei (Democratic Youth League) also had spectacular success, as did other affiliated organizations. The Party became far more effective than the Socialists in situations which demanded activism, such as labour union disputes, anti-Government campaigns about foreign policy issues, environmental pollution or rising prices. On the other hand, it studiously adhered to moderate positions in relation to student unrest and other areas where political violence was common. Its moderate line and effective organization led to charges of 'bureaucratism' from rival left-wing elements.

The independence which the JCP managed to establish in relation to major foreign Communist parties was not bought easily. To simplify a very complex story, the JCP supported

Chinese opposition to the Partial Nuclear Test-Ban Treaty of 1963, and entered a period of alignment with Peking when its relations with Moscow were strained. Defections from the JCP followed, and a rival pro-Soviet party (the 'Voice of Japan') was formed, but never attracted a substantial following. In 1965, however, the JCP sent a delegation to Peking, which urged the Chinese leaders to sink their differences with Moscow so as to co-ordinate their assistance to North Vietnam. The JCP leaders were rebuffed, and from then on relations between the JCP and China have been quite hostile. The split with China also involved defections from the JCP itself, but did not critically affect its basic cohesion. Attitudes to the Sino-Soviet dispute also involved the internal politics of the left-wing movement within Japan, and particularly relations with the JSP. The JCP, however, came through the struggles of the 1960s with high morale and apparently poised for further advances.

By the early 1980s, in contrast, the JCP was barely holding its own electorally, the sales of its publications were falling, the future of its leadership was in doubt, and it occupied an isolated position shunned by other parties. There were three principal reasons for this: one was that in 1976 Miyamoto came under attack in the Diet and elsewhere for alleged involvement in the killing of a police spy in the 1930s. The Party vigorously attempted to refute the allegations, but some of the mud stuck. Secondly, by 1981 Miyamoto, whose organizational ability had been crucial to the Party, was a sick man and there was no obvious successor. Thirdly and most importantly, despite the substantial modification of its policies that had taken place in the 1970s in order to dissociate itself from the Soviet Union, it was adversely affected by a conservative and strongly anti-Soviet mood in the electorate. Despite all this, however, the JCP could be expected to survive as a vigorous and heterodox voice in Japanese political debate, not unlike the 'Eurocommunist' parties of Italy and elsewhere in Western Europe (see tables 17 and 23).

The New Liberal Club was originally a splinter from the LDP that formed itself as a political party during the Lockheed scandals in 1976. It had a spectacular success, particularly in the Tokyo area, at the 1976 elections, but performed disastrously in 1979 and staged a partial recovery in 1980. After the initial euphoria of the 1976 result this new-style conservative Party fell into internal wrangling on matters of policy and suffered some defections. By the early 1980s there were signs that it was establishing its own identity rather more successfully, and in particular it was developing a coherent foreign policy line based on a positive defence of the spirit of the 1947 Constitution. With only twelve Lower House members, however, its long-term viability as a separate party was questionable, and it was expected to participate in moves towards the formation of a broad-based party of moderates (see tables 18 and 24). The Social Democratic League, with only three Lower House members, (see tables 18 and 24), merged with the NLC in September 1981, to form the New Liberal Club Democratic League.

It can be seen from the above that a model of alternating party politics has hitherto been singularly inappropriate to the Japanese context. Voting patterns have been stable rather than swinging, and so far as past experience at least would indicate, the electorate can be seen as consisting of a number of exploitable segments. Each segment is the actual or potential clientele of a given political party (or set of candidates). When that segment has been fully exploited by a party, it is difficult for the party to progress any further, and, losing the momentum of its appeal, it is likely to begin to decline. As the JSP, and to a lesser extent the LDP, lost electoral support, so other parties moved in to exploit the situation thus created. However, this meant a proliferation of Opposition parties. Given the existing electoral system, each of them was able to get some representation from its limited 'segment' of national support. During the 1970s and early 1980s, the earlier electoral trends away from the LDP stabilized and began to be reversed, while the Opposition continued to fragment. Faced, therefore, with a situation of retreat rather than advance, the Opposition parties were beginning to regard unification as a difficult but pressing necessity. Even though the scope of such unification efforts was likely to be problematical (in particular the JCP would certainly be excluded), the possibility of substantial progress in this direction was not to be dismissed. If the Opposition could unite, as the fragmented conservative parties united in 1955, or if the JSP could substantially broaden its base of support, the face of Japanese politics might ultimately change.

Table 14

JSP Members of the House of Representatives, 1980 Election

Electorates	Total Number	Average Age (years)	Sitting Members		Previous Members		New Members		Average No. of Times Elected	Graduated University		Did Not Graduate University		Graduated Tokyo University	
			No.	%	No.	%	No.	%		No.	%	No.	%	No.	%
A	23	55·1	21	91·3	1	4·3	1	4·3	4·8	14	60·9	9	39·1	4	17·4
B	15	56·8	11	73·3	2	13·3	2	13·3	4·7	8	53·3	7	46·7	0	0.0
C	33	58·3	26	78·8	3	9·1	4	12·1	5·1	9	27·3	24	72.7	1	3.0
D	26	58·5	20	76·9	5	19·2	1	3·8	5·2	8	30·8	18	69·2	3	1·2
E	10	55·2	9	90·0	1	10·0	0	0·0	4·3	6	60·0	4	40·0	1	10·0
Total	107	57·2	87	81·3	12	11·2	8	7·5	4·9	45	42·1	62	57·9	9	8·4

Source: As for table 13.

Table 15
Kōmeitō Members of the House of Representatives, 1980 Election

Electorates	Total Number	Average Age (years)	Sitting Members No.	Sitting Members %	Previous Members No.	Previous Members %	New Members No.	New Members %	Average No. of Times Elected	Graduated University No.	Graduated University %	Did Not Graduate University No.	Did Not Graduate University %	Graduated Tokyo University No.	Graduated Tokyo University %
A	23	50·0	23	100·0	0	0·0	0	0·0	4·9	9	39·1	14	60·9	1	4·3
B	6	51·7	6	100·0	0	0·0	0	0·0	4·5	2	33·3	4	66·7	0	0·0
C	2	45·5	2	0·0	0	0·0	0	0·0	3·0	1	50·0	1	50·0	0	0·0
D	2	55·5	1	50·0	1	50·0	0	0·0	2·5	1	50·0	1	50·0	0	0·0
E	0	—	0	0·0	0	0·0	0	0·0	—	0	0·0	0	0·0	0	0·0
Total	33	50·2	32	97·0	1	3·0	0	0·0	4·6	13	39·4	20	60·6	1	3·0

Source: As for table 13.

Table 16

DSP Members of the House of Representatives, 1980 Election

Electorates	Total Number	Average Age (years)	Sitting Members		Previous Members		New Members		Average No. of Times Elected	Graduated University		Did Not Graduate University		Graduated Tokyo University	
			No.	%	No.	%	No.	%		No.	%	No.	%	No.	%
A	13	55·2	13	100·0	0	0·0	0	0·0	4·4	9	69·2	4	30·8	1	7·7
B	7	52·1	7	100·0	0	0·0	0	0·0	4·0	6	85·7	1	14·3	2	28·6
C	8	54·1	8	100·0	0	0·0	0	0·0	3·5	3	37·5	5	62·5	0	0·0
D	4	51·0	4	100·0	0	0·0	0	0·0	5·0	3	75·0	1	25·0	0	0·0
E	0	—	0	0·0	0	0·0	0	0·0	—	0	0·0	0	0·0	0	0·0
Total	32	53·8	32	100·0	0	0·0	0	0·0	4·2	21	65·6	11	34·4	3	9·4

Source: As for table 13.

Table 17

JCP Members of the House of Representatives, 1980 Election

Electorates	Total Number	Average Age (years)	Sitting Members		Previous Members		New Members		Average No. of Times Elected	Graduated University		Did Not Graduate University		Graduated Tokyo University	
			No.	%	No.	%	No.	%		No.	%	No.	%	No.	%
A	19	52·7	18	94·7	0	0·0	1	5·3	3·3	10	52·6	9	47·3	4	21·1
B	6	48·3	5	83·3	0	0·0	1	16·7	3·0	4	66·7	2	33·3	0	0·0
C	3	64·7	3	100·0	0	0·0	0	0·0	5·7	2	66·7	1	33·3	1	33·3
D	1	59·0	1	100·0	0	0·0	0	0·0	5·0	0	0·0	1	100·0	0	0·0
E	0	—	0	0·0	0	0·0	0	0·0	—	0	0·0	0	0·0	0	0·0
Total	29	53·3	27	93·1	0	0·0	2	6·9	3·6	16	55·2	13	44·8	5	17·2

Source: As for table 13.

Table 18

NLC Members of the House of Representatives, 1980 Election

Electorates	*Total Number*	*Average Age (years)*	*Sitting Members*		*Previous Members*		*New Members*		*Average No. of Times Elected*	*Graduated University*		*Did Not Graduate University*		*Graduated Tokyo University*	
			No.	%	*No.*	%	*No.*	%		*No.*	%	*No.*	%	*No.*	%
A	9	49·9	3	33·3	4	44·4	2	22·2	2·9	8	88·9	1	11·1	4	44·4
B	1	39·0	1	100·0	0	0·0	0	0·0	6·0	1	100·0	0	0·0	0	0·0
C	0	—	0	0·0	0	0·0	0	0·0	—	0	0·0	0	0·0	0	0·0
D	1	42·0	0	0·0	0	0·0	1	100·0	1·0	1	100·0	0	0·0	0	0·0
E	1	42·0	0	0·0	0	0·0	1	100·0	1·0	1	100·0	0	0·0	0	0·0
Total	12	47·7	4	33·3	4	33·3	4	33·3	2·8	11	91·7	1	8·3	4	33·3

Source: As for table 13.

Note on the SDL

The Social Democratic League elected 3 members at the 1980 House of Representatives elections. One was from a category A electorate, one from category B and one from category C. Their average age was 48. Two of them were sitting members and one was newly elected. They had been elected an average of 5·0 times and all three had graduated from university, though none from Tokyo University.

Table 19
Number and Percentage of Seats Held by All Opposition Parties in Three Consecutive Lower House Elections, According to Type of Constituency

Electorates	*Total No. of Seats*	*1976* *No. of Seats*	*1976* *% of Seats*	*1979* *No. of Seats*	*1979* *% of Seats*	*1980* *No. of Seats*	*1980* *% of Seats*
A	138	91	65·9	99	71·7	88	63·8
B	86	42	48·8	42	48·8	36	41·9
C	135	60	44·4	55	40·7	46	34·1
D	101	33	32·7	34	33·7	34	33·7
E	51	15	29·4	14	27·5	12	23·5
Total	511	241	47·2	244	47·7	216	42·3

Sources: As for table 12.

Table 20
Number and Percentage of Seats Held by JSP *in Three Consecutive Lower House Elections, According to Type of Constituency*

Electorates	*Total No. of Seats*	*1976* *No. of Seats*	*1976* *% of Seats*	*1979* *No. of Seats*	*1979* *% of Seats*	*1980* *No. of Seats*	*1980* *% of Seats*
A	138	28	20·3	25	18·1	23	16·7
B	86	19	22·1	15	17·4	15	17·4
C	135	38	28·1	31	25·9	33	24·4
D	101	26	25·7	25	22·8	26	25·7
E	51	12	23·5	11	21·6	10	19·6
Total	511	123	24·1	107	20·9	107	20·9

Sources: As for table 12.

Table 21
Number and Percentage of Seats Held by Kōmeitō in Three Consecutive Lower House Elections, According to Type of Constituency

Electorates	*Total No. of Seats*	*1976* *No. of Seats*	*1976* *% of Seats*	*1979* *No. of Seats*	*1979* *% of Seats*	*1980* *No. of Seats*	*1980* *% of Seats*
A	138	28	20·3	32	23·2	23	16·7
B	86	11	12·8	12	14·0	6	7·0
C	135	11	8·1	11	8·1	2	1·5
D	101	4	4·0	1	1·0	2	2·0
E	51	1	2·0	1	2·0	0	0·0
Total	511	55	10·8	57	11·2	33	6·5

Sources: As for table 12.

Table 22
Number and Percentage of Seats Held by DSP in Three Consecutive Lower House Elections, According to Type of Constituency

Electorates	*Total No. of Seats*	*1976* *No. of Seats*	*1976* *% of Seats*	*1979* *No. of Seats*	*1979* *% of Seats*	*1980* *No. of Seats*	*1980* *% of Seats*
A	138	12	8·7	15	10·9	13	9·4
B	86	7	8·1	7	8·1	7	8·1
C	135	8	5·9	9	6·7	8	5·9
D	101	2	2·0	4	4·0	4	4·0
E	51	0	0·0	0	0·0	0	0·0
Total	511	29	5·7	35	6·8	32	6·3

Sources: As for table 12.

Table 23
Number and Percentage of Seats Held by JCP in Three Consecutive Lower House Elections, According to Type of Constituency

Electorates	*Total No. of Seats*	*1976* *No. of Seats*	*1976* *% of Seats*	*1979* *No. of Seats*	*1979* *% of Seats*	*1980* *No. of Seats*	*1980* *% of Seats*
A	138	12	8·7	24	17·4	19	13·8
B	86	1	1·2	6	7·0	6	7·0
C	135	2	1·5	4	3·0	3	2·2
D	101	1	1·0	4	4·0	1	1·0
E	51	1	2·0	1	2·0	0	0·0
Total	511	17	3·3	39	7·6	29	5·7

Sources: As for table 12.

Table 24
Number and Percentage of Seats Held by NLC and SDL in Three Consecutive Lower House Elections, According to Type of Constituency

		1976				*1979*				*1980*			
	Total	*No. of Seats*		*% of Seats*		*No. of Seats*		*% of Seats*		*No. of Seats*		*% of Seats*	
Electorates	*No. of Seats*	*NLC*	*SDL*	*NLC*	*SDL*	*NLC*	*SDL*	*NLC*	*SDL*	*NLC*	*SDL*	*NLC*	*SDL*
A	138	11	—	8·0	—	3	0	2·2	0·0	9	1	6·5	0·7
B	86	4	—	4·7	—	1	1	1·2	1·2	1	1	1·2	1·2
C	135	1	—	0·7	—	0	0	0·0	0·0	0	0	0·0	0·0
D	101	0	—	0·0	—	0	0	0·0	0·0	1	0	1·0	0·0
E	51	1	—	2·0	—	0	1	0·0	2·0	1	1	2·0	2·0
Total	511	17	—	3·3	—	4	2	0·8	0·4	12	3	2·3	0·6

Sources: As for table 12.

10 Some Problems of the Constitution

Japan cannot yet be said to have developed a national consensus about the present Constitution. Although its basic provisions command a wide measure of popular support, and although successive conservative governments have learned to operate within its framework, it continues to be regarded by a substantial body of – mostly right-wing – opinion as a foreign import, which ideally should be rewritten to conform with Japanese society and traditions.

Debate over the Constitution was at its height in the 1950s and early 1960s. From the Ikeda period, however, less and less was heard of it, and in the *hakuchū* period of the 1970s it appeared as if the idea of revising the Constitution had been all but forgotten. The LDP success at the 1980 elections, however, put constitutional revision once more on the political agenda. The apparent lack of interest in revision for such a long period was not because the fundamental issues have been satisfactorily solved, but because there is a stalemate between the opposing sides. On the one hand, the stalemate favours the Constitution's supporters, because it is impossible, in present circumstances, to revise it,[1] and in the absence of revision it becomes progressively more embedded in the national consciousness. On the other hand, however, it has proved adaptable to the demands of those who are less than wholehearted in its defence. The Liberal Democrats, during their long tenure of office, have been able to water down, through practice and interpretation, the more radical or inconvenient constitutional provisions. The resultant gap between theory and practice is a constant source of political friction, and undoubtedly contributes to a rather widespread disillusionment with politics and politicians.

There is a sense of paradox about attitudes to the Constitution. Liberal Democrats, championing throughout the Cold War period the closest of links with the United States, have been lukewarm about their 'American-imposed' Constitution. Socialists and members of other Opposition parties constantly attack the United States, and yet wholeheartedly support a Constitution which the Americans apparently engineered.

American actions have an even more paradoxical appearance. The Constitution was introduced under the auspices of General MacArthur – not generally regarded in the United States as a particularly radical or left-wing figure – and yet it was full of New Deal concepts and contained the famous 'peace clause' (article 9), which on the face of it banned armed forces for Japan in perpetuity. Later this was to prove a serious embarrassment to the American Government in its policies towards Japan, and in 1953 Vice-President Nixon even went so far as to urge the Japanese to scrap it. It is possible, of course, to argue that article 9 was an example of American 'imperialism', since it was designed to keep Japan militarily subdued in the period before the Cold War really began. Those who argue thus, however, are brought up against the fact that its most vociferous champions are the left-wing 'anti-imperialist' forces in Japan itself, while it is the right-wing 'reactionaries' who want to revise it.

The origin of the 1947 Constitution is crucial to an understanding of the subsequent controversies about it. The allegation that General MacArthur 'imposed' the Constitution on Japan while creating the fiction that it had been accepted voluntarily, or even that it was an indigenous Japanese product, has been the most emotive and powerful charge levelled against it by its opponents. As a result of the labours of the Commission on the Constitution (Kempō Chōsakai) between 1957 and 1964, it is now possible to give a moderately confident judgement about the reasonableness of this charge.[2] The Potsdam Declaration gave positive sanction for a major reform of the Meiji Constitution. It was hardly surprising, therefore, that the Americans, left virtually in complete charge of the Occupation of Japan because of the conflicts that emerged among the former Allied powers once the war in the Pacific had ended, should have placed constitutional revision high on their agenda. It was also obviously desirable that a matter so fundamental as constitutional reform should emanate from the Japanese political process itself, and should benefit from adequate popular discussion.[3] In accordance with the latter principle, the Shidehara Government was invited to submit proposals for reform late in 1946. A committee was set up under a Cabinet minister, Dr Matsumoto Jōji, and had worked out the draft of a revised constitution by the beginning of February 1946.[4] This however conceded few changes in the text of the Meiji Constitution, and was rejected by SCAP as too conservative.

On 7 January 1946 General MacArthur had received a document called SWNCC-228 from the State-War-Navy Co-ordinating Committee in Washington. This document urged that the Japanese should be encouraged to reform the Constitution along democratic lines, but warned the Supreme Commander against a coercive approach, on the unimpeachable grounds that this would seriously prejudice the ultimate acceptability of a constitution introduced under pressure from the occupying power.[5]

There was little evidence of haste in MacArthur's attitudes towards constitutional revision until the beginning of February, when something apparently happened to make him drastically revise his priorities and his strategy. On 3 February 1946 the Supreme Commander summoned his Government Section and gave them instructions to prepare, with the utmost despatch, a draft constitution to be presented to the Japanese Cabinet as a 'guide' to their work for constitutional revision. Among the items which MacArthur specifically ordered to be included in the draft were a clause to the effect that the emperor should be 'at the head of state', but that his duties and powers should be 'exercised in accordance with the Constitution and responsible to the basic will of the people as provided therein', and one specifying that the right to wage war and to maintain the means of waging it should be abolished.[6] The Government Section, under Major-General Courtney Whitney, worked under great pressure from 4 February and completed their draft (now usually known as the 'GHQ draft') in the staggering time of six days. It was presented to Cabinet on 13 February, and Cabinet was persuaded to accept it 'in basic principle' by 22 February, which, by a strange coincidence, was Washington's birthday.

Ward acidly comments: 'This awesome display of speed and "efficiency" without a doubt represents the world's record time for the devising and acceptance of a constitution for a major modern state.'[7]

It is now well established that the reason for this haste was the prospective establishment of the Far Eastern Commission in Washington, decided upon at the Big Three summit conference in Moscow in December 1945. The Far Eastern Commission, on which representatives of eleven nations were to sit, could have its decisions vetoed by any of the United States, the United Kingdom, the USSR or China, which on the face of it gave the Americans a fairly free hand if they were prepared to use the veto. From MacArthur's point of view, however, the crucial difficulty lay in the following provision: 'Any directives dealing with fundamental changes in the Japanese constitutional structure or in the regime of control, or dealing with a change in the Japanese Government as a whole, will be issued only following consultation and following the attainment of agreement in the Far Eastern Commission.'[8]

As late as 30 January 1946, General MacArthur met the Far Eastern Advisory Commission (precursor of the Far Eastern Commission) and told them that, because of the Moscow Agreement, he no longer had authority to take action on constitutional reform, which he hoped would be carried out on Japanese initiative.[9] It is striking that it should have been only four days later that MacArthur gave his historic instructions to the Government Section. The precise motivation for such a sudden reversal at this point remains somewhat unclear, but the most crucial factor was the knowledge that the Far Eastern Commission would begin to operate on 26 February, after which it was likely to become much more difficult to implement constitutional reform than it would be before that date. Experience with the Matsumoto Committee no doubt also convinced him that constructive measures of reform were hardly to be expected from the current Government, operating on its own initiative.

What exactly happened when the GHQ draft was presented to a shocked and disbelieving Cabinet on 13 February has never been completely cleared up. What is certain is that substantial pressure was brought to bear upon the Cabinet by the officials of Government Section, including Whitney himself. The precise nature of that pressure however has been a subject of some dispute, and upon it hangs in part the controversy about whether the Constitution was 'imposed' or 'written in co-operation'. According to one account that has gained wide currency, Whitney told members of the Cabinet that if the Japanese Government did not present a revised constitution similar to the GHQ draft, the *person* of the Emperor could not be guaranteed.[10]

This account was the basis of the later charge by Dr Matsumoto, whose constitution-drafting efforts have already been mentioned, that the Americans threatened to indict the Emperor as a war criminal if Cabinet did not accept the GHQ draft as the basis for a new constitution. If the statement was actually made, however, a more likely interpretation would appear to be that it was meant as a warning, to the effect that without drastic action to forestall the Far Eastern Commission, SCAP would find it difficult to stave off demands from the Soviet Union and other countries for the Emperor to be tried in person.[11] It has, moreover, been doubted whether Whitney ever actually spoke in such terms. Whitney in his own published account of the meeting nowhere mentions it,[12] and Professor Takayanagi Kenzō, later Chairman of the Commission on the Constitution, casts doubt on the reliability of the original account.[13]

Even if Takayanagi's doubts can be sustained, however, it is extremely difficult to agree with his thesis, courageously and persistently argued during the hearings of the Commission on the Constitution, that the new constitution was a 'collaborative effort' between the Americans and the Japanese.[14] Even Whitney's own account reveals a calculated plan of coercing the Cabinet into virtually accepting the GHQ draft as its own, effected with relentlessness and precision. Apart from his gratuitous remark about 'atomic sunshine', Whitney by his own account threatened to place the draft before the people over the heads of Cabinet if they refused to accept it.[15] As Ward commented in 1956, 'Given the traditional distrust of Japanese officials for popular sovereignty in any form, rendered particularly acute at the moment by the country's desperate and tumultuous economic and social circumstances and the unprecedented scale of left-wing political activities, it is difficult to conceive of any more ominous development from the standpoint of Japanese officialdom than a constitution formulated in the "marketplace".'[16]

After the meeting on 13 February, the Cabinet made one more attempt to persuade SCAP to accept the Matsumoto draft as a basis for negotiation, but this was flatly rejected.[17] Finally, the Cabinet capitulated and hammered out a draft constitution, following closely the GHQ draft. This was delivered to SCAP on 4 March. There followed an extraordinary session, some thirty hours long, in which Cabinet and the Government Section arrived at a mutually acceptable draft. Here also the Americans kept up a relentless pressure upon the Japanese Government. Whitney gave an ultimatum that he would 'wait till morning' for a final draft to be produced, and then proceeded to reverse most of the changes which the Japanese had attempted to introduce into the GHQ draft. The only significant concession made at this point by the Americans was the substitution of a bicameral for a unicameral assembly.[18] The document was published on 6 March, and subsequently went through the normal processes of debate in the Diet. The House of Representatives passed it on 24 August by 421 votes to 8 (6 of the dissenters being Communists), it was agreed to by the House of Peers on 6 October and the Privy Council on 29 October. During this process some changes were made to the text, but for the most part they were not of great importance, and in any case they were all cleared by SCAP. The overwhelming affirmative vote in the House of Representatives seems to have been in part an index of active support (by that time many of the more conservative Diet members had been removed by the purge edict), but also to have reflected a realization that no real alternative course of action was practicable.

It seems clear enough on the evidence, therefore, that the charge that the postwar Constitution was imposed by the Americans upon the Japanese Government is valid. To put it at its mildest, SCAP 'twisted the arm' of the Japanese Cabinet by writing a constitutional draft based on popular sovereignty and threatening to take it to the people if Cabinet should fail to sponsor it as its own creation. A fiction was then maintained that the new Constitution was a 'Japanese product'.[19] Whether such a course of action was justified in the light of the impending establishment of the Far Eastern Commission with the opportunities it seemed likely to provide for Soviet interference, or indeed in the light of the later history of the Constitution, are separate questions.

The Americans ensured the survival of the Constitution by making it very difficult to revise. The accusation that it was 'imposed by the Americans' has never gained sufficient impetus as the basis of a political movement to surmount the legal obstacles to revision. On the contrary, there has developed impressive support for the fundamental principles of the Constitution, although this has been stronger on the left than on the right.

There is however another charge that revisionists have used, namely that six days is insufficient time to write a constitution for a modern state, and that the document is basically ill-considered, and ill-suited to Japanese social and political reality. As Ward put it: 'The Government Section patched together an almost ideally democratic constitution, one that could scarcely have gained serious consideration if advanced for adoption in the United States. It had even less relevance to the traditional and dominant political aspirations or practices of Japan.'[20] To this it could be replied that Japan was ripe for radical political change, and a dramatic new approach was needed. In any case, successive governments have not found it difficult to interpret its provisions with flexibility.[21] The declamatory element in the Constitution, it could be argued, was necessary in order to provide an impetus for change.

A curious and unusual thing about the Japanese Constitution is that a high proportion of the constitutional argument that has taken place, especially at the popular and intellectual levels, concerns one article – the peace clause – which involves matters that would be peripheral in most constitutions. The fact that it is frequently called the 'peace Constitution' is an indication of the dramatic impact and controversial nature of this particular clause.

Both the origin and the subsequent history of the peace clause are interesting and important. It is apparent that it did not originate in instructions received by MacArthur from Washington. The document SWNCC-228, for instance, merely required that 'the civil be supreme over the military branch of the government'.[22] It was natural to assume, therefore, that the author and originator of the clause was MacArthur himself. The idea of having Japan renounce war and the means of waging it through a clause in the body of her Constitution[23] could be seen perhaps as appealing to the visionary element in MacArthur's temperament, and also as part of the calculated attempt to forestall interference from the Far Eastern Commission, mentioned above. With the Soviet Union and others calling for the Emperor to be put on trial as a war criminal, a Constitution which was so radical that it not only replaced imperial by popular sovereignty, but even went so far as to remove from Japan the right to engage in military activities, *and yet retained the Emperor* (something which MacArthur apparently regarded as vital to the success of the Occupation), was an attractive stratagem. If this version of events and motivations were correct, then revisionists could argue with force that the obnoxious peace clause was very specifically 'imposed'.

Unfortunately for this version, MacArthur in his testimony to a United States Senate Committee in May 1951 claimed that not he, but the man who was Prime Minister in 1946, Shidehara, was the originator of the peace clause.[24] According to MacArthur, Shidehara had come to see him on 24 January 1946, and had proposed that a new Constitution should incorporate a renunciation of war. This was substantially corroborated in Shidehara's biography,[25] and was used by Takayanagi in his argument against the 'imposed Constitution' thesis.[26] Shidehara allegedly said nothing of this at the time to his Cabinet colleagues, and since no third person was present at the meeting (and both parties to it are now dead), it is impossible to be sure exactly what happened. Not all of Shidehara's colleagues were prepared to accept this account of events.[27]

The wording of the peace clause went through a number of changes between its initial enunciation by MacArthur in his instructions to the Government Section on 3 February 1946, and the final version. All the versions contained two paragraphs, the first renouncing the right to war, and the second stating that armed forces would not be maintained.

General MacArthur's initial version read as follows:

War as a sovereign right of the nation is abolished. Japan renounces it as an instrumentality for settling its disputes and even for preserving its own security. It relies upon the higher ideals which are now stirring the world for its defense and protection.

No Japanese Army, Navy or Air Force will ever be authorized and no rights of belligerency will ever be conferred upon any Japanese force.[28]

In the GHQ draft worked out by the Government Section and presented to the Japanese Cabinet on 13 February 1946 the sentence about 'higher ideals' was dropped, as, more significantly, was the phrase 'even for preserving its own security'. There was a further change in the text of the agreed draft published on 6 March, the first paragraph of which read: 'War, as a sovereign right of the nation, and the threat or use of force, is forever renounced as a means of settling disputes with other nations.' This version, in which instead of war being simply abolished as a sovereign right of the nation, it is renounced *as a means of settling disputes with other nations*, could conceivably be regarded as permitting defence against invasion, or participation in international sanctions.[29]

The most important change to the wording of the article was introduced on the initiative of Ashida Hitoshi (later to be Prime Minister) during the course of debates in the Diet. An additional phrase was tacked on to the beginning of each of the two paragraphs of the article, ostensibly to reinforce and clarify its pacifist purpose. The final version, therefore, read as follows:

Aspiring sincerely to an international peace based on justice and order, the Japanese people forever renounce war as a sovereign right of the nation and the threat or use of force as means of settling international disputes.

In order to accomplish the aim of the preceding paragraph, land, sea and air forces, as well as other war potential, will never be maintained. The right of belligerency of the state will not be recognised.

The real significance of the additional phrases (as Ashida admitted later) was one of qualification rather than reinforcement. Now that the 'aim' of the first paragraph was 'an international peace based on justice and order', the ban on land, sea and air forces in the second paragraph could be regarded as qualified insofar as it was now designed to 'accomplish the aim' of the first. Presumably in an imperfectly peaceful world, other aims, such as defence preparedness against aggression, could be regarded as legitimate.

There is evidence that this interpretation was understood at the time by SCAP, which did not disapprove.[30] If this is the case, it tends to reinforce the conclusion that article 9 was intended initially as a stratagem, to forestall criticism and interference from the Far Eastern Commission, and that later on, even before the onset of the Cold War had started to change American foreign policy priorities, SCAP was content to see the original purport of the article emasculated. It is ironic indeed that despite this it should have become a potent weapon in the hands both of left-wing opponents of American foreign policy within Japan, and of conservative politicians such as Yoshida, who could use it to combat American pressure for heavy Japanese defence spending, exerted during the period of Japan's economic recovery in the 1950s.

The existence of the peace clause in the postwar Constitution has not prevented the emergence of substantial armed forces, under the somewhat euphemistic title of the Ground, Maritime and Air Self-Defence Forces. A measure of rearmament (though it was not called such) was sanctioned by General MacArthur as early as 1950, after the outbreak of the war in Korea. The National Police Reserve, formed at that time to supplement American troops which had left Japan for Korea, was subsequently strengthened and took on the title of 'Self-Defence Forces' in 1954.

There has been much debate, within and outside Japan, about how far Japanese governments have been inhibited in their defence policies by the existence of article 9. The question is more complicated than it seems, because quite plainly Liberal Democratic governments have used the existence of the article and the popular support which it enjoys as a means of countering American pressure for substantially increased expenditure on defence. Apart from the defence and foreign policy aspects of this issue (see Chapter 12), it raises the crucial question of the constitutional relationship between the various branches of government. One of the most important innovations of the 1947 Constitution was the granting to the judiciary of the power of judicial review. Article 81 of the new Constitution reads as follows: 'The Supreme Court is the court of last resort with power to determine the constitutionality of any law, order, regulation or official act.'

Given the doubtful constitutional position of the Self-Defence Forces, it has often been asked why, in view of article 81, the Supreme Court has apparently been so reluctant to take a strong stand on this matter. To answer this question it is necessary to examine in general terms the present relationship between the political and judicial branches of government and the use made by the Supreme Court of its power of judicial review.

Under the Meiji Constitution the courts had no power whatever of reviewing governmental acts. Constitutional issues were politically, not legally, determined. This is not to say that the prewar courts were subject to substantial political interference in the conduct of their cases (although the Ministry of Justice determined judicial appointments, among other things), but that the notion of judicial review of political acts was absent.[31]

The introduction of judicial review in the postwar Constitution had a strong American ring about it, and was obviously derived in large measure from Marbury *v.* Madison. Initially, there was a debate among Japanese legal scholars about whether the American practice should be followed whereby the Supreme Court only ruled on constitutionality where a specific case came before it, or whether it should act as a 'constitutional court' to determine matters of constitutionality in the abstract. The notion of a constitutional court, derived from continental European models, was effectively disposed of by the Supreme Court in the Suzuki case of 1952.

The Suzuki case is of particular interest because it led the Supreme Court to commit itself on the way it proposed to handle its new power of judicial review, and also because it signalled its longstanding reluctance to interfere in matters of delicate political significance, specifically in this case the peace clause of the Constitution.

Suzuki Mosaburō, Chairman of the Left Socialist Party, called on the Supreme Court to declare the National Police Reserve (precursor of the Self-Defence Forces) unconstitutional under article 9. The Court, in dismissing the case, ruled that '... a judgment may be sought in the courts only when there exists a concrete legal dispute between specific parties'.[32] If, the Court argued, it had the power to 'issue abstract declarations nullifying laws, orders, and the like', then it would be in danger of assuming 'the appearance of an organ superior to all other powers in the land, thereby running counter to the basic principle of democratic government: that the three powers are independent, equal, and immune from each other's interference'.[33]

This use of the separation of powers doctrine as a principal reason for refraining from judging constitutional issues in the abstract has extended to a general reluctance to assert itself in the whole sphere of judicial review. Indeed, until 1973 the Supreme Court had held only two statutes to be unconstitutional. The first such case, in 1953, concerned the constitutionality of some interim laws, enacted after the Peace Treaty to extend the validity of SCAP regulations. The second, in 1962, concerned a Customs Law, under which goods which were discovered being smuggled out of the country, but which belonged to a third party, had been confiscated without the third party being given due notice and a chance to be heard.[34] As may be guessed from the limited and marginal scope of these two cases, the Supreme Court had proved remarkably reluctant to exercise with any vigour its power of judicial review conferred by article 81 of the Constitution.

A much more important ruling was brought down in April 1973, when the Supreme Court reversed its own previous decision of October 1950 and ruled unconstitutional article 200 of the Penal Code, which provided heavier penalties for the crime of patricide than for that of homicide, on the ground that it contravened article 14 of the Constitution which stipulates that '[a]ll people shall be equal under the law ...' The treatment of patricide as a worse crime than ordinary homicide stemmed from the traditional respect for the father as head of the family, and therefore the Supreme Court's decision could be seen as a rejection of part at least of the traditional morality as a basis for legal enactments.

Since 1973 the willingness of the Supreme Court to rule laws or regulations unconstitutional appears to have increased only slightly. Thus in 1975 the Court ruled unconstitutional a law which restricted the distance between pharmacies, on the grounds that it infringed article 22 of the Constitution, which guarantees freedom of occupation.[35] In a judgment with far more political significance, the Court in 1976 ruled that the discrepancy in the value of a vote in different constituencies in the 1972 House of Representatives elections was so extreme as to constitute an infringement of articles 14 and 44 of the Constitution. This differed in effect from the Court's 1964 ruling that the distribution of Diet seats was a matter for the Diet itself to decide, so long as 'extreme inequality' (undefined) was not created. In this context it is worth noting that in December 1980 the Tokyo High Court brought down a judgment that a discrepancy of 'more than about two to one' in the value of a vote between different constituencies infringed article 14 (equality before the law) of the Constitution. In addition to Supreme Court rulings, there have been a number of instances where lower courts have judged laws or administrative acts unconstitutional in freedom of religion controversies and other areas.

There are two further doctrines that have been evolved by the Court as justification for its highly cautious approach. One is the 'political question' doctrine, and the other is the 'public welfare standard'.

The 'political question' first became an issue in the extremely important Sunakawa decision of 1959, which was the first to involve the peace clause of the Constitution. In 1957 seven demonstrators were charged with breaking into the United States Air Force base at Tachikawa, west of central Tokyo, following a protest against the extension of a runway on to agricultural land. The penalty they faced, under a law derived from the Administrative Agreement accompanying the Japan–United States Security Treaty of 1951, was heavier than it would have been had they been found guilty of trespass on to other property.[36] The Tokyo District Court acquitted the defendants, on the specifically constitutional grounds that the Security Treaty, and thus the Special Criminal Law based on the Administrative Agreement, was illegal under article 9. The Tokyo Public Prosecutors' Office immediately appealed to the Supreme Court, which quashed the lower court decision.

There was a wide variety of opinions expressed by the fifteen judges, but the formal judgment used the doctrine of the 'political question'. The judgment pointed out that the Security Treaty was of a 'highly political nature' in the context of the present case, and possessed 'an extremely important relation to the basis of the existence of our country as a sovereign nation'. Arguing, therefore, that it was Cabinet, the National Diet and ultimately the 'sovereign people' that should decide on matters such as this, the Court most significantly concluded that 'the legal decision as to unconstitutionality . . . falls outside the right of judicial review by the courts, unless there is clearly obvious unconstitutionality or invalidity.'[37]

The use of the 'political question' doctrine by the Supreme Court as a reason for refraining from judging governmental acts unconstitutional has been heavily criticized by Japanese legal experts, especially those whose training has been in the postwar period. One writer, for instance, discussing the Sunakawa decision, comments: 'The American courts from which the Court borrowed the "political questions" doctrine have of recent years never been as unsophisticated as this in their approach and have not contented themselves with the stark statement that the subject matter is highly political.'[38]

In any case, the Supreme Court has made use of the doctrine in quite a number of cases. For instance, when in 1962 a former member of the House of Representatives sued the state for loss of parliamentary salary as a result of what he alleged was a wrongful dissolution of the House, the Court dismissed his appeal on the grounds that: 'an act of state of a highly political nature which is directly connected with the fundamentals of government is beyond the jurisdiction of the courts, even where it becomes the subject of legal controversy and where, accordingly, it is legally possible for its validity to be adjudged'.[39] It appears that in this case the Court was adhering to the pragmatic position (formulated specifically at the academic level) that the political consequences of invalidating an election long after it had taken place outweighed the possible legal merits of the appellant's claim.[40]

At first sight, therefore, it would seem that the 1976 Supreme Court judgment declaring unconstitutional the vote value discrepancies existing at the time of the 1972 Lower House elections represents a significant breakthrough. In practice, however, although there was some redrawing of boundaries following that election (but before the Supreme Court decision), no remediary administrative action appears to have resulted from the Court's judgment.

If the Supreme Court has been cautious (some critics would say wilfully timid) in its exercise of judicial review where it judges that 'political questions' are involved, it has also been fairly conservative in its approach to cases concerning constitutional rights and freedoms. Its evolution of the notion of the 'public welfare standard' is particularly interesting because it raises some of the most difficult political problems which Japan's abrupt transition to a constitution based on popular sovereignty has produced.

The rights guaranteed by chapter 3 of the 1947 Constitution are both more extensive and less qualified by concomitant duties of the individual than in the corresponding section of the Meiji Constitution. Of the thirty-one separate articles in chapter 3, only four are qualified by consideration of the 'public welfare'. Articles 12 and 13 provide general qualifications, and read as follows:

> Article 12: The freedoms and rights guaranteed to the people by this Constitution shall be maintained by the constant endeavor of the people, who shall refrain from any abuse of these freedoms and rights and shall always be responsible for utilizing them for the public welfare.
>
> Article 13: All of the people shall be respected as individuals. Their right to life, liberty and the pursuit of happiness shall, to the extent that it does not interfere with the public welfare, be the supreme consideration in legislation and in other governmental affairs.

Whereas the 'public welfare' in articles 12 and 13 presumably refers to the whole of chapter 3, in articles 22 and 29 it qualifies specific freedoms, namely that of choosing one's place of residence and occupation (article 22), and the right, as defined by law, to own property (article 29).

As early as 1949 the Supreme Court used the 'public welfare' as the reason for upholding a Cabinet order forbidding incitement of farmers not to deliver certain agricultural products to the Government. This was a time of acute food shortage, and the reasonableness of the order in the conditions of the time seems manifest enough, but it is more surprising that it should have been used as a precedent for many later decisions. In view, also, of the very specific guarantee of freedom of expression contained in article 21, some Japanese legal experts have found it difficult to see why incitement to disobey a regulation should be treated in exactly the same way as disobedience itself.[41] The precedent was later followed in cases of incitement (where the issue was the right of public employees to strike) and the non-payment of taxes, among others.[42]

The 'public welfare' has been admitted by the Supreme Court as adequate grounds for curtailing a number of constitutionally guaranteed freedoms, including the right to choose one's occupation and the right to move to a foreign country. Particularly striking was a case dismissed by the Supreme Court in 1958, where a former Left Socialist Diet member appealed against the denial to him of a passport to attend an international economic conference in Moscow in 1952. A blatantly political criterion for refusing a passport had been applied by the Government, and the Supreme Court upheld the Government's contention that freedom to travel abroad could legitimately be restricted where even the possibility existed that acts harmful to the interests and security of Japan might be performed. (At that time Japan was engaged in negotiations with the Soviet Union for a peace treaty, and for the release of prisoners of war and fishermen whom the Soviet Union was holding.)[43]

One area of fundamental political importance on which the Supreme Court has had to pronounce is the regulation of demonstrations. Given the seriously divided nature of the Japanese polity, and the widespread use of demonstrations by dissenting groups as a means of expressing opposition to government policies, the guarantee of freedom of assembly contained in article 21 of the Constitution has given rise to much contentious argument.[44]

From the late 1940s a series of cases arose involving the regulations of local authorities governing demonstrations. In 1954 a case concerning the Niigata Prefectural Public Safety Ordinance came before the Supreme Court. The Court upheld the Ordinance, but maintained that prior restraints under a 'general system of licensing rather than a system of simple notification' were 'against the intent of the Constitution and impermissible'. This, however, was immediately qualified by the statement that a licensing system 'concerning the place and procedure under reasonable and clear criteria in order to maintain public order and to protect the public welfare against serious harm from such activities' was constitutional. What was unacceptable was a blanket set of regulations which served to restrict demonstrations and similar activities in general. The Niigata regulations did not, according to the Court, fall into this category.[45] It was possible, however, to detect a discrepancy between the Court's statement of constitutional principles and its flexibility in applying them.[46]

What appeared to many critics to be a somewhat tougher and more restrictive decision was brought down by the Supreme Court in 1960, when it upheld the Tokyo Ordinance, which had been declared unconstitutional on more than one occasion by the Tokyo District Court. The background was one of very serious demonstrations over revision of the Security Treaty and other issues, and the failure of Kishi's attempted revision of the Police Duties Law in 1958. Some critics even maintained that what the Government had failed to achieve by legislative means had been achieved on its behalf by the Supreme Court.[47]

The decision, which was complex, played down the distinction between a 'licensing' and a 'notification' system, stressed the dangers of crowd psychology and mob violence and denied the contention of the lower court that the ordinance was too general in its expression. As Beer points out, however, the Tokyo decision was not so inconsistent with the Niigata decision as many critics have maintained.[48] There would appear to be room for a relatively liberal interpretation of the Tokyo decision, although it certainly does not leave local authorities without the means to handle demonstrations.

More recently, employment relationships have been the subject of a number of Supreme Court rulings, and one distinguished commentator sees a disturbing trend towards a more rigidly conservative approach among Supreme Court judges in the 1970s.[49] In the Post Office Employees case of 1966, which concerned activities by some postal employees which were illegal under laws restricting the organizational rights of public service workers, a majority of Supreme Court judges ruled that only a 'necessary minimum' of restrictions on labour should apply, and therefore overturned the lower court's conviction of the defendants. In a rather similar case in 1974, however, the Court upheld a strict restriction of the legal limits to the political activities of public employees. In another case a year earlier, the Court upheld the right of a firm to dismiss an employee for failing to disclose his political activism when he was a student. The commentator cited above sees this conservative trend as resulting from a turnover of Supreme Court judges, with conservatives tending to replace liberals.[50]

In the judiciary, as in other areas of government and politics in Japan, there has been no lack of controversy over the basic issues of national politics. As we have seen, the Supreme Court has been cautious and conservative for the most part in handling its newly found power of judicial review and in defending constitutional provisions against administrative erosion. This is perhaps scarcely surprising since Supreme Court judges are appointed by Cabinet, and nearly all governments have been conservative in political orientation.[51] In contrast, younger judges in some of the lower courts have in some cases been much more radical in their approach. The decisions of the Tokyo District Court in the Sunakawa case and over the Tokyo Public Safety Ordinance (both subsequently reversed by the Supreme Court) are an example.

In 1969 a lengthy and acrimonious controversy arose between judges who are members of Seihōkyō (Seinen Hōritsuka Kyōkai, or Young Lawyers' Association), a left-of-centre group which strongly opposed constitutional revision and particularly revision of the peace clause, and more conservative members of the bench. The controversy began with a dispute between the president of the District Court of Sapporo (Hokkaidō) and one of the judges of that court over the Naganuma Nike missile site case, which concerned article 9. Later it was taken up by organs of the Liberal Democratic Party, and by the Judges Indictment Committee of the Diet. Although, largely because of Socialist pressure within the Committee, no proceedings for the removal of any judges was instituted, the Supreme Court failed to reappoint one judge when his ten-year term expired, and another resigned in protest.[52] In this case, the issue of the political impartiality of judges was raised in a most acute form, but it could be suggested that those who raised it against the members of Seihōkyō were scarcely less politically committed than those against whom it was raised. Given the still controversial nature of the Constitution, it was difficult to see how this could be otherwise. In September 1973, when the Sapporo District Court duly handed down a judgment in the Naganuma case holding the Self-Defence Forces unconstitutional, the Prime Minister was moved to restate in forthright terms his conviction that they were perfectly constitutional.

While, as we have seen, the Supreme Court has remained sparing in its use of its power of judicial review, there is evidence that the judiciary as a whole since the early 1970s has become a more important actor in the political system. There are two principal reasons for this. One is the increased willingness of ordinary citizens and groups representing them to take their grievances to the courts, especially where these concern problems of environmental pollution and personal loss of amenities or violation of rights. Examples are the cases relating to mercury poisoning in Minamata Bay, and protests concerning the construction of *Shinkansen* (super-express) railway tracks through residential areas, as well as protests against the siting of airports and of nuclear power stations. The second reason is the number and complexity of political corruption cases being pursued through the courts. The most widely publicized of these is the Lockheed case, which was still continuing in 1981, but there have been several others. As a result of increased litigation in these two areas, the courts have found themselves faced with a variety of matters of profound political significance.

Surprising as it may seem when one considers the inauspicious origins of the Constitution and its radical rejection of much in the Japanese political tradition and experience, serious attempts to revise its text were shelved for many years, though in the early 1980s there is some renewed pressure among conservatives for revision to be attempted. After the end of the Occupation in 1952 there was a relatively brief period of intense activity in conservative circles with a view to initiating constitutional revision. Most accounts written at that period tended to assume that revision was only a matter of time, since the Japanese would inevitably wish to write a constitution of their own genuine authorship, and thus reassert both national identity and continuity with their own traditions.

Paradoxically it was the peace clause, the most radical and controversial (its enemies would say the most quixotic and absurd) single element in the whole Constitution, which above all else ensured that not a single ideograph of the text of this hastily written document should be amended in thirty-four years of its operation. By the late 1950s the Opposition had sufficient numbers in the Diet to block any attempt at revision, and even if the required two-thirds majority of all *members* of each House had been obtainable, it is doubtful whether the revisionists could have secured one-half of the votes in a subsequent national referendum. The one thing, however, that galvanized opponents of revision was the thought that if they were not stopped the conservatives would destroy the peace clause, embark on a major programme of rearmament and bring back the armed forces as a major element in politics. This was a quite plausible fear, given the extent of American pressure on Japan to rearm, although Yoshida's policy had been to utilize the peace clause as a means of forcing the Americans to accept only small-scale rearmament so as not to prejudice Japan's economic recovery or political stability. On the other hand Hatoyama, and particularly Kishi, were known to be enthusiastic advocates both of constitutional revision and of accelerated rearmament.

The peace clause therefore became the talisman of the Opposition parties and associated groups, who benefited electorally from strong anti-war feeling among the population at large. The result however was that proposals to revise any part of the Constitution were seen as an attack on article 9. In many cases, of course, this was a perfectly correct inference, since it could be demonstrated that constitutional revisionists numbered in their ranks the most 'reactionary' of government supporters. On the other hand, the ultimate effect was to place the Constitution beyond the bounds of any rational and limited amendment process.

One wonders how General MacArthur and his aides would have reacted in February 1946, had they been able to foresee that the Constitution of their devising would become virtually immune to the possibility of amendment to its text largely because of the support gained for a declamatory clause introduced in part as a tactic to secure freedom from international interference in the Occupation of Japan.

Moves for constitutional revision within the conservative parties resulted in the establishment of the Commission on the Constitution, which began hearings in 1957 and delivered its final report in 1964. From the outset the Socialists refused to sit on the Commission, which they saw as a device by the Government to give respectability to the revisionist cause.[53] What on the face of it is surprising about the Commission on the Constitution is that, given the Socialist boycott, it should have produced such a wide variety of views about amendment. After much argument, it was agreed that a report incorporating both majority (pro-revision) and minority (anti-revision) views should be drawn up. It is also interesting that, while there was majority support for the amendment of article 9, only one member actually advocated a return to imperial sovereignty on the model of the Meiji Constitution.[54] Indeed, the most emotive and persistent demand within the Commission was for a Constitution 'written in Tokyo'.

Ward summarizes the general effect of the revisionist proposals in the following terms (thus abstracting from differing and even contradictory proposals within the revisionist group): to strengthen the prime minister and Cabinet at the expense of the Diet and the political parties; to strengthen the national government at the expense of the localities; to strengthen public and collective rights against private and individual rights and claims; to expand and legitimize the present powers of the national government in the conduct of military and political aspects of foreign relations; to change the relationship of the two Houses by enhancing the House of Councillors; and to diminish somewhat the ambit of judicial powers through administrative courts, and perhaps also to circumscribe somewhat the powers of judicial review.[55]

These are obviously conservative proposals. Some, though not all, have already been in part attained by flexible constitutional interpretation, as we have seen. To some extent they may be seen as merely a recognition of the process whereby the Executive has tended to become progressively stronger in a number of major technically advanced nations.[56]

Following the LDP election victory of June 1980, some LDP Diet members and others showed renewed interest in constitutional revision. In April 1981 the Constitution Committee of the LDP announced that it was preparing a concrete set of revision proposals. The Committee foreshadowed that it would propose revisions in respect of article 9, individual rights (where it would propose a formulation to ensure that individual rights did not clash with the 'common welfare'), and the status of the emperor. These proposals had a strong sense of *déja vu* about them, and indeed there is remarkably little variation in the way revisionist arguments have been formulated since the early 1950s. Campaigning throughout the country by the supporters of constitutional revision has also markedly increased, and this in turn has engendered a counter-reaction from the Constitution's defenders. There is little indication as yet that constitutional revision is seriously being pursued by mainstream leadership groups in the LDP, and it remains, of course, technically very difficult to revise. Nevertheless, the political atmosphere in relation to the Constitution has shifted somewhat, and at least two of the Opposition parties (the DSP and the Kōmeitō) are rather less vigorous in its defence than they used to be. The argument that Japan needs a constitution of its own rather than an 'imposed constitution' has an emotive impact on certain sections of the population, even though many public opinion polls have shown a substantial majority in favour of the Constitution as it is.

Constitutional revision is not an issue that can easily be resolved. Indeed, the absence of consensus about the Constitution has meant that, as with other really difficult political issues in Japan, a head-on clash is carefully avoided. This is not something that appeals to those who like clear-cut, unambiguous or bold solutions. It is however a politically sensitive outcome, in which there is some balancing of the different opinions involved. The anti-revisionists have the text of the Constitution intact, and apparently immune to tampering. They are fairly secure in the knowledge that the document is expounded in the schools, commands majority popular support and has become entrenched in administrative practice. The revisionists, on the other hand, can take comfort from the fact that significant 'democratic' safeguards in the Constitution have been already eroded through administrative and judicial interpretation and through the political fact of conservative dominance.

How stable this situation really is in the changing world of the 1980s remains to be seen.

11 Domestic Political Issues

Despite the prior concern of many foreign observers with fundamental issues such as the Constitution, or with foreign policy and defence, the Japanese electorate as a whole is understandably more interested in 'bread and butter' questions of domestic policy. It is true that perennial issues, such as the relationship with the United States and the problem of defence, are given enormous publicity in the mass media, and command considerable attention among reasonably articulate and sophisticated people, but insofar as the average Japanese is vitally interested in politics, his interest tends to lie with matters affecting his pocket, or more broadly his way of life. Indeed, even in such a sensitive political area as the siting of nuclear power stations, it tends to be locally affected fishing and farming groups that are most vigorous in protest, rather than nationally based political organizations which do not have to sell a product in a volatile market.

In this, there is little evidence that the Japanese are much different from electorates in other parts of the world; indeed, economic motivation appears to govern Japanese behaviour to a marked degree. It is therefore at first sight surprising that questions of the redistribution of wealth, such as those which have been at the centre of party politics in countries like Great Britain or Australia, have played a less prominent (though still far from negligible) role in the appeals of political parties in Japan.

Two reasons stand out as explanations for this. The first is the system of 'vertical loyalties', which has in recent times bound an employee to his place of employment rather than to his fellow-workers in the same occupation of craft but in other establishments. The role of the labour union is thus primarily to secure the interests of the employees of the company to which the labour union is confined, and for the most part the union will refrain from doing anything that would put the firm at a serious disadvantage in relation to its rivals. Although many labour unions belong to union federations, they are jealous of their own rights when it comes to day-to-day bargaining with employers. Overall wage-fixing agreements affecting large segments of industry are thus highly unusual, although by the device of the annual 'Spring Struggle' the campaigns of individual unions are quite well co-ordinated. It follows that the 'us-versus-them' mentality is less prominent in the working class in Japan than in some Western countries, though it is by no means absent. Indeed, it is often very strong within declining industries and among government employees. Left-wing parties, notably the Socialists and the Communists, use a declamatory 'class-war' rhetoric, but particularly with the Socialists it is at a level of abstraction which suggests that it is removed some distance from reality.

This is not to argue that Japan has a particularly docile work force, or one that is slow in the pursuit of its own interests.[1] During the inflationary period of 1973–4 workers achieved wage increases which ranged from twenty to over thirty per cent, though this was only a temporary phase following the OPEC oil crisis. Since the middle 1970s wage rises have been held down to around seven to eight per cent, in line with the lower economic growth of the recent period. The principal reason why wage costs have not been allowed to get seriously out of line with productivity and economic growth is that employees bargain for improvements in their wages and conditions almost entirely within individual firms, in whose continued profitability they have a direct and continuing interest. Employers tend to take a similarly parochial line, concerning themselves with the task of maintaining and if possible expanding their firm's share of the market. This means that their relations with other similar firms can be acutely competitive. Both labour and management maintain their own national organizations, which confront each other in the national arena; but to an extent which would be surprising elsewhere, issues of wealth distribution and even of welfare are determined outside the sphere of politics, by arrangement within separate firms. It should not be assumed that such a system would have been voluntarily agreed to by workers if they had really had a choice. The disadvantages suffered by a worker leaving one place of employment to seek work elsewhere are so manifold that from necessity most workers simply accept the normality of the permanent employment system. Indeed, it has been cogently argued that the system originated from oligopolistic co-operation between large employers faced with an acute shortage of skilled labour, which, had employers not agreed to act in concert, could have exploited its scarcity through craft or industrial unions to extract disproportionately high wages.[2] Reinforced by a group-centred tradition from which employers could draw examples, and by the experience of prewar and wartime mobilization, the system survived and was strengthened during the high economic growth period from the 1950s.

The second reason for the relatively low priority given within politics to the class distribution of national wealth is the rate at which that wealth has been increasing. The rate of economic growth between the 1950s and early 1970s was so high that distributional problems, though objectively far from negligible, assumed secondary significance as general prosperity rapidly and visibly increased. The economic climate has been much harsher since the 1973–4 oil crisis, but except for a period of two or three years in the middle 1970s, growth rates have averaged five or six per cent per year. Thus, although real income per head and the store of social capital remains lower than in a few other advanced nations, Japan has the third largest economy in the world and essentially Western European levels of prosperity. Among the political effects is a dampening of the tensions, which might otherwise have become acute, over problems of wealth distribution between social strata. The turbulent industrial scene during the first postwar decade, when wages were extremely low and rising very slowly, is an indication of what might have been in store politically had Japan not become a high-growth economy.

The argument, however, that economic wellbeing creates political quiescence ought not to be taken too far. Economic growth as a complete panacea for political conflict is certainly not borne out by the Japanese case. The untrammelled dynamism of Japanese industrial growth has brought in its train a number of serious social, economic and political problems whose solution has proved far from easy. Prominent among these is the issue of environmental pollution, which for a while in the late 1960s and early 1970s appeared to be completely out of hand, but which with slower economic growth and tougher government action in the more recent period has been brought under control to some extent. Other issues include a lower standard of social amenities and welfare provisions than in some Western-type countries; extremely high land prices and what, by Western standards, is cramped and poor-quality housing; a slate of problems in the educational field; the difficulty of maintaining a population balance between the cities and the countryside, and of preserving a reasonable income balance between large-scale industry on the one hand, and small-scale industry and agriculture on the other; and finally the perennial problem of discrimination against minority groups.

To put the nature of these problems, and reactions to them, into focus, we need to make three basic points. First, the Government is less involved in the provision of services to the individual than has been the case in Western Europe and Australasia, and by contrast the private sector has been much more involved. This is true of welfare, where government spending has been relatively low by relevant international standards (though rising), but where places of employment provide extensively – sometimes extremely generously – for the welfare of their employees, especially those on their permanent staff. It is also true in education, where the Government is cheeseparing in its provision of educational facilities, particularly in the tertiary sector, but where there is a very substantial private contribution. It is clear that this offends against any principle of the equal provision of services for equality's sake. Thus an employee of a major firm will have access to company-provided housing, hospital facilities, holiday homes and so on, which will not be available to somebody who is self-employed or who works for a much smaller organization. The latter will not be without all welfare services, since government services are available, as are facilities for private insurance, but the standard available is likely to be lower and the financial burden for the individual much higher. In education, the individual whose parents cannot afford to send him or her to the best schools may still succeed in entering Tokyo University or one of the few Government-financed élite universities, since the entrance examinations are quite strictly meritocratic. On the other hand competition for entrance is intense, and those whose parents can afford the best tuition are at an advantage. Moreover, failure to enter the best State universities means that the only avenue to an élite-style tertiary education is by entry to a leading private university, where fees are substantial, and where also, of course, there is a highly competitive entrance examination. It is difficult to deny that in practice this discriminates against children from poorer families, even though some of them do manage to achieve the best possible education, and although with widespread prosperity the number of those who can afford the expenses involved is quite large.[3]

One consequence of low government spending on welfare and education, in a society where private contributions in these (and other) areas are large, is that objectively the best way for the under-privileged individual to better his lot is in many cases to join the system rather than to resist it. One way is to save to an extent where it is possible to afford an expensive education for one's children. Another is to achieve employment in an organization which will enable one to secure superior levels of security and welfare. Since it is difficult to change jobs once a person has been hired by a respectable firm, the pressure on parents and children alike to ensure entry to an educational 'stream' that will lead to the right sort of firm is intense. It is also a much-discussed source of social and psychological problems. On the other hand the Western alternative of joining a class-based trade union movement does not exist for most people as a realistic alternative. Some who, for whatever reason, are incapable of 'joining the system', find solace in a new religion such as the Sōka Gakkai, but this again is a minority phenomenon.

Another important result of relatively low levels of government expenditure, combined with a high personal savings rate, is that fairly low levels of personal taxation are accepted as the norm, and the political consequences for a government of attempting to increase taxation levels substantially can be severe.[4] Governments of the late 1970s and early 1980s were facing serious budgetary problems as a result. The fact that the Suzuki Government in March 1981 announced that it would pursue 'administrative reform' in the interests of 'small government' suggests that it appeared to the Government politically easier to tackle its budgetary problems from the expenditure side rather than from the revenue side. A minor but well-publicized aspect of this was the proposal by the National Railways to close many of its local lines in country areas on the grounds that they were making a loss. Protests from adversely affected local communities appeared unlikely to have much more than token effect. On the other hand it was very difficult for Government, for political reasons, to make savings where they would really have made a difference to the budget, such as by slashing subsidies to agriculture.

The second point is that whereas during the whole period of LDP rule the Government had pursued a policy of relatively low (though increasing) financial commitment to public welfare, it remained profoundly interested in the problem of control. We have earlier discussed the extent of bureaucratic power within the political system as a whole. Across a range of policy areas government ministries and agencies have striven to retain a high level of control over their areas of jurisdiction, both by use of their statutory powers and through the cultivation of networks of alliances. In this, of course, they have been immeasurably assisted by the fact that a party that is essentially content with the system as it exists has been continuously in power. To put it broadly, what the bureaucracy has been mainly interested in achieving – and concerned to extend its control in order to achieve – is an ordered society. In areas such as gun control they have been not only extraordinarily successful, but thoroughly in tune with popular sentiment. In the field of local government, on the other hand, attempts to regain the kind of central control that used to be in the hands of the old Ministry of Home Affairs in the prewar period have clashed – more or less, at different periods – with the collective choices of local communities. The power of the purse, however, has been strong, and locally elected authorities of a radical bent have only shown limited success in changing policy away from the directions desired by the central authority in Tokyo. Again, although important changes have taken place during the 1970s and early 1980s, central government control over financial markets has remained sufficiently strong seriously to inhibit the emergence of a free market of the kind that exists in New York or

London.[5] Faced with the possibility of an acute energy shortage in the 1980s or 1990s the Government (principally MITI) has had remarkable success in enforcing energy conservation and the development of sources alternative to oil, even though continued success may be problematical in the longer term. In education, the Ministry of Education has worked assiduously to develop and maintain a degree of control over the whole education system that is regarded as dangerous and undemocratic by its opponents. This extends to control over the content of textbooks, a highly controversial issue which reminds the Ministry's critics of prewar precedents.

In all these policy areas, and others as well, the principal concern of the bureaucrats has been to minimize unstructured or unduly disruptive activity. Citizens' movements, because of their generally fragmented nature, have proved more difficult to manage than, say, the Agricultural Co-operative Association (Nōkyō), which has a sophisticated organization and is geared to working with government.

This leads us to the third point, namely that policies are differentially influenced by the relative power and effectiveness of relevant interest groups. The unique importance of the large-firm sector of the economy has been referred to in chapter 8. What can broadly be described as the agricultural interest is also capable of influencing policy profoundly because of the LDP's dependence on the agricultural vote. In other policy fields, however, it is the coincidence of changing government priorities with pressure from interest groups that are not necessarily regarded as formidable opponents by the bureaucracy that has resulted in changes of policy. The progressive tightening of regulations concerning the environment during the 1970s reflected not only pressure from a wide variety of concerned groups, but also a realization that the problems that had developed were too serious to be left to the uncontrolled workings of the market-place. These points will be illustrated in the various examples that follow.

Ironically, one of the most troubled areas from the point of view of the bureaucracy has been in its relationship with its own employees. Strained relations between the Government and the public service unions have a history which goes back to the Occupation period. Part of the reason for this is that wages and conditions in the public sector have not kept up with those in the private sector. More important is that the rights of trade unions in the public sector are specifically curtailed by legislative statute and are considerably inferior to those in the private sector. This legislative deprivation has resulted in chronic ill-will between public enterprise unions and Government, with unions engaging in industrial action in order to assert their right to act in ways which are forbidden them by law.

The political repercussions of this situation were disproportionate. About two-thirds of the unionists affiliated through their unions with the largest and most militant trade union federation, Sōhyō, belong to the public sector. These unions have practically no representation in any other federation. Sōhyō has for many years been the principal backer of the main Opposition party, the Japan Socialist Party, and the closeness of their relationship may be regarded as a key reason for that Party's narrow sectionalism, ideological militancy and failure to broaden its political appeal.

The position of the public sector unions was highlighted by the controversy over Japan's tardiness in ratifying Convention no. 87 of the International Labour Organization (ILO). ILO Convention no. 87 was drawn up in 1948, and concerns freedom of association and protection of the right of organization. Among other things it guarantees to workers (as well as to employers) the right to form associations of their choosing, without requiring permission beforehand, and to join any such association, limited only by the rules of that association. This was of particular relevance in the context of Japanese industrial relations, because of the prevailing enterprise union structure. This provision of the Convention went against the desire of some employers to formalize the enterprise union structure in ways that would have formally restricted the freedom of a worker to belong to a union of his choice. On the other hand, it was in tune with the aspirations of elements in the union movement at the national level to promote industrial unionism. The other relevant provision of the Convention was that which gave freedom to labour unions (as to associations of employers) to select their representatives for bargaining purposes. This implied that the representatives did not have to be currently employed by the company concerned.

The controversy over Convention no. 87 did not get under way until 1958, but stemmed from legislation to control the activities of labour unions in the public sector, brought down by the Government (prompted by SCAP) in 1948. After a period of intense industrial unrest in the public service and in government instrumentalities, the liberalized labour legislation of the immediate postwar period was amended in respect of employees of the public sector.[6] Public service and government corporation workers were put into two separate categories. Public service workers were no longer subject to the Labour Union Law, which had guaranteed them extensive trade union rights, and were now, under the revised National Public Service Law, deprived of the rights to strike and to bargain collectively. The determination of their wages and conditions was left almost entirely in the hands of the National Personnel Authority. Workers in government corporations and enterprises were placed under the Public Corporation and National Enterprise Labour Relations Law[7] and although they could still organize and bargain collectively they were forbidden to strike.

This legislation also circumscribed the membership and bargaining rights of public sector workers in two respects which appeared to clash directly with the provisions of ILO Convention no. 87.[8] First of all, article 4, paragraph 3 of the Law meant that union membership was confined to the employees of a single organization, and the union was forbidden to select its officers or bargaining representatives except from among the union membership. Coupled with the ban on strike action, this served to penalize those militant unions whose officials had been dismissed from government employ because of their leadership of strikes or similar activities. Since a union could choose as an official only somebody who was currently employed by the government instrumentality to which the union belonged, the provision become a source of constant friction between the Government and the public sector unions. In many cases it served to increase, rather than decrease, union militancy. It also meant that the unions came to see ILO Convention no. 87 as indirectly relevant to their battle for the right to strike, although the Convention does not actually mention the right to strike.[9]

The other major problem, from the unions' point of view, was that the Public Corporation and National Enterprise Labour Relations Law included the term 'appropriate bargaining units' in order to decentralize the process of bargaining. The intent seems to have been to prevent bargaining from falling into the hands of labour union militants at the national level, and also to weaken the labour union impact by putting its unity under the strain of having to work exclusively through local units. This was principally relevant to Nikkyōsō, the extremely militant teachers' union, which fell under this law. The polarization of view between the Ministry of Education and Nikkyōsō in the period since the Occupation was notorious in Japan, and there were few areas of industry where industrial relations were so bad as they generally were in the area of education. For the Ministry of Education, the Public Corporation and National Enterprise Labour Relations Law was a means of justifying its refusal to enter into regular bargaining with Nikkyōsō at the national level. Instead, it insisted on bargaining with the union at the prefectural level. This was natural at a time when educational administration was in the hands of locally elected boards of education, but since education has been progressively recentralized it gives an obvious advantage to the Ministry, which now had effective control over the local education committees. Nikkyōsō fought consistently for the right to bargain centrally with the Ministry of Education, only to find its approaches rebuffed. Another issue affecting Nikkyōsō was whether 'managerial and supervisory personnel' were eligible for union membership. The Government wished to debar school headmasters and supervisors from membership of Nikkyōsō, whereas the union saw them as an important element in its membership.[10]

In 1958 some of the public sector unions affiliated with Sōhyō appealed to the ILO against article 4, paragraph 3, of the Public Corporation and National Enterprise Labour Relations Law, on the ground that it violated ILO Convention no. 87. Thus began a series of appeals to the ILO by Japanese trade unions, criticisms of Japanese labour legislation by the ILO, promises of action by the Japanese Government, tortuous manœuvring between the Government, the JSP and the labour unions, and repeated delays. Finally, in January 1965, nearly six and a half years after the original appeal, the ILO sent a high-level commission to Japan which, after extensive discussions with all the interested parties, urged the newly formed Satō Government to ratify the Convention immediately. This it did in April 1965, over union protests that the situation had not been properly rectified from the union point of view. Some of the contentious legislation was however repealed, including article 4, paragraph 3 of the Public Corporation and National Enterprise Labour Relations Law, and similar provisions in other laws. This was a substantial gain for the unions, but industrial relations in the public sector continued to be unhappy in the extreme, and the public sector unions never regained the right to strike.

The issue revealed among other things the complexity of relationships between the public sector unions, the leadership of the Sōhyō federation (some two-thirds of whose membership was from the public sector) and the Japan Socialist Party in their bargaining with the Government and the Liberal Democratic Party. For instance, in 1963 a compromise was worked out between Kuraishi Tadao, on the Liberal Democratic side, and Iwai Akira, acting for Sōhyō, which on several points was more favourable for the unions than the solution which finally emerged. The compromise, however, became entangled with other issues, and with the internal politics of both the JSP and the LDP, so that another two years of wrangling were necessary before the problem was patched over under unprecedented pressure from the ILO.

Ratification itself precipitated a Socialist boycott of the Diet for several days, and the Socialists were induced to return only by means of a compromise mediated by the Lower House Speaker, Funada Naka. The compromise included reference of some contentious points that remained to a committee including representatives of the Government, the employers and the unions. It was agreed that the committee should report back before 14 June 1966, the date at which ILO Convention no. 87 was to take effect. The committee, however, failed to reach agreement, and its final report was drawn up in the absence of the union representatives.[11] The Government, while accepting its report, allowed the committee further time to sort out its internal differences; but since the unions refused to return to it, and the Chairman 'accepted responsibility' by tendering his resignation, the Government insisted that its proposals that had been held over should go into effect in December 1966.[12]

As we have seen, Nikkyōsō had its own special reasons for concern about the ratification of ILO Convention no. 87. This reflected a legacy of bad relations between the union and the Ministry of Education, which stemmed back to the immediate postwar period. Indeed, education has been one of the most conflict-ridden areas of domestic policy in Japan since the Occupation. The issues have already been touched upon in chapter 5. The Americans essentially attempted three things. They sought to 'democratize' education by throwing open its benefits to as wide a segment of the population as possible. They attempted a drastic ideological reform of its content, replacing the old emphasis on nationalism and obedience with a stress on individualism, rational scientific thought and democratic internationalist values. And finally, they tried to decentralize its administration.

The third policy was the least durable of the three, and was rapidly reversed during the 1950s. Its reversal however was the occasion for much of the bitterness that developed between the Ministry of Education and Nikkyōsō. The issue of the 'appropriate bargaining unit' sprang directly from the recentralization that the Government had imposed. Ideological questions, however, added greatly to the mutual suspicion with which the two sides regarded each other, while the radical changes in the structure of the school system from primary right up to tertiary level caused extensive confusion, whose ramifications were slow to disappear.

The ideological dimension was the most conspicuous during the 1950s and 1960s. Nikkyōsō from the outset was a strongly Marxist, militant union, whose enthusiasm for the teaching of democracy in schools spilled over into a belief that teachers should be regarded as 'labourers', engaged in the struggle for the victory of the working class against the forces of reaction. Conversely, the Ministry of Education took a consistently tough stand, and succeeded in steadily expanding its own control over both the administration of schools and the content of courses. The dispute about the Ministry's introduction of a 'teachers' efficiency rating' system in 1957 and 1958 stemmed largely from the fact that it was using it quite specifically as a means of getting rid of the influence of Nikkyōsō militants from the schools. Refusal of the Ministry to bargain centrally with the national leaders of Nikkyōsō was similarly motivated to cut down the union's influence.

The polarization of view between the Ministry and the union was sharply revealed by their dispute about the reintroduction of ethics courses into schools in the early 1960s. For the union, it was a dangerous and reactionary reversion to prewar practices of teaching 'ethics' as a form of indoctrination to reinforce militaristic control by the State. For the Ministry (at least according to its official view), ethics courses were required in order to go some way towards filling the 'spiritual vacuum' into which Japan had fallen since the war, leading to serious social problems such as juvenile delinquency. The content of the ethics courses were of course quite different from those before the war, and emphasized such practical moral problems as road safety, but Nikkyōsō could argue with some plausibility that they were the thin end of the wedge, and should be regarded as one small part of a concerted government programme of gradually subverting the postwar political, social and economic reforms.

One educational *cause célèbre* of the 1960s was over the question of government control over textbooks. A professor called Ienaga Saburō wrote a history textbook which was referred back by a Ministry of Education panel on the grounds that certain passages in it were biased or distorted.[13] After making some alterations he resubmitted the textbook, but it was rejected since he was not prepared to change some passages which the Ministry had objected to. (One of these was that the history of the early emperors was all invented in the interests of the emperor system.) The Tokyo District Court found in his favour when he brought a suit alleging that the decision was illegal and unconstitutional, but this verdict may later be overturned by the Supreme Court. The Ministry of Education, whose control over textbooks had tightened substantially since the postwar period (though it fell far short of that exercised before the war), fought the case with vigour, arguing that supervision of textbooks was required as a check upon accuracy and suitability, given the duties of the State in regard to education.

Since the early 1970s the educational arena has been rather less troubled by the kind of uncompromising ideological conflict that had bedevilled it over the previous two decades. To a very considerable extent government educational policy has come to focus on matters such as expanding the scope of technological education and providing a greater variety of educational institution than was in the system inherited from the Occupation. Meanwhile, the policies of Nikkyōsō have become somewhat less rigid (though its political loyalties still lie with the JSP and to some extent with the JCP) than they were a decade earlier. Nevertheless, the early months of 1981 saw a revival of the textbook issue, with proposals emanating from the LDP and the Ministry of Education for the revision of textbooks containing 'biased' material. Predictably, the offending passages concerned issues such as defence and the role of business where conservative and radical perspectives were at loggerheads.

If education at primary and secondary levels was for long an arena of political conflict, at tertiary level it was at times even more politically troubled. The campus riots of 1968 and 1969 coincided with an upsurge of student radicalism across the world, but also reflected some specifically Japanese circumstances. There is a long history of student radicalism in Japan,[14] and the experiences of prewar students at the hands of the authorities tended to condition the movement towards total distrust of authority, whether that of the Government or that of the university. Nearly all student radicals in Japan were strongly influenced by Marxism.

The great expansion of university education put in train during the Occupation brought with it many problems, not the least of which was the woefully inadequate facilities for teaching in many of the newer (and some of the older) tertiary institutions. University facilities in general remain much inferior to those of private industry. Although a much higher proportion of the population than before was able to embark upon a university education, the hierarchy of institutions, with Tokyo University at the apex, remained much as before, and competition to enter the best universities was intense. Finally, the Ministry of Education exercised tight control over the administration of the national universities, although the private universities had their own autonomy. Faced with rapidly rising costs, however, private universities were forced to rely on enrolment expansion (often beyond what their facilities could properly cope with) in order to survive.[15] Another aspect of the same problem was the series of scandals in the early 1980s where private university administrators stood accused of requiring illegal or excessive 'contributions' from students on admission.

In the 1960s a combination of a radical tradition, poor conditions, effective inequality of institutions and bureaucratic control finally produced an explosive situation, and in the late 1960s universities erupted into violence across the country. In Tokyo University, for instance, some clumsy handling by the university administration was paralleled by an astonishingly rapid resort by student organizations to extreme measures.

The Universities Control Bill of August 1969, which as the ultimate sanction enabled the minister of education (with the advice of the Provisional Council for University Problems) to suspend any university department in which a dispute had continued for more than nine months,[16] was effective in persuading university administrations to act decisively to settle outstanding disputes. In many cases this involved calling in the police to remove students engaged in sit-ins. While the Bill was certainly well timed in terms of its impact on public opinion, there is evidence that the student movement was in any case rapidly running out of steam, as the less committed radicals began to lose interest in constant political agitation. Lasting reform of universities, however, was much slower to materialize, though the establishment of Tsukuba University, near Tokyo, was an interesting example of attempts by the Ministry of Education to establish a new pattern of tertiary education which should be less susceptible to radical political activity than the older universities.

Although much has been achieved in Japanese tertiary education, the concept of universities being institutions free to criticize society has not been wholly accepted by the political and bureaucratic Establishment. Though in general such freedoms exist to a large extent, their further restriction could well provoke political struggles in the future.

Conflict over the extent and nature of central government authority was thus the stuff of educational politics in Japan. Similarly, in the general area of local government and politics, questions of the distribution of authority were of crucial importance. Here, challenges to central authority were increasing in intensity and effectiveness from the late 1960s, although the original devolution of local authority put into effect by the Occupation was radically attenuated during the 1950s. The challenge came in the form of a serious erosion of Liberal Democratic support at the local level in the most urbanized areas. Much of this can be attributed to the serious dislocations of life caused by unchecked industrial expansion and the growth of huge unplanned metropolitan centres such as Tokyo and Ōsaka, and the consequent politicization of a population previously rather apathetic to local political issues.

By 1973 Tokyo, Ōsaka, Kyōto, Nagoya, Yokohama and other major cities in Japan had elected left-wing mayors or governors. Although by the late 1970s a number of the major cities had returned to conservative control, the changes in the political atmosphere wrought by the earlier advent of progressive local regimes was hard to eradicate.[17]

From the point of view of the Liberal Democrats and the government bureaucracy, the existence of a large number of progressive local authorities represented a challenge to some of its basic notions of how local governments should work. It will be recalled that the American Occupation introduced a radical measure of decentralization in local government. This ran completely counter to the centralizing trend of Japanese governments since the Meiji Restoration, and against the prevailing concept of local administration as essentially an extension and agency of the central government. After the Occupation ended, its reforms in this area were among the first to be challenged by the newly independent Yoshida Government, and by its immediate successors. Control over education and the police were recentralized, and the old Home Ministry, which had exercised almost total powers over local administrations before the war, was partially reconstituted in 1960 as the Local Autonomy Ministry. These reforms, as well as the extreme dependence of local administrations upon central government funds, made it difficult for them to play anything but a subordinate role. Attempts, however, by the Yoshida and Hatoyama Governments to make prefectural governorship once more appointive rather than elective failed, and, as we have seen, a very large number of positions at all levels remained subject to election.[18]

The structure of local government is complex, and has not

entirely kept pace with the tremendous shifts of population into the major cities. Formally speaking, it is based upon articles 92–5 of the Constitution, from which stem a number of laws, notably the Local Autonomy Law, the Local Public Service Law, the Local Taxation Law and the Public Offices Election Law.

The system consists of two levels, the prefectural and the municipal. The first level is that of the prefecture, which is roughly equivalent in geographical area to an English county or a French *département*. Prefectures were set up, replacing a previous system, after the Meiji Restoration, and still reflect the population geography of that period. There are now forty-seven prefectures (forty-six before the reversion of Okinawa in 1972), which are known collectively as *to-dō-fu-ken*.[19]

At the municipal level the local unit of administration may be a city (*shi*), town (*chō* or *machi*) or village (*son* or *mura*), being so designated according to population and degree of urbanization.[20] Some functions which are prefectural in areas where the municipal authority is a town or village are performed by city administrations in areas under their jurisdiction. There are, moreover, a small number of 'designated cities', whose administrations have wider functions than those of ordinary cities. They all have populations over half a million.[21] In such cases, the powers of the prefecture over the region covered by the city area are correspondingly reduced. So far as towns and villages are concerned, they all have identical functions, at least in principle. Since the end of the Occupation there has been widespread amalgamation of existing areas of administration into larger and presumably more effective ones. The new units, however, by no means always reflect actual communities, and amalgamations often reflect central bureaucratic convenience rather than any local demand. Plans for amalgamation of prefectures into large-scale regional units have not yet made much progress.

All the categories of administrative unit mentioned above are termed, in the jargon of the Local Autonomy Law, 'ordinary local public bodies'. There is, however, a kind of residual category, which reflects the confused history of local administration in Japan, called a 'special local public body'. This term in fact denotes several quite different things, which appear to have in common only the fact that they are exceptions to the normal administrative structure.[22] The first meaning is that of any facility (such as a hospital or port) which is run jointly by two or more ordinary local public bodies. Co-operation of this kind is permitted up to the point of total amalgamation.[23]

The second is what is known as a 'property ward'. A property ward may be set up when two ordinary local public bodies (say, two villages) are amalgamated, but when one of them does not wish to allow some facility that it has owned (for instance an area of forest) to become the common property of the larger unit. In this case it may continue to belong, as a property ward, to the original village, even though that village is no longer an administrative unit for other purposes.[24] One important function of the property ward has been to grant some degree of legal recognition to the *buraku* (hamlet), despite the fact that legal recognition was specifically denied it in the Occupation's reforms of local government. The *buraku* remains the most natural indigenous unit of local association in many parts of rural Japan, but because of its use during and before the war as a local instrument of government control, the Occupation authorities decided that its influence should be curbed so far as possible.[25] The smallest unit of rural administration therefore became the village, but since in many cases 'villages' were distinctly artificial creations the influence of the *buraku* has persisted. The device of property wards has thus served to allow local rural communities to revert to something approaching the *status quo* in administrative matters.

Finally, the most important type of 'special local public body' exists within the Tokyo Metropolis, i.e. the twenty-three wards of the Metropolis which comprise the central and inner suburban areas of the city, but not its outer suburban and rural areas.[26] This special designation[27] is occasioned by the huge size of Tokyo, the complexity of its administrative problems and the fact that it is the main centre of Japan's commercial and economic affairs and the seat of the national Government. The twenty-three special wards each have powers which are similar to, though a little less than, those of cities elsewhere in Japan. On the other hand the Metropolitan Government (remembering that the Tokyo Metropolis is equivalent to a prefecture) has substantial powers of co-ordination over the special wards, and whereas the mayor of a city, town or village is elected directly by the local electors, between 1952 and 1974 the head of a special ward in Tokyo was selected by the ward Assembly with the consent of the governor of the Tokyo Metropolis. In 1974, however, the Local Autonomy Law was amended to make the headships of the Tokyo special wards once more elective positions. The first elections under the new legislation were held in April 1975.[28]

Local government in Tokyo is complicated by the unusual administrative structure. The Metropolitan Government does not have the same degree of control over the outer surburban areas, largely on the western side of the city, as it does over the twenty-three special wards. The result has been a good deal of unco-ordinated development, particularly in the San-Tama (three Tamas) area, a commuter area of vast new housing estates. The sheer size and population of Tokyo has made it a problem area from the point of view of administration, but the fact that it is in addition the nation's capital also ensures a high degree of politicization. Whether it be in the area of pollution control, land prices, commuter services or policy towards anti-Government demonstrators, what happens in Tokyo is noted carefully in other parts of the country.

Until 1965 both the Tokyo Metropolitan Assembly and the Tokyo governorship were firmly in Liberal Democratic hands. In that year however they suffered a severe defeat in the Assembly elections because several of their Assemblymen were involved in a serious corruption scandal. Subsequently, in 1967, Minobe Ryōkichi, standing as an Independent but backed by the Socialist and Communist parties, defeated a moderate conservative candidate to become Tokyo's first 'progressive' governor. Once in office, Minobe went on to attract enormous popularity, largely, it seems, as a result of his flair for publicity, his humanitarian image and his anti-Government, anti-business stand on quality-of-life issues. When he stood again for election in 1971, he overwhelmed a conservative candidate and won with a huge majority.[29] In this election Minobe attracted the support of many voters who would not normally have voted for progressive candidates, and clearly the votes he managed to attract did not simply depend on the organizational support of the Socialist and Communist parties. In part, his popularity at the polls may be attributed to his charisma (perhaps an unusual phenomenon in Japanese politics), but even more importantly to his proclaimed policies of providing satisfactory amenities, social services, and, in his words 'minimum standards of wholesome and cultured living'.[30] The concept of a 'civic minimum', which should be higher than the minimum standards set by the national Government, was central to his whole approach, and this struck a responsive chord in the Tokyo electorate.[31] The provision of pedestrian overpasses at dangerous intersections and the improvement of parks in a city where greenery had long been losing the battle with concrete was one side of his programme. The other was to upgrade welfare provisions for old people, mothers of small children and in general those who tended to be disadvantaged in the highly competitive business-orientated environment of big-city Japan. In Tokyo and other big cities of the early seventies this was extremely popular.

The later history of the Minobe administration was less happy than the earlier. The central reality of local government remained the fact that local administrations were dependent on central government funds to implement their programmes. When central government funds became tight following the 1973–4 oil crisis, Minobe and other progressive local governors found their funds dwindling and their political credibility therefore at risk. He also lost popularity for two other reasons. The first was the emergence of a dispute in 1975 between Socialists and Communist parties in his support organization over control of the Burakumin liberation movement.[32] The other was the problem of expectations raised over Minobe's policy of consultation with local citizens' movements. Preferring negotiation rather than coercion, Minobe found himself in trouble over a number of issues, particularly over where to locate garbage disposal facilities.[33] The 1975 Tokyo gubernatorial election, held in the shadow of the Burakumin controversy, was won by Minobe with a clear majority of votes, but was not the runaway victory of 1971. His principal rival was the novelist-politician Ishihara Shintarō, who stood ideologically on the far right of the LDP. In 1979 Minobe did not contest the election, preferring to retire from the political scene. With his retirement the twelve-year period of progressive local administration in Tokyo came to an end. His successor was Suzuki Shunichi, a conservative, who stood for election with the support not only of the LDP, but also of the DSP and Kōmeitō. The former Chairman of Sōhyō, Ōta Kaoru, backed by the left, was no match for him at the elections. Under Suzuki, the administration of Tokyo has been of a more traditionally conservative kind.

Two other examples of progressive local government deserve mention. One is that of Yokohama, where the former JSP Diet member Asukata Ichio was first elected mayor in 1963, and remained in that post until his retirement to become national Chairman of the JSP in 1977. Asukata's policies in relation to pollution control were of great significance, and formed the model for local government policies in other parts of the country. Given the extreme nature of the pollution problem in the Yokohama area in the 1960s, it is hardly surprising that these problems should have proved popular with the electorate. Essentially the policies were based on agreements with local firms.[34]

The other example is that of Kyōto, where the durable regime of the progressive governor Ninagawa Torazō has already been mentioned in chapter 5. The twenty-eight years of the Ninagawa administration (1950–78) were notable for a range of progressive policies, for the advance of Communist influence in his organization from the late 1960s, and perhaps most interestingly for his ability to cultivate successfully a range of interests not normally associated with left-wing politics in other parts of the country. Kyōto under Ninagawa may even be regarded as an interesting 'alternative model' for Japanese politics. Failure of Ninagawa's left-wing support base to remain united led to its replacement by a conservative administration after his retirement in 1978.[35]

Even though many of the progressive local authorities reverted to conservative (or conservative-moderate) control at the end of the 1970s, it would be wrong to see this as simply a reversion to the *status quo ante*. Not only had a fundamental shift in electoral behaviour in the cities taken place which no local authority could ignore, but also many of the policies (for instance on pollution) pioneered by progressive governors and mayors had been assimilated to a considerable extent by conservative regimes at both national and local level. In the early

1980s the main constraint affecting policy choice and policy innovation was financial restriction imposed by the centre and the influence of 'small government' ways of thinking. This, however, was something that necessarily affected all local administrations, conservative and progressive alike.

One of the most important and well-publicized issues of recent years in Japan has been that of environmental pollution. The unprecedented speed of economic growth in the 1960s, coupled with *laissez-faire* policies on the part of government, imposed an intolerable strain on the environment, and this, after an interval, placed the issue squarely in the political arena. Of the many human tragedies resulting from lax control over pollution, the Minamata case has a symbolic, as well as a real, significance. The case was one of mercury pollution in Minamata Bay in Kyūshū; mercury waste from a nitrogenous fertilizer company located on the shores of the Bay entered the food chain over a long period, and seriously affected fish which were eaten by local residents. What became in a sense 'symbolic' about the case for citizens' movements fighting pollution was that despite the fact that the cause of the pollution was reasonably well established at quite an early stage, it took several years for the company to cease pouring its waste mercury into the Bay. Moreover, the company's labour union supported the company management in its stand, taking the view, essentially, that the maintenance of jobs in the district was its prime responsibility and the interests of pollution victims ought to be subordinated to this basic aim. It was after a series of court cases ultimately found in favour of the victims, and the company was obliged to pay compensation, that the company was forced into submission.

The Minamata case was merely the best known of a large number of essentially similar cases. The political results, however, are highly significant, since from these cases sprang the citizens' movements which have done so much to politicize local politics in Japan; and as we saw in chapter 10, the courts come into the picture in a big way in the resolution of disputes arising from pollution-related cases. Moreover, government policy itself has been much affected by the pollution problem. Since the Environment Agency within the Prime Minister's Office was established in 1971, regulations have been tightened and serious obstacles have been placed in the way of highly polluting industries.[36] The thrust of industrial policy in general has in any case been away from heavy industry into the 'knowledge-intensive' industries which create less pollution, while slower economic growth also takes the pressure off the environment to some extent. Nevertheless, it would be foolish to suggest that Japan has yet solved its many pollution dilemmas or that the political impact of the issues involved has subsided.

Agriculture too is by no means free of worrying economic and social problems which spill over into the political sphere. The reverse side of the coin of urbanization during the period of rapid economic growth was the flight of population from the countryside. The rural population stabilized somewhat during the 1970s, and the rapid decline of the earlier period in numbers of people engaged in agriculture was stemmed. The problem remains, however, that part-time farming, and farms run by women and old people, are widespread.

The Agricultural Co-operative Association (Nōkyō), to which practically all farmers are affiliated, is an effective pressure group with close links to the Government and the LDP. The Ministry of Agriculture, whose influence is bolstered by the large number of Liberal Democratic Diet members who represent over-weighted rural constituencies, has fought with a great deal of success for the maintenance of agricultural subsidies and price support schemes which have encouraged gross over-production of rice. The Ministry has also fought long and hard against the liberalization of agricultural imports, and its success in this field has contributed to an unreasonably high cost of food to the domestic consumer. Its stand is usually justified in terms of reducing the inequalities of urban and rural incomes, but the alternative solution of allowing economic forces to produce an even faster move out of agriculture than has actually occurred is resisted. Reduced employment opportunities in the cities and the trend towards city firms relocating their factories in country areas now makes the spectre of rural depopulation seem rather less urgent. Both the levelling of incomes and the aim of maximum national food self-suffiency as part of national security policy influences government policy towards agriculture, but the key factor is undoubtedly the amount of political leverage which agricultural interests are able to exercise. The

Nōkyō, which can be likened to a huge agricultural conglomerate operating a range of services throughout the country for farmers and others who may have relatively little connection with agriculture, may in some ways be regarded as the single most effective pressure group in Japan.[37]

In the field of social welfare Japan still spends a lower proportion of her GNP on welfare, so far as government provision is concerned, than most other comparable nations, but the population in general is much better covered than it has been at any time in Japan's history. The situation is long past where the family was expected to take the main burden of providing financially for its aged and sick members. Participation by the State in social welfare schemes was retarded by the fact that industrial firms and other employers of labour were (and are) expected to provide for the welfare of their employees. Implicit in this system of industrial paternalism has been a range of inequalities. While the large firms, with their 'élite' work force, have been able to provide lavish benefits for their permanent employees in the form of subsidized housing, subsidizing shops, health schemes, superannuation schemes, cheap holiday accommodation and so on[38] (as well as twice-yearly bonuses, which may amount to 50 per cent of basic salary), those outside the élite, such as temporary workers, women or employees in smaller and less affluent establishments, are provided for much less lavishly. The system therefore could be said to provide social welfare on a generous scale for what may broadly be termed the most productive part of the work force and very much less generously for the rest.

Whatever the benefits of such a division in terms of overall economic dynamism and efficiency, the political implications of such entrenched inequalities became too obvious for the Government to ignore. A series of legislative changes, principally in 1973, led to substantial improvements in the previously backward area of pensions, both increasing the level of pension and introducing the principle of indexation. In the early 1980s welfare provisions in the areas of health and of pensions were quite advanced by international standards, though housing was the sphere in which welfare could be said to lag most conspicuously behind. By far the most difficult problem facing Japan's social welfare planners was that of the 'ageing society'. The demographic structure of the population was such that the numbers in receipt of pensions and other old age welfare benefits was destined sharply and steadily to increase. In the cost-cutting political atmosphere of the early 1980s, the Government was inclined to think of ways of curtailing benefits, but was at the same time well aware of the adverse political effects such a programme might have on its electoral chances.[39]

A much-discussed policy area during the 1970s and early 1980s was the status and role of women, both at home and in the work force. Social norms restricting the roles which it was acceptable for women to play were slower to die in Japan than in other comparable countries. Differential treatment in terms of wages, retirement provisions, responsibilities and promotion remained widespread throughout industry, while in many cases women were compulsorily retired on marriage. Nevertheless, there was some indication of change in the status and treatment of women in the work force, particularly in the area of pensions.[40] To some extent the problems of women paralleled the problems of small and medium industry, in that workers in smaller firms had less advantageous access to welfare provisions provided by the private sector, as well as less job security.

An even more seriously disadvantaged group was the indigenous minority caste called Burakumin ('Village People'), who during the 1970s became highly politicized, as we have already noted in connection with Minobe's 1975 election campaign.[41]

All these policy areas confronted the Government with problems of great complexity, and they had all become questions in which politics was closely involved. We should note, however, that the problem of inflation was managed in Japan with considerable skill and reasonable success. Although retail price inflation briefly reached wholly unacceptable levels in 1973–4, it was subsequently brought under control, and remained at single figures in the late 1970s and early 1980s. The magnitude of this achievement can be appreciated when Japan's extreme dependence on oil imports, and the oil price rises of 1973–4 and 1979–80, are taken into account. It was achieved by a series of measures, including energy saving and the search for alternatives to oil; the curbing of wage increases; and the maintenance of a competitive edge in international markets, as well as in the domestic market against international competition. This last, by the early 1980s, was causing Japan acute problems in her relations with America and Europe, as we shall see in the next chapter.

12 Issues of Foreign Policy and Defence

The rapidity of Japanese economic growth in the past quarter of a century has given rise to a mixture of expectations and anxieties about her future role in world politics. However, even from the perspective of the early 1980s it is difficult to argue that Japan has already emerged on the world scene with a clearly definable and positive role. In part, however, this may be because the most commonly proposed ideas for a positive Japanese role in world affairs tend to have American authorship and envisage greatly enhanced military capacity and responsibilities. From a Japanese perspective a fairly limited capacity – in terms of international comparisons – to wage war has not necessarily been seen as a barrier to positive involvement in world affairs in other, particularly economic, ways. Even though since the late 1970s there has been a perceptible shift in the climate of official opinion in favour of a more positive defence policy, it is still too early to say that there has been a 'breakthrough' or a conclusive departure from past attitudes and practices.

At the same time Japan is now clearly an important factor in international affairs, with a fairly complex foreign policy. She is not a 'superpower' in the generally recognized sense of that term, but being both a major (and highly successful) trading nation and the second largest economy in the non-Communist world, her ability to affect events is considerable. Whether, as is sometimes argued, she would acquire greater capacity to influence events in her own interest were she to become a major military power is highly debatable.

By far the most salient factor in Japan's foreign policy since the Occupation has been her relationship with the United States. As events in the early part of 1981 clearly demonstrated, the American connection remained both the most central and the most problematical part of Japan's relations with the outside world. The possibility of any decisive break with the United States was extremely slight, but Japan in the early 1980s could be seen as searching for a way of reconciling American demands for enhanced Japanese participation in the maintenance of global security with a domestic preference for maximum freedom of action and minimum military commitment.

As Japan's economy has grown, her relationship with the United States has naturally evolved into something different from what it was in the early postwar period. Having been under American rule between 1945 and 1952, she remained in a kind of tutelary relationship for a number of years. The ramifications of this were extensive. Through the Security Pact of 1951, revised in 1960 as the Mutual Security Treaty, Japan received guarantees of protection in case of attack at fairly low cost in terms of her own defence expenditure. The continued American occupation of Okinawa not only provided the United States with its most important strategic base in the western Pacific, but gave the Americans a hostage to Japanese good intentions, which they did not give up until May 1972. Japan also received considerable American aid (including military aid), profited greatly from the 'Korea boom' in special procurement orders for the UN forces fighting in Korea, also did well economically out of the Vietnam war, and has a massive trade with the United States. When one remembers that for several years including the Occupation period Americans were practically the only foreigners with whom even the Japanese élite came into contact, it is easy to see that the relationship must have had a profound and no doubt often uncomfortable effect.

One crucial aspect of the Japan–US relationship after the Occupation was that it entailed a radical restructuring of Japan's international relations away from the pattern that had developed from the Meiji period onwards. Up to 1945, Japan had been largely an Asian power, with an extensive overseas empire which included Korea and Taiwan, and with ever-growing interests in China. In the 1930s Manchuria became a Japanese puppet state, and from 1937 Japan began to occupy large areas of China proper. For many years she was in close and largely hostile contact with Russian (later Soviet) interests in Northeast Asia. Finally, for a brief period beginning in 1941, Japan held in her possession a huge colonial empire in Southeast Asia.

With defeat, Occupation and the onset of the Cold War, all this suddenly changed. Japan was now a weak and defeated nation co-opted as a not very significant American ally in the fight against 'international communism'. For many years her interaction with her principal neighbours on the continent of Asia was minimal. Diplomatic relations were not established with the Soviet Union until 1956, but even then the two countries could not agree on a peace treaty or on the northern territories issue. (Both of these issues remain unresolved.) Formal relations with South Korea were not entered into until 1965; with North Korea they are still to be established; and with the People's Republic of China, despite enormous pressure from within Japan itself, they were not established until 1972. Japanese businessmen, helped by a series of reparations and aid agreements, soon penetrated the markets of Southeast Asia in strength, but relations with most Southeast Asian countries remained on a strictly economic level, with few specifically political initiatives being recorded.

It followed from the closeness and one-sidedness of Japanese–American relationships stemming from the Occupation period that any development of Japanese foreign policy could only be in the direction of greater independence from the United States. It was scarcely surprising if the two countries should have given the appearance of drawing somewhat further apart simply by virtue of the fact that Japan was developing a wider range of international contacts. Nevertheless, mutual co-operation held remarkably firm until the early 1970s, although it was shaken very briefly by the 1960 crisis revision of the Security Treaty.

When change came it came suddenly and, from the Japanese point of view, in a curiously disconcerting manner. In July 1971 President Nixon took a dramatic new initiative, without prior reference to the Japanese Government, by announcing his coming visit to Peking. This was followed the next month by his announcement of a series of economic measures, including the floating of the dollar in terms of gold and a 10 per cent surcharge on imports entering the United States. A principal target of these measures was the exchange parity of the yen, since it was calculated by the American Government that the lifting of the surcharge could be traded for an upward revaluation of the Japanese currency, and thus make Japanese exports less competitive in the American market. The 'second Nixon shock' (as it came to be called in Japan) eventually succeeded in this objective and in the new era of floating exchange rates the yen became a much more expensive currency.

The two Nixon shocks precipitated an intensive debate among articulate Japanese about the future direction of foreign policy, and there was a great deal of questioning about the long-term viability of a policy of continuing as a military satellite of the United States. Although the Japanese reactions to the Nixon shocks were curiously similar to later reactions to American initiatives, relations between the two Governments at that time had also been poisoned by a lengthy wrangle over textiles, in which personal ill-will between President Nixon and the Japanese Prime Minister, Satō Eisaku, was an exacerbating factor.[1]

More broadly, at about this time protectionist pressures had been building up in the United States, with Japan as the chief target – a problem that was to recur later – while in Japan, foreign policy makers were beginning to explore a wider range of options than they had needed to contemplate before.

Only just over a year after the Nixon shocks, Japan under a new prime minister recognized the People's Republic of China. This was widely heralded as a turning point in Japan's foreign policy, marking the end of passive adherence to American policies. Clearly, President Nixon's visit to Peking was a major reason why the new Tanaka Government was so eager to shift diplomatic relations from Taipei to Peking, and thereby reverse the strong stand in favour of Taipei that the Satō Administration had taken for so long.

Another important development of the early 1970s was the return of Okinawa. Although the reversion of Okinawa to Japanese sovereignty had been agreed on two and a half years previously, and although American bases remained there after reversion, it was highly symbolic that the Americans no longer held control of a piece of Japanese territory accounting for nearly one million people. It also substantially extended the area of Japanese defence responsibilities, and raised doubts about whether the Americans had in fact removed their stock of nuclear weapons from what was now Japanese territory.

While the Nixon shocks and the return of Okinawa seemed major events at the time they occurred, they were dwarfed by the impact of the first 'oil shock' of 1973–4. The quadrupling of the oil price had a massive and immediate impact on an economy in which inflationary pressures were already building up, and temporarily halted economic growth. Psychologically the impact was also very great. Resource vulnerability came to be seen as Japan's most pressing international problem, and politics designed to reduce dependence on oil imports in particular were devised and put into effect with urgency and skill. The policies included the search for alternative energy sources (including nuclear), and the reduction of wasteful usage. On raw material generally, Government and industry sought as far as possible to avoid excessive dependence on one source of supply and rather to develop resource flexibility. The Government, as we have seen, following the economic disruption of the first oil crisis, was able rather quickly to put the economy back on the rails, and when the oil price was once again increased substantially in 1979–80 the disruptive effect was much less. The Government was now much better able to handle the second oil crisis because of its experience in handling the first, and because of the long-range policies to cope with resource vulnerability that had been coming into operation since the mid-1970s. Nevertheless, the potential for economic disaster posed by severe interruptions in supply, especially of oil, continued to be a source of great anxiety for policy-makers.

In the specifically diplomatic area, the most important event of the late 1970s was the much-delayed signature of a peace and friendship treaty with the People's Republic of China in 1978. The significance of this may be regarded as both less and greater than was commonly supposed at the time. First of all, the confident expectations that a trade bonanza for Japan would stem from the friendship treaty (and an associated trade agreement) soon had to be scaled down in the face of manifold difficulties of economic modernization in China. On the other hand fears about an adverse Soviet reaction to the treaty proved rather exaggerated, though relations between Japan and the Soviet Union have been anything but happy. The other side of the picture, however, is that a key issue which had long divided the Government and Opposition in Japan was largely removed from the arena of contentious political debate. Undoubtedly this has contributed to a certain coming together of political forces in Japan in their views on foreign policy in general.

The Soviet invasion of Afghanistan in December 1979 wrought substantial changes in US Government policy towards the Soviet Union, and as a consequence of this, led to increased pressure upon Japan to contribute more to an American-led security system whose main purpose was to counter what was seen as an unacceptably rapid Soviet arms build-up. The reactions to this of the Ōhira Government were quite positive, and a number of measures taken by Japan in the first half of 1980, including the boycotting of the Moscow Olympics, were noted with appreciation in Washington. Relations with the United States under Suzuki, however, have been less smooth. Following official talks between the Japanese Prime Minister and President Reagan in May 1981, Suzuki's Foreign Minister, Itō Masayoshi resigned in disagreement with the Prime Minister's refusal to admit that there was a military content in the 'alliance'[2] referred to in the communiqué issued after the talks. Suzuki had also publicly expressed dissatisfaction at the way in which the communiqué had been drawn up.

On the day after the Foreign Minister's resignation, a former ambassador to Japan, Professor Edwin Reischauer, revealed that for many years US naval vessels had been calling at Japanese ports with nuclear weapons on board. Since this flatly contradicted repeated Japanese Government assurances that this was not the case, it caused a major political storm in Japan. The Government, in the short term at least, refused to change its official stand on the matter, despite confirmation of the essence of Professor Reischauer's remarks from a number of high-level, but unofficial, sources in the United States. When actual and proposed levels of defence spending were examined it was difficult for Americans to avoid thinking that the Japanese Government under Suzuki was less positive towards its military 'obligations' to the United States than it had been under Ōhira.

Clearly, Japan is in the early 1980s a power of great importance in world affairs, and almost unrecognizable from what she was in 1952 when the Occupation ended. Nevertheless, if one examines Japanese foreign policies since the 1950s, a sense of continuity of development is very evident. This should not be too surprising given that the same political party has been in power since the 1950s, that it is ideologically conservative and business-oriented, and that under its leadership Japan has enjoyed a sustained high rate of economic growth. Although significant changes in the leadership of the LDP have taken place, there has been no large shift in the domestic balance of political power such as might have entailed any really fundamental reorientation of foreign policy. Changes in foreign policy have tended to come from shifts in the external environment, and from the need to adjust to becoming a major economic power.

The basic continuities in Japanese foreign policy can be reduced to three long-term trends, all of which have developed with some consistency over a number of years. It would perhaps be an exaggeration to say that they represent aims of policy which have been specifically and consistently pursued, since many policy decisions have been prompted more by short-term considerations of expediency than by any long-term plan. Nevertheless, as trends they are clear enough.

The first such trend has been the development of a multilateral diplomacy within, and to some extent constrained by, the framework of the security relationship with the United States. Though it is arguable that there was more rhetoric than substance to the phrase 'multilateral diplomacy'[3] used by governments in the late 1970s, it did have substance in the sense that there was a pragmatic broadening of international contacts and a strong reluctance to maintain a foreign policy which could be seen as having been dictated by the United States. At the same time, however, this exercise was carried out strictly within the strategic assumption that the Japan–US Security Treaty would continue and that Japan's military security would be looked after by the United States in co-operation with the Japanese Self-Defence Forces. Pressures upon Japan, especially after the Soviet invasion of Afghanistan, to contribute more to the 'alliance' created difficulties for the policy and strains within the Government. Nevertheless, there seemed little alternative other than to continue a balancing act of this kind. The theoretical alternative of breaking with the United States was seen as far too expensive and dangerous, while the other alternative of simply following the American line and becoming part of a full-fledged military alliance against Soviet expansionism, though favoured by some, was also strongly opposed by many within the Government. In these circumstances it looked as though Japan would continue to pursue a kind of multilateral diplomacy while attempting to retain a special relationship with the United States. It was unlikely that the future course of the policy would be smooth.

The second trend has been the consolidation of Japan's position as a major trading power, with an increasingly important role to play in world trading arrangements. The status of Japan as an accepted member of the 'club' of first-class economic powers is now generally accepted, but a considerable amount of positive diplomacy was required over the years to establish it. In this respect 1964, the final year of the Ikeda administration, was a key year, for it was then that Japan gained entry to the Organization for Economic Co-operation and Development (OECD) and had her status under the International Monetary Fund (IMF) changed from that of an article 14 nation (with substantial exchange controls) to an article 8 nation (moving to a convertible currency). She also entered the General Agreement on Tariffs and Trade (GATT) at this period, and negotiated the ending of discrimination against her exports authorized by article 35 of GATT.

More recently, Japanese interest in the economic development of third world countries, particularly those in Southeast Asia, led to her heavy involvement in the Asian Development Bank, and to an interest in proposals for the establishment of some kind of Asia–Pacific, or 'Pacific Basin', community.[4] During the 1970s Japan in a sense acquired global economic interests, and having previously established her credentials as a leading advanced economy, became involved in North–South problems. Much of this was, not surprisingly, motivated by national interest, and in particular by the advance of her capital into Southeast Asian countries. The rather blatantly self-interested nature of Japanese economic policy towards the third world, especially as reflected in her foreign aid policies,[5] adversely affected her popularity, if not her influence, in some third world countries.

Liberalization of trade and capital imports was a feature of Japanese trading policy in the 1960s and early 1970s, but Japan continued to be the object of complaints from foreign companies and governments that it remained far too difficult for foreign interests to operate effectively inside the Japanese market. Since Japanese imports also remained out of balance with exports, the problem of 'friction' in trading relations between Japan on the one hand and the United States and the European Community countries on the other remained a continuing obstacle to the full acceptance of Japan as an equal partner in the world economy. To some extent, as has been suggested earlier, this kind of criticism reflected factors other than deliberate obstacles imposed by Japan to the penetration of her market.[6]

Thirdly, there has been a slow but steady trend towards the development of more sophisticated and better equipped defence forces. The whole issue of defence is one of great political delicacy in Japan, with Opposition parties and substantial sections of public opinion having opposed any increased expenditures on defence, and even at times arguing that the existing Self-Defence Forces should be abolished. The controversy over article 9 of the Constitution has been discussed in chapter 10 and elsewhere. Public opinion now shows majority support for the existence of the Self-Defence Forces, but broad uncertainty about their role, and support for the present Constitution which includes the peace clause remains strong.[7] Of the Opposition parties, the Democratic Socialists now favour a clearer statement of defence policy, while there has been some shift of view in that direction on the part of the Kōmeitō. The Socialists and Communists, however, are still strongly opposed to increased spending on defence, and within the LDP itself, as was evident from the controversy following the Suzuki–Reagan talks of May 1981, there are divisions of opinion on the desirable rate of military build-up.

Despite the lack of consensus on defence, however, Japan already has substantial, well-trained, and comparatively well-equipped armed forces. They do not compare remotely with the forces of the United States or the Soviet Union, and they conspicuously lack nuclear weapons. Their role in the defence of Japanese territory has nevertheless been increasing, and participation by units of the Maritime Self-Defence Forces in the RIMPAC exercises in 1980, as well as in joint naval exercises with the US Navy in May 1981,[8] was part of this trend. Japanese involvement in sea-lane protection was under active discussion during the first half of 1981. As a proportion of Gross National Product (GNP), Japanese defence expenditure fell from over two per cent in the 1950s to slightly under one per cent, which is much the lowest of any advanced country, although there may be some 'hidden' expenditures as well. On the other hand, GNP has also been rising faster than that of any other major nation, so that Japan clearly could quite rapidly effect a massive expansion of her military capacity if the political decision were taken. In March 1981 General Takeda, the retiring Chairman of the Self-Defence Forces Joint Staff Council, was disciplined for suggesting in a magazine article that military spending should be upgraded to three per cent of GNP.[9] The prospect of this happening under the Suzuki Government seemed remote, partly because of the Government's concern with budget deficits. As of 1981, the Government still maintained its ban on the export of arms, and actively prosecuted firms contravening the ban. The definition of what constituted 'arms' was of course a problematic point in the policy. The absence, however, of a large and powerful economic constituency for military spending (though a modest constituency of this kind did exist) suggested that the theory that there was a 'military-industrial complex' with the potential to pressure government into a precipitate military build-up was exaggerated.[10] Conscription was also regarded as politically out of the question in present circumstances.[11]

Japan signed the Nuclear Non-Proliferation Treaty in 1970, but did not ratify it until 1976, during the time of the Miki Government. Slowness to ratify the Treaty was attributable to a number of factors,[12] but it should not be taken as an indication of any likelihood that Japan may 'go nuclear' in the foreseeable future. Official government policy since the Satō period remains that Japan will not 'possess, manufacture or introduce' nuclear weapons, though the meaning of 'introduction' has been rendered uncertain by the controversy over the May 1981 Reischauer statement mentioned above. In purely technical terms, Japan's peaceful nuclear programme and her advances in rocketry, together with the technological sophistication of her industry as a whole, appeared to make some level of nuclear armament quite feasible. On the other hand, the political obstacles at home and the alarm that would be created abroad were powerful inhibiting factors. Furthermore, the extreme vulnerability of Japan's highly concentrated population to a preemptive strike by the Soviet Union or China during the period when a nuclear weapons system was being developed seemed to make any such enterprise a perilous one. Moreover, it has been persuasively argued that if Japan were nuclear-armed, it might in certain circumstances find the American nuclear umbrella less reliable than when it does not pose a nuclear threat to the USSR.[13]

Thus it has been towards multilateral diplomacy within the framework of a security relationship with the United States, consolidation of her position as a major global trading nation, and a reasonable level of national security (regarded broadly in an economic as well as a military sense) that Japanese foreign policy has been moving. It will be observed that these trends have not been formulated here in terms of anti-Communism versus Communism, nor of any specifically recognized philosophy of international relations. It is true that the groups which have been predominant in the LDP have been deeply anti-Communist, and this has affected policy on a number of issues, but particularly the question of relations with the USSR. The anti-Communism of the LDP did not ultimately prevent (though it delayed) the establishment of normal diplomatic and trading relations with the People's Republic of China.

The domestic debate on foreign policy has also often taken on the appearance of a debate about the merits of alignment with Communist or anti-Communist blocs, with non-alignment presented as a third alternative. On closer inspection, however, successive governments in Tokyo appear to have been extremely reluctant to commit themselves to a positive and active identification with the anti-Communist side in disputes within the Asian area. The lukewarm support given by the Satō Government (usually thought of as an especially right-wing administration) to the American and South Vietnamese side in the Vietnam war is a case in point. Another is Prime Minister

Suzuki's refusal to agree that there was military content to the term 'alliance' in the Suzuki–Reagan communiqué of May 1981. The emerging policies of the Ōhira administration during the early months of 1980 constitute a partial exception to this, but it is as well to remember that the issue of defence was one of the reasons cited in the non-confidence motion which ultimately brought down his government. Certainly, of course, Japanese governments have not been consciously neutralist, nor have they attempted to follow the principles of non-alignment, and there has been little real attempt to identify with the aspirations of 'developing countries'. It is difficult, in fact, to characterize Japanese foreign policy except in terms peculiar to Japan's own circumstances.

As already indicated the achievement of greater equality and independence within the relationship with the United States has been a persistent theme of Japanese foreign policy debates since the early 1950s.[14] Thus Yoshida's policy of resisting American demands for a massive Japanese military commitment had considerable success, although under the 1951 Security Treaty and the Mutual Security Assistance Agreement of 1954 Japan found her freedom of action in the sphere of defence and foreign policy quite severely restricted by the American presence. Negotiations for revision of the Security Treaty between 1958 and 1960 were motivated on the Japanese side largely by the search for greater equality within the framework of continuing security guarantees. Although it was obscured at the time by the domestic political discord which the whole issue aroused, it was Kishi's achievement to have obtained, through tough bargaining with the Americans, a number of quite significant concessions which in effect placed Japan in a more equal and favourable position than she enjoyed under the old Treaty.

The first concession, which had a considerable symbolic significance, was that the Americans agreed to renegotiate the Treaty at all. Thus the stigma that attached to the old Treaty, of having been entered into by Japan when she was technically an occupied power and thus not fully a free agent, was removed. Two specific restrictions on Japanese freedom of action (however academic they may seem in retrospect) were also allowed to lapse. One was the 'internal disturbance' clause in article 1 of the 1951 Treaty. This had provided that American forces stationed 'in and about Japan' might 'be utilized to contribute to the maintenance of international peace and security in the Far East and to the security of Japan against armed attack from without, including assistance given at the express request of the Japanese Government to put down large-scale riots and disturbances in Japan, caused through instigation or intervention by an outside power or powers'. The other was the provision of article II that Japan would not grant, 'without the prior consent of the United States of America, any bases or any rights, powers or authority whatsoever, in or relating to bases or the right of garrison or of maneuver, or transit of ground, air or naval forces to any third power'.

On the positive side, the most important achievement from Japan's point of view was the inclusion of article IV of the new Treaty, the 'prior consultation' clause. This read as follows:

> The parties will consult together from time to time regarding the implementation of this Treaty, and, at the request of either Party, whenever the security of Japan or international peace and security in the Far East is threatened.

What this article was supposed to mean in practice was spelled out in the important exchange of notes between Kishi and Secretary of State Herter of 19 January 1960 (the date on which the revised Treaty was signed):

> Major changes in the deployment into Japan of United States armed forces, major changes in their equipment, and the use of facilities and areas in Japan as bases for military combat operations to be undertaken from Japan other than those conducted under Article V of the said Treaty, shall be the subjects of prior consultation with the Government of Japan.[15]

The exact interpretation of this understanding, as well as its propriety, were subjects of recurring dispute between the Government and the Opposition parties. One of the main reasons which the Socialists put forward in 1960 for opposing the revised Treaty was that the 'prior consultation' clause did not provide the Japanese Government with a veto over potentially dangerous military activities by the American forces stationed in and around Japan. The prior consultation clause was also at issue in the controversy following the Reischauer statement in May 1981. The Suzuki Government, like its predecessors, maintained that the 'introduction'[16] of nuclear weapons to Japan was subject to the prior consultation clause, and that if it received a request from the American side to 'introduce' nuclear weapons, its policy was always to refuse. The problem was, however, what was meant by 'introduction'. According to Reischauer and others, the American side had consistently interpreted the word as excluding the berthing at Japanese ports of US naval vessels with nuclear weapons on board, whereas the official Japanese view was that 'introduction' included just such an event. Since the established American policy was never to comment when asked whether its vessels were loaded with nuclear weapons, the Japanese Government could still argue that, in a legal sense, it was complying with the prior consultation clause, and also adhering to the three non-nuclear principles inherited from the Satō Government. Since, however, there was a suggestion in the Reischauer statement that the Japanese Government had in fact been aware all along that there were nuclear weapons on board many US vessels calling at Japanese ports, its credibility was seriously at risk, even though its spokesmen vigorously denied the charge.[17]

A futher indication of the greater equality which Japan achieved – at least on paper – in the new Treaty was the fact that she assumed greater obligations to contribute to a mutual defence effort. Article III of the 1960 Treaty in effect committed Japan to a continuing programme of rearmament, though the phrase 'subject to their constitutional provisions' was a ritual obeisance by the Americans to the peace clause of the Japanese Constitution. There was a similar proviso in article V, which provided that the two countries would act together in the event of 'an armed attack against either Party in the territories under the administration of Japan'.

The 1960 Treaty contained three separate references to the 'peace and security of the Far East'.[18] This was the subject of a lengthy debate in the Diet during the early months of 1960 about the precise geographical definition of the term 'Far East'. Government spokesmen at the time came out with differing answers to the question, but it seemed to be accepted that it included not only the Japanese islands themselves, but also South Korea and Taiwan, at the minimum. As the Government subsequently interpreted the Treaty, however, there was no question of Japanese forces being sent overseas in joint defence with the United States of the 'peace and security of the Far East'. Government ministers repeated frequently that the despatch of troops overseas would be in violation of article 9 of the Constitution, and this ban was extended even to cover participation in UN peacekeeping operations.

It need not be supposed that the Japanese Government was acting here out of a scrupulous regard for the Constitution as such. But a combination of domestic political pressures, suspicion of Japanese intentions on the part of other countries in the area and a preference not to be too closely identified with American policies in the Asian region all contributed to an official interpretation of the Security Treaty which virtually confined the Japanese contribution to a role in the defence of Japanese territory, while providing facilities for American operations elsewhere.

The Kishi and Eisenhower administrations in 1960 agreed that the revised Treaty should run for ten years (that is, until June 1970), after which it was open to either party to give one year's notice of termination. This led to widespread fears of a '1970 crisis' over the Security Treaty paralleling that of 1960, but this failed to materialize. The two Governments agreed that the Treaty should continue for the time being, and since then no revisions to the text have been made.

One of the most serious issues at stake between Japan and the United States during the 1960s was the future disposition of the island of Okinawa and the surrounding Ryūkyū group to the southwest of Japan. They had been under American administration since they were won in 1945 in some of the bloodiest battles of the war in the Pacific. After the end of the Occupation the Americans were unprepared to allow the islands to revert to Japan, although John Foster Dulles conceded to Japan an undefined 'residual sovereignty'.[19] For the United States, Okinawa became a military base of key strategic importance to the pursuance of its policies in East and Southeast Asia. It was generally accepted, though never formally acknowledged by the United States, that nuclear weapons were stockpiled on the island.

Within Japan and in Okinawa itself there was always an undercurrent of agitation for reversion of the islands, which had been a Japanese prefecture before the war. In the mid-1960s, however, Okinawa began to turn into a major issue of domestic Japanese politics. The use of the bases on Okinawa in connection with the Vietnam War fanned the flames of anti-Americanism in Japan, and the war itself contributed among other things to an extremist trend in the left wing during the late 1960s. With the Okinawa problem becoming more and more troublesome domestically, Satō tried but failed to obtain a promise of its return at his summit meeting with President Johnson in November 1967 (though some other small islands were to be returned), but he was more successful two years later, at the Satō–Nixon talks in November 1969.

In these latter talks President Nixon agreed to transfer the administration of Okinawa back to Japan some three years later, during 1972. (In the event it was returned in May 1972.) Japan, apparently as a *quid pro quo*, agreed to a phrase in the joint communiqué which stated that 'the security of the Republic of Korea is essential to Japan's own security', and that 'the maintenance of peace and security in the Taiwan area is also a most important factor for the security of Japan'. It appears that this was intended to signify that a Japanese government would consider facilitating American operations from Japan in the case of a major conflict in the Korean peninsula or over possession of Taiwan. It almost certainly did not indicate any commitment of the Self-Defence Forces to overseas operations. It was, nevertheless, taken up by China in a series of denunciations of 'resurgent Japanese militarism', a campaign which was continued virtually unabated until Tanaka replaced Satō as Prime Minister in 1972.[20]

With the return of Okinawa and the Ryūkyūs to full Japanese sovereignty in May 1972, Okinawan affairs became of local, rather than international, significance. The reversion of Okinawa, and the normalization of diplomatic relations with China, greatly reduced the domestic political importance of two most divisive issues of the 1960s, and paved the way for somewhat less abrasive relations between Government and Opposition in foreign policy matters than had been the case in the past.

In the earlier stages of establishing independent relations with neighbouring states following the Occupation, Japan experienced a lengthy period of difficult adjustment. The case of Korea is particularly interesting, because of the time it took to overcome the legacy of past bitterness. Until 1945 Korea had undergone some forty years of harsh and unpopular rule at the hands of the Japanese, who, though they had done much to develop the Korean economy, had done little to make their rule agreeable to the Koreans. In the Korean war, Japan was a staging post for American forces engaged in the United Nations operation against North Korea. President Syngman Rhee of South Korea, as an ardent nationalist, in exile for many years before 1945, harboured almost as strong anti-Japanese as anti-Communist sentiments, and no progress was possible towards normalization of Japan–South Korea relations until after his overthrow in 1960. The regime of Pak Chung-Hee, established after a brief interregnum, was much less fanatically anti-Japanese, and the Ikeda Government in Japan was able to make some progress towards a settlement. It was, however, left to the Satō Government in 1965 actually to normalize diplomatic relations, an event which led to serious anti-Government demonstrations in both South Korea and Japan.[21] Since 1965 the South Korean economy has experienced rapid though not uninterrupted growth, with the Japanese growth strategies used to a considerable extent as a model. Japanese capital has come to play an important part in this process. At the political level, the fate of the South Korean opposition leader, Kim Dae-Jung, periodically bedevilled relations between the two countries. Kidnapped in Japan in 1973 and spirited to Korea, allegedly by South Korean Embassy officials, Kim was later released, rearrested, and condemned to death by a South Korean court in 1980, following the earlier riots in the city of Kwangju. This became a *cause célèbre* among political groups in Japan, and Japanese protest, official and unofficial, may have been a factor influencing the suspension of his sentence in February 1981. It is likely, however, that the reactions of the newly elected Reagan Government in Washington were more important.

The turbulent politics of the Korean peninsula are a perennial source of anxiety to Japanese government officials, partly because of the possibility of war developing, and partly because of the presence in Japan of a substantial Korean minority with loyalties divided between North and South. Indications early in President Carter's term of office that he was considering a major withdrawal of American troops from South Korea met a hostile reaction in Tokyo, and the later decision to leave most of them in place was greeted with relief. The different style of politics in South Korea from that in Japan creates tensions between the two governments, even though relations are infinitely closer than obtain between Japan and North Korea. The existence of a small but vocal South Korea lobby within the LDP is also a divisive factor in that Party, while corrupt connections between conservative politicians and South Korean businessmen are not infrequently alleged by the Opposition parties and the mass media.

If the issue of Korea has divided political opinion in Japan, that of China did so for a long time in a much more fundamental way. Until the normalization of diplomatic relations with the Peking regime in 1972 (and even to some extent until the peace and friendship treaty of 1978) the issue of China was central to the longstanding debate between supporters of the alliance with the United States and advocates of some form of non-aligned, or broadly more independent, foreign policy. It also touched upon a cultural complex which is formed out of a Japanese sense of indebtedness to China for the origins of its culture.[22] A sense (sometimes in the past greatly exaggerated) of the potential importance to Japan of China as a market has been a key factor in the enthusiasm of certain sections of the business world for improved relations with China. On the other hand, the right wing of the LDP and associated business interests, which were able to make their views prevail throughout the Satō period from 1964 to 1972, were extremely reluctant to prejudice relations with Taiwan or with the United States for the sake of what they saw as dangerous political entanglements with the mainland.

Until President Nixon's shock announcement of July 1971, Japanese tended to see the problem of relations with the People's Republic of China as the reverse side of the problem of relations with the United States. Shortly after the San Francisco Peace Treaty came into force in 1952 the Yoshida Government, under pressure from the United States, signed a separate peace treaty with the Chiang Kai-shek regime on Taiwan acting in the name of 'China'. This ended the state of war with 'China', but was of course regarded as evidence of hostile intentions by the regime in Peking. A long and complicated period of political manœuvring between Peking and Tokyo followed, with China making the best use she could of the substantial pro-China sentiment in Japan. Four successive 'unofficial' trade agreements during the 1950s brought about a certain amount of trade between the two countries, but in 1958 the Chinese cut off trade completely following an alleged slight to their national flag in Nagasaki. Following this setback, trade (which had never been substantial in terms of Japan's total trade) was slow to revive, but the advent of the Ikeda Government in 1960 provided a somewhat more favourable atmosphere. By 1964 serious predictions could be made that Japan–China relations might be established on a better and more permanent footing. The Satō Government, however, was less well disposed, and little progress was made towards a settlement while Satō remained Prime Minister.[23]

The official line of the Japanese Government at this time was that 'politics should be separated from economics', in other words that trade on an unofficial basis was acceptable provided that nothing was done to imply political recognition of the Peking regime. The Chinese responded by treating trade (which by the mid-1960s had become quite substantial) as a political instrument. Much of the trade was conducted through Japanese firms which the Chinese regarded as 'friendly', which for the most part meant that they had a sympathetic trade union. The control of 'friendly firm' trade became an important element in the shifting international allegiances of the JCP and the left wing of the JSP at this period. A smaller part of the trade, however, stemmed from annual negotiations between the Chinese side and 'unofficial' (but in fact semi-official) teams on the Japanese side. This was known as 'L–T Trade' from the Liao–Takasaki agreement of 1962.[24] Each time the annual negotiations came round, they were an occasion for intense political pressure by the Chinese, who on several occasions forced the Japanese negotiators to sign communiqués highly critical of the Japanese Government, as the price of continuing trade. The procedure became more and more of a charade as time went on, and was increasingly embarrassing to the Satō Government because of the strength of sentiment within Japan favouring better relations with China. During the Cultural Revolution, however, it was deemed advisable by the Japanese promoters to keep the annual negotiations going for as long as possible, so as to keep some sort of semi-official channel open to the Peking Government.

Further pressure upon Japan was applied by the Chinese in 1970, with the announcement of Chou En-lai's four principles under which Japanese firms would be acceptable for trade with China.[25] This made things very difficult for those firms with interests in South Korea or Taiwan which wished to enter the China market. The new Chinese policy resulted in a notable upheaval as many firms came to accept the Chinese terms.

For this and other reasons, Satō found himself increasingly isolated in his China policy during his last year in office. His decision to co-sponsor the unsuccessful American resolution at the UN in October 1971, designed to keep Taiwan within the world body, was apparently taken on his own initiative. Although it may have helped reassure the Americans about Japanese intentions it caused a storm of criticism at home, which scarcely abated until Satō stepped down a few months later.

Considering the strained condition of Japan–China relations during Satō's prime ministership, the rapidity and smoothness with which Tanaka's new approach was accepted in Peking is remarkable. In the agreement for restoration of diplomatic relations, Japan apologized for the damage she caused China before 1945, and the Chinese agreed to waive reparations. Japan 'fully understood and respected' the Chinese position on Taiwan, and a reference to article 8 of the Potsdam Declaration (which restricts Japanese sovereignty to the main Japanese islands and 'such minor islands as we shall determine') signified the renunciation of any Japanese claim to Taiwan. There was no reference to the Japan–Republic of China peace treaty of 1952, and no new peace treaty was entered into between Tokyo and Peking, although there was a reference to 'the termination of the state of war'. Japan was not required to sever *de facto* relations with Taiwan, nor was the Japan–US Security Treaty or the contentious 1969 Nixon–Satō communiqué referred to. In other words, Japan appeared to have obtained slightly better conditions for a settlement than had been widely anticipated.[26]

It was to be six years before the problems inherent in the new relationship were to be ironed out satisfactorily. Although the problem of who owned some small islands between Taiwan and Okinawa (the Senkaku Islands) was easily disposed of, Japan's continued *de facto* connections with Taiwan were more difficult to reconcile with the Peking relationship. When Ōhira, as Foreign Minister in the Tanaka Government, signed an airlines agreement with Peking, Taipei responded by cancelling Japan Airlines' landing rights in Taiwan for an indefinite period. Eventually a face-saving formula was found which permitted air services to be operated between Japan and both the PRC and Taiwan.

It took much longer to bring about a satisfactory solution of the issue of 'hegemony'. At an early stage in the negotiations for a peace and friendship treaty, the Chinese side indicated that it wanted the treaty to contain a clause stating that both sides opposed 'hegemony' (in Japanese, *haken*) in international affairs. Since this was Chinese shorthand for the international policies of the Soviet Union, the Japanese Government refused to accede to this requirement. Ultimately, during the tenure of the Fukuda Government in 1978, a formula was agreed on in which 'hegemony' was mentioned in one clause, but its exclusive applicability to the Soviet Union denied in another.[27] The Japan–China trade agreement signed earlier the same year provided the formal basis for a substantial expansion of trade between the two countries. Economic and political problems in China itself, however, meant that economic intercourse between them was slower to develop than many had anticipated.

Relations between Japan and the Soviet Union have not had the same cultural overtones as relations with China. Since 1956, when diplomatic relations were entered into but no peace treaty was signed because of the northern islands dispute,[28] the two countries have regarded each other coolly. Memories of the way Stalin unilaterally broke the Neutrality Pact in August 1945 and of the treatment of Japanese prisoners after the war have not entirely disappeared, and the two countries have had little in common either culturally or politically. Nevertheless, relations at the economic level have gradually developed in recent years, largely as a result of Japanese interest in the natural resources of Siberia. Although the grandiose Tyumen project to supply oil from Western Siberia through a pipeline to the Pacific coast was still-born, other more modest projects in eastern Siberia have been pursued.

The northern islands dispute appears no closer to solution than it was in 1956, and no Japanese government has been prepared to act on the suggestion of Miki Takeo's adviser Hirasawa Kazushige during the former's prime ministership, that the question of Etorofu and Kunashiri (the southernmost two islands of the Kurile chain) be shelved until the twenty-first century.[29] Proposals from the Soviet side for a treaty between the two countries always run up against a Japanese refusal to consider such a treaty until the northern islands are returned.

In 1976 a Soviet military jet was flown by a defector under Japanese radar to land at Hakodate airport in Hokkaidō. Subsequent delays by the Japanese side in handing back the aircraft (which American military personnel were allowed to inspect) called forth a stiff reaction from the Soviet side. The Soviet invasion of Afghanistan, and subsequent events in Poland, made any improvement of relations even more difficult, and there was genuine anxiety in Tokyo about Soviet naval strength around Japan. This was of course an essential factor involved in the Japanese defence debate of the early 1980s and in controversies about the application of the Japan–US Mutual Security Treaty. In general within the Government and outside it the Soviet Union was regarded with fairly intense apprehension and dislike, but attempts to establish a working economic relationship with it were not being entirely discounted. The decision by President Reagan, early in 1981, to lift the grain embargo on exports of grain to the USSR – a decision taken without consulting Tokyo – created some renewed interest in Japan in improving trade ties with Moscow.

If relations between Japan and her near neighbours on the mainland of Asia were greatly complicated by political factors, her contacts with the countries of Southeast Asia were largely dominated by economics. In part on the basis of reparations agreements with a number of Southeast Asian countries, Japanese firms were quickly able to establish trading links with the area, and as the Japanese economy grew, trade with Japan became a dominant factor in the external trade of practically every Southeast Asian country.[30] The series of riots against Tanaka, when as Prime Minister he toured Southeast Asian capitals in January 1974, prompted a certain degree of reconsideration of the role of Japanese businesses in the region, but the central point that the Japanese economy is enormously dominant in Southeast Asia remains. Apart from the important Japanese role in the Asian Development Bank, the impact of Japanese capital investment and Japanese-based multinationals has been increasingly important. Politically, Japan has maintained close relations with the ASEAN nations. So far as possible she has avoided becoming entangled in the international politics of Indochina.

Large-scale contracts for the sale to Japan of iron ore, bauxite and other minerals were the basis for a major trade expansion from the 1950s between Japan and Australia (wool has been the other major factor). On the whole the relationship developed without serious frictions, aided no doubt by the fact that Australia has had a consistent trade surplus with Japan. The Basic Treaty of Friendship and Co-operation between Australia and Japan, signed in 1976, gave Japan what was essentially most favoured nation treatment in matters of entry and stay, as well as investment. The changing structure of the Japanese economy in the 1970s and 1980s was requiring substantial adjustments to the mutual economic relationship. Moreover, there was a certain impetus between the idea of sorting out economic problems in the Asian and Pacific area – an area of rapidly increasing regional economic exchange – in a multilateral rather than a purely bilateral context.[31]

Japan's economic relations with Western Europe have also greatly increased, but the 'friction' entailed by an excess of Japanese exports to Europe over imports from Europe was far from resolution as of early 1981.

From the above picture it can be seen that, whereas Japan's economic impact on much of the rest of the world has been spectacular, her foreign policy remains fairly unassertive and 'low key', even though changes have taken place since the 1960s. A number of explanations have been advanced to explain this caution. One is that Japan, having known the bitter taste of defeat and the horrors of atomic attack, and possessing a 'peace Constitution' which commands widespread respect among the electorate, cannot aspire to more positive, nationalistic or adventurous foreign and defence policies because this would not be acceptable to public opinion. Another explanation is that politics in Japan is seriously fragmented, with the politics of factional advantage and the constant search for a watered-down consensus of what can be agreed between rival groups inhibiting clear and sustained policy initiatives. A third explanation is that, by concentrating on building up the economy and developing a strong position in international trade, Japan has maximized national advantage at minimal cost, and that the policy is continued because it is successful and recognized as such.

All these three explanations contain a considerable element of truth, but they need to be looked at critically, and also tested against Japan's changing domestic and external situation of the early 1980s.

The anti-war sentiment based on the Constitution is still a factor to be reckoned with in the Japanese electorate, although the fervent pacifism of the postwar years has declined, and the existence of the Self-Defence Forces is more readily accepted than it was. The Opposition parties remain generally hostile to rearmament and continue to champion the Constitution, though the Democratic Socialists in particular had changed by the early 1980s to a more forward attitude on defence. The Liberal Democrats, having been returned in 1980 once more with a comfortable majority, may not be too much inhibited by Opposition attitudes, but the prospect of disruption of Diet proceedings and popular demonstrations in the streets, has in the past tended to encourage caution.

Factionalism and consensus politics have also in the past tended to make it hazardous for the Government to pursue obviously innovative policies in ideologically charged areas of foreign policy and defence. The crisis which Kishi faced in 1960 over revision of the Security Treaty is the classic case of this, but there have been a number of examples since, including the passage of the non-confidence motion which led to the downfall of the Ōhira Government. Nevertheless, one ought not to exaggerate the degree to which foreign policy-making has been hamstrung by internal division during the long period of Liberal Democratic rule. Taken in broad perspective, Japan's foreign policy-making processes have been cautious and conservative not solely because they are the product of compromise, but because the Liberal Democrats, together with influential businessmen and civil servants, have seen advantage to lie in the policies actually pursued.

This leads on to the third explanation, that the successes hitherto of a foreign policy emphasizing economic development rather than military strength or political assertiveness have been such as to convince a generation of decision-makers that it is worth while. The Government, by concentrating on economics, or more specially by allowing businessmen the freedom to pursue their natural interests for growth, while itself working vigorously for maximum resource security and a stable economic environment, has succeeded in establishing Japan as a global economic power without resort to military power politics.

On the whole, this third explanation appears to be the most convincing, although the other two should certainly not be discounted. The three are of course connected, in the sense that the line of least resistance, of avoiding controversial political decisions because of the domestic complications they involve and the resistance of public opinion, has through a combination of luck and astute judgement been made to work in such a way that it has paid off.

Whether it will continue to pay off, however, is more problematical. Japanese foreign policy is already having to contend with some difficult and important political problems. Perhaps the most worrying long-term issue is the nature and credibility of Japan's security arrangements with the United States. All things considered, Japan is likely to depend for a long time upon security guarantees given by the United States simply because she has no real alternative. Short of a massive shift of the ideological balance within Japan itself, she has no other obvious ally. How long, however, the United States will be prepared to underwrite the security of a nation as economically advanced and independent-minded as Japan is problematical. Under the late Carter and early Reagan presidencies Japan has come under greater pressure than ever before to stop 'taking a free ride on the Security Treaty' and to contribute more to the 'alliance'. Moreover this corresponds with the increasing prominence of such sentiments in some sections at least of the Japanese Establishment.

One course of action that is open is to embark upon a substantial build-up of Japanese armed strength, and to an extent this is already happening.[32] In military terms however Japan has a long way to go before she can remotely match the superpowers, and the cost of attempting to do so could well be grave in terms of alienating her neighbours, promoting political instability at home and imposing strains upon her own economy and environment. The nuclear option would be the most striking instance of this kind of dilemma, and to take it would be for Japan a step with the very gravest of implications. Indeed, one may well question whether anything recognizable as a democratic system of government would be likely to survive a decision for massive rearmament including the development of nuclear weapons.

Japan has succeeded in weathering the international economic crisis of the late 1970s and early 1980s with her economy in remarkably good shape in comparison with the economies of many other countries. Despite the perennial problems of resource vulnerability, it is at least arguable that Japan is headed for a situation where her economic leverage is internationally so great that she can afford to 'write off' particular markets and sources of supply because she has adequate supplies and markets elsewhere.[33] Oil is an obvious exception to this scenario, but as we have seen, Japan's dependence on external sources of oil for her vital energy supplies has been diminishing under government guidance. The continued competitiveness of her most advanced industries, and the flexibility of her industrial structures as a whole, mean that nothing short of massive international protectionism could stop her in her tracks. And it needs to be remembered that Japan herself is an integral part of the world economy, so that serious harm to the Japanese economy tends to affect adversely the international economy as well.

There is a sense, however, in which the Japanese economic success story has been achieved at the expense of the outside world. Americans and Europeans, not to speak of Southeast

Asians, are not entirely without reason when they argue that Japan has done well economically because of a light defence burden, the 'free ride on the Security Treaty', low spending on genuine foreign aid (as distinct from aid designed to further the commercial success of Japanese industries overseas), and official policies encouraging exports and discouraging imports. Even though such views are frequently expressed in exaggerated form, they contain the proverbial grain of truth. It is therefore in the interests of the outside world generally, to encourage Japan to develop more internationalist attitudes, and within Japan itself there is a distinct trend in this direction.

One thing, however, that is often overlooked about Japan's foreign policy record in discussions such as these is that while in one sense she has been 'reluctant to bear a defence burden commensurate with her economic capacity', this very fact has been an integral part of her economic success. While other nations groan under an excessive defence burden and their economies fail to recover from 'stagflation', Japan with her concentration on economic efficiency amd motivation rather than international politics has continued to expand and prosper. Moreover, whether her military security has actually suffered as a result of these policies is a more difficult question than it sounds. Perhaps the only way of resolving it is to ask what Japan would look like today if since the war she had been spending a similar proportion of her GNP on defence (including presumably nuclear weapons) as the United States, the major European countries or the two Koreas. Quite apart from the domestic political impact of such a policy, one needs to ask whether, had it been pursued, China and the Soviet Union might not have developed strategies of Asian defence directed primarily against Japan rather than primarily against each other. Of course, had that been the case, Japan would have been forced into still greater military efforts, and one wonders how her economy would have fared in that case.

While the foreign policy and defence policy problems of Japan in the 1980s may well be complex and difficult to resolve, the caution and restraint which have been characteristic of Japanese policy for several years have put down deep roots, and are unlikely to be abandoned lightly.

13 Conclusions and Dilemmas

In Japanese politics since the 1950s three things stand out above everything else. These are the emergence of Japan as an economic power of the first rank, continuous rule by a single conservative party, and unresolved differences within the polity on fundamental political issues. If the first and the second are more widely recognized outside Japan than the third, it is largely because successive governments have been clever enough or fortunate enough in their handling of both economics and politics to prevent existing political divisions from getting out of hand. Nevertheless, even though the lines of division are not quite so clearly marked as they were at the beginning of the 1970s, on some basic issues of politics there has been so little agreement or meeting of minds between proponents of opposing philosophies and attitudes as to negate what are usually taken as the requirements for pluralist democracy.

The most celebrated division in Japanese politics has been in policies towards defence and foreign affairs. At times, indeed, this has looked like the overwhelming concern of the politically aware. As we have seen in chapter 12, the lines of division here are not simply between a militarist Government and a pacifist Opposition. Differences within both camps are substantial, and involve rival interpretations of national interest as well as pacifism and anti-nuclear feeling versus 'realistic' views on defence.

At a more fundamental level, however, crucial differences within the Japanese polity remain unresolved. The dominant position of the government bureaucracy under Liberal Democratic Party rule has meant that statist concepts of government have been pitted against ideas of democratic pluralism stemming from the Occupation. This is particularly evident in local government and in education policy, as we saw in chapter 11, but at a quite different level it can be seen in official policy towards financial markets, which to a marked degree remain 'managed' rather than 'free'. It is rather misleading to interpret this division – as has so often been done – simply in terms of a difference between 'tradition' and 'modernity'. When we reflect on the fact, referred to in chapter 11, that permanent employment and the enterprise union were a relatively late development of Japanese industrialization, we see how problematic this dichotomy in fact is.

One feature of Japanese political and social life which we have frequently encountered in this book is the importance of the family-like group as a focus of loyalty and activity in political organizations and in the workplace. Indeed, some writers on Japanese politics have seen this as the key feature of the system as a whole. We contend, however, that it is necessary to look beyond the phenomenon, at the nature of its impact, both on policy-making and on political activity. While it has undoubted implications both for economic dynamism and for consensus-making, it also creates a tendency towards fragmentation and division. When we examined political parties, we noted that fragmentation has hurt the Opposition much more than the LDP, but that the internal politics of the LDP has been informed by constant factional conflict of a not infrequently disruptive kind.

Differences of political ideology are as important in Japan as in other political systems, with radical nationalists, conservatives, liberals, democratic socialists and Marxist–Leninists competing on the political stage. The traditional notation, however, of a spectrum of views stretching in a single line from the far right to the far left is not perhaps the most enlightening way of understanding divisions of political opinion in the Japanese case. The Communists, for instance, may be seen as having a less pacifist (and therefore more right-wing?) defence policy than the Socialists, while Miki's attempt to put teeth into the Anti-Monopoly Law in the interests of free capitalist competition (a right-wing policy?) was successfully resisted by some who regarded it as likely to reduce government control over the economy.

Another most important division within the Japanese polity concerns the distribution of wealth. Although by international comparative standards Japan lacks extreme divisions of wealth between rich and poor, the divisions are greater than would be suggested by merely looking at statistics of income. The existence of lavish private welfare services provided to permanent employees of private firms, but not available to employees in smaller establishments, creates notable inequalities, while poor and expensive housing is a much lamented cause of inequality.[1] Much of this, however, is obscured by the lack of a horizontal and class-based labour union system such as exists in most Western countries. Japanese enterprise unions for the most part represent the interests of the more affluent part of the work force, while the worse off segments have to do as best they can by belonging to local and work-centred personal networks. Because of the structure of industry and of the union system, this fundamental divison of economic distribution has been reflected politically in a somewhat fragmented fashion.

Finally, as we saw in chapter 9, the nation's basic law, the Constitution of 1947, remains a matter of controversy in respect of several of its most important provisions. Although it is extremely difficult to revise, and revision is certainly not to be expected in the foreseeable future, lack of agreement about it, particularly within the LDP, is at the root of Japan's divided polity.

The political impact of these divisions has been partially blunted by the long Liberal Democratic ascendancy. Indeed, the achievement of the Liberal Democrats ought not to be underestimated. They have presided over a major transformation of Japanese society and of Japan's world status. They have remained together for the common purpose of staying in office, despite the potent centrifugal forces exerted by faction, interest and to a lesser extent ideology. The Party has acted as a kind of central political clearing house, co-operating closely with the government ministries and the major business interests. The tradition of bureaucratic dominance has remained strong, though constantly under challenge from powerful interest groups.

For the Liberal Democrats and their allies between the 1950s and the early 1970s rapid economic growth was the most natural policy to pursue, for a number of reasons. First of all, the structure of the economy was well suited to a high and continuous level of capital investment, so that the Government essentially had to provide a favourable environment for the capital investment that industrial firms were in any case determined to carry out. Although Government and business co-operated closely in providing such an environment, and in some respects the Government could be said to exercise control, the basic impetus sprang from industry rather than Government.

Secondly, the high rate of economic growth was attractive as a policy because it enabled material wants to be satisfied in a way that took much of the wind out of the sails of the Opposition. The Socialist Party in particular lost electoral ground during the 1960s because many of its potential supporters were enjoying rapid increases in their standard of living.

The third reason was that the rapid growth of the economy provided much the most attractive means of satisfying the Liberal Democrats' own rather heterogeneous base of support. Although economic growth benefited the cities more immediately and directly than the countryside, it also provided the revenue with which the Government could stabilize the prices of agricultural produce and thus prevent rural income from falling too far behind urban levels.

Fourthly, by framing a political appeal in terms of the rapid accumulation of national and personal wealth, it was possible for governments to play down the more divisive political issues, such as those of the Constitution, defence, relations with China, the position of the emperor, education and the bargaining rights of workers in the public sector. These, it must be remembered, were divisive issues not only between the Government and the Opposition, but also within the LDP itself, where any contentious issue was capable of being exploited for the purposes of factional advantage. The Security Treaty revision crisis of 1960 was in retrospect a landmark in the formulation of this 'economics first' approach, since Ikeda, learning from the mistakes of his predecessor, deliberately played down issues likely to cause acute political division. The broad approach adopted by Ikeda was to be continued with modifications by Satō, although with both decreasing consistency and diminishing success towards the end of his long period in office.

From the Liberal Democratic point of view the successes of this policy made it attractive, but it also created serious problems. One was the massive problem of environmental pollution, which in turn created a new and potent oppositional force, in the shape of citizens' movements and their backers in local government and some political parties. Another was the ambiguity that it left in the status of the Self-Defence Forces and in the implementation of the Security Treaty. A third was the increasing lack of susceptibility to government influence of the larger industrial concerns as they expanded their operations internationally. Fourthly the LDP in the 1970s was forced to rely for its parliamentary majority upon a grossly gerrymandered electoral system. The fact that the gerrymander had resulted negatively from lack of action to correct it rather than by any positive attempt to distort the value of votes made it no more acceptable. Despite the fact that some improvement was made before the 1976 Lower House elections, this did not stop the courts becoming involved in the issue, to an extent which was embarrassing for the LDP, though it did not precipitate significant change.

Thus the Government and the LDP survived the many economic and political dilemmas of the late 1970s and early 1980s better than many had predicted, but the Lockheed scandals, the fall of the Ōhira Government, and controversies within the Suzuki Government over the Japan–US Security Treaty showed that politically sensitive issues and controversies were never far below the surface.

Seen in historical perspective, Japanese politics exhibit a tension between stability and instability, cohesion and division. This is reflected in the widely differing analyses which have been attempted by foreign writers. Some emphasize the cohesive nature of 'consensus politics' and explain Japan's 'economic miracle' and other phenomena of the past hundred years in terms of a national capacity for subordinating individual gratification to the common good. Others are more impressed by the constant faction fighting, the apparent lack of agreement between left and right on the basic rules of political competition and the ready resort by many groups either to behind-the-scenes deals of questionable legality and dubious morality or to extra-parliamentary demonstrations, riots and other anomic activities. This is the central paradox of Japanese politics, which it is hoped this book will have gone some way to explaining.

From the perspective of 1981 it appeared that in the 1980s there were many issues over which political battles would be fought. Whether Japan could maintain the economic, foreign and defence policies of the past, whether she would retain her economic edge over competitors and whether resource vulnerability could be truly overcome, were questions which other countries would watch with interest.

It is, however, possible to end on a more encouraging note. Despite all its problems, Japan in 1981 was a highly 'modern' society, enjoying a sophisticated range of social, economic and political institutions, a highly developed structure of authority, a competent and experienced economic bureaucracy, near-total literacy and the habit of attaching enormous importance to education, a meritocratic selection process for positions of responsibility in government and elsewhere, and an urban population that was increasingly articulate on political matters. Although Western history has shown that 'modernity' of this kind is no guarantee against the emergence of the more disreputable and dangerous forms of politics, Japan at least lacks many of the intractable political problems facing many developing countries. In considering the outlook for Japanese politics over the next few years, perhaps particular attention should be paid to the emergence of viable alternatives to the kind of business-oriented conservatism that has left such an indelible mark upon Japanese politics in recent years. While at present the prospects for alternative government seem highly problematical, future governments will have to be particularly responsive to the demands and sensitivities of a broad-based and predominantly urban electorate if the health of Japanese politics is to be maintained.

Notes

Chapter 1 Introduction

1 See Kazushi Ohkawa and Henry Rosovsky, *Japanese Economic Growth: Trend Acceleration in the Twentieth Century*, Stanford, Stanford University Press, 1973, pp. 217–50.
2 Ibid., p. 235.
3 Ibid., pp. 236–7.
4 One who makes use of this notion is Zbigniew Brzezinski, *The Fragile Blossom: Crisis and Change in Japan*, New York, Harper and Row, 1972.
5 See for instance Richard Halloran, *Japan: Images and Realities*, New York, Knopf, 1969.
6 The political management of the vast industrial expansion that Japanese economic growth rates implied has led to Japan being regarded as something of a model for developing countries, particularly in Asia. South Korea and Taiwan especially have followed the Japanese path in recent years. In the early stages of Japan's economic development, however, international trading conditions, the state of technology and popular political expectations, among other factors, were very different from those confronting developing nations today. See E.S. Crawcour, 'Japanese Economic Experience and Southeast Asia', in D.C.S. Sissons (ed.), *Papers on Modern Japan 1965*, pp. 70–82.
7 For a view which emphasizes the importance of business links with Government, see James C. Abegglen and the Boston Consulting Group, *Business Strategies for Japan*, Tokyo, Sophia University in co-operation with TBS Britannia Co. Ltd, 1971. On the Meiji period, see William W. Lockwood, *The Economic Development of Japan*, Princeton, Princeton University Press, 1954. Lockwood maintains that Government control over the economy was relatively small until the 1930s.

Chapter 2 Historical Background

1 See R. Dahrendorf, 'Out of Utopia: Toward a Reorientation of Sociological Analysis', in Lewis A. Coser and Bernard Rosenberg (eds), *Sociological Theory*, London, Macmillan, 3rd edn, 1969, pp. 222–40.

2 For a readable account of the events leading up to the Meiji Restoration, see W.G. Beasley, *The Modern History of Japan*, London, Weidenfeld and Nicolson, 3rd edn, 1981.

3 With the overthrow of the Bakufu, the emperor's court was moved from Kyōto to Edo (where the Shōgun had previously resided) and the name Edo was changed to Tokyo, or 'Eastern Capital'.

4 It may be noted that two postwar prime ministers, Kishi Nobusuke and Satō Eisaku, came from Yamaguchi Prefecture, the area of the former Chōshū *han*.

5 The last serious revolt against the authority of the Meiji regime was that of Saigo Takamori, which was suppressed in 1877, thus demonstrating the superiority of the new conscript army to élitist *samurai* forces. Beasley, op. cit., pp. 118–19.

6 George Akita, *Foundations of Constitutional Government in Modern Japan, 1868–1900*, Cambridge, Mass., Harvard University Press, 1967.

7 Article 38: 'Both Houses shall vote upon projects of law submitted to it by the Government, and may respectively initiate projects of law.'

8 Article 39: 'A bill, which has been rejected by either the one or the other of the two Houses, shall not be again brought in during the same session.'

9 Japanese names are given throughout this book in their original order, with the surname first and the given name second.

10 Akita, op. cit., pp. 76–89.

11 Banno Junji, *Meijo Kempō taisei no kakuritsu* (The Establishment of the Meiji Constitutional System), Tokyo, Tokyo University Press, 1971.

12 John K. Fairbank, Edwin O. Reischauer and Albert M. Craig, *East Asia, The Modern Transformation*, Cambridge, Mass., Harvard University Press, 1965, pp. 554–63.

13 For an analysis of the role of the Genrō in Japanese politics see Roger F. Hackett, 'Political Modernization and the Meiji Genrō', in Robert E. Ward (ed.), *Political Development in Modern Japan*, Princeton, Princeton University Press, 1968, pp. 65–97.

14 For an analysis of the Manchurian 'Incident', see Sadako N.

Ogata, *Defiance in Manchuria: The Making of Japanese Foreign Policy, 1931–1932*, Berkeley and Los Angeles, University of California Press, 1964.

15 For an analysis of army factionalism in the 1930s see Richard Storry, *The Double Patriots*, London, Chatto and Windus, 1957.

16 Frank O. Miller, *Minobe Tatsukichi, Interpreter of Constitutionalism in Japan*, Berkeley and Los Angeles, University of California Press, 1965.

17 Gordon M. Berger, *Parties out of Power in Japan 1931–1941*, Princeton, Princeton University Press, 1977.

18 Gary D. Allinson, *Japanese Urbanism: Industry and Politics in Kariya, 1872–1972*, Berkeley, Los Angeles and London, University of California Press, 1975.

Chapter 3 Social Background

1 Ezra F. Vogel, *Japan as Number One: Lessons for America*, Berkeley, Los Angeles and London, University of California Press, 1979.

2 Chie Nakane, *Japanese Society*, London, Weidenfeld and Nicolson, 1970.

3 Takeo Doi, *The Anatomy of Dependence*, Tokyo, Kodansha International, 1973.

4 Ross Mouer and Yoshio Sugimoto, *Some Questions Concerning Commonly Accepted Stereotypes of Japanese Society*, Australia–Japan Economic Relations Research Project Research Paper No. 64, Canberra, Australian National University, 1979. See also Alan G. Rix, *An Analysis of Japanese Responses to Foreign Societies: A Critique of Nakane's Work on Japanese Mentality and Social Structure*, Australia–Japan Economic Relations Research Project Research Paper No. 26, Canberra, Australian National University, 1975.

5 David H. Bayley, *Forces of Order: Police Behaviour in Japan and the United States*, Berkeley, Los Angeles and London, University of California Press, 1976.

6 Ross Mouer, Yoshio Sugimoto, and Shōko Yoneyama, *Some Further Research on Stereotypical Images of Japanese Society: Report on a Content Analysis of 'Japan as Number One' and 'The Japanese'*, Third National Conference of the Asian Studies Association of Australia, Griffith University, Brisbane, 1980.

7 For an up-to-date discussion of the Japanese family, see Yuriko Kitaoji, 'Family Systems in Australia and Japan', in Peter Drysdale and Hironobu Kitaoji (eds), *Japan and Australia: Two Societies and their Interaction*, Canberra, London and Miami, Australian National University Press, 1981.

8 Hironobu Kitaoji, 'The Structure of the Japanese Family', *The American Anthropologist*, vol. 73, no. 5 (October 1971), pp. 1036–57.

9 This may be illustrated by the example of the two postwar prime ministers, Kishi Nobusuke (prime minister 1957–60) and his younger brother Satō Eisaku (prime minister 1964–72). Kishi Nobusuke's father was originally adopted by the Satō family to marry a daughter of that family. He thus took the name Satō, as did his subsequently begotten children, including Nobusuke and Eisaku. Satō Nobusuke, as he then was, was adopted in his teens by a sonless uncle to marry one of the uncle's daughters, and thus adopted the surname Kishi. Satō Eisaku, on the other hand, retained his father's adopted surname.

10 Hironobu Kitaoji, op. cit.

11 Chie Nakane, *Kinship and Economic Organisation in Rural Japan* (London School of Economics Monograph on Social Anthropology No. 32), London, Athlone Press, 1967, p. 21.

12 Ibid., p. 172.

13 Ibid.

14 Kazuko Tsurumi, *Social Change and the Individual: Japan Before and After Defeat in World War II*, Princeton, Princeton University Press, 1970, pp. 93–4.

15 There is also a tradition of 'common interest associations', which exhibit a relatively egalitarian pattern of internal relationships. Today's agricultural co-operatives have something of this nature. See Edward Norbeck, 'Common-Interest Associations in Rural Japan', in Robert J. Smith and Richard K. Beardsley (eds), *Japanese Culture: Its Development and Characteristics*, Chicago, Aldine, 1962.

16 Ruth Benedict, *The Chrysanthemum and the Sword: Patterns of Japanese Culture*, Boston, Houghton Mifflin, 1946.

17 Ibid., p. 116.

18 Dore, op. cit., p. 374.

19 Ibid., p. 254.

20 L. Takeo Doi, 'Amae: A Key Concept for Understanding Japanese Personality Structure', in Smith and Beardsley (eds), op. cit., pp. 132–9.

21 Tsurumi, op. cit., pp. 91–2.

22 For the building of a new Japan,
Let's put our strength and mind together,
Doing our best to promote production,
Sending our goods to the people of the world,
Endlessly and continuously,

Like water gushing out of a fountain.
Grow, industry, grow, grow, grow!
Harmony and sincerity!
Matsushita Electric!

Quoted in Herman Kahn, *The Emerging Japanese Superstate: Challenge and Response*, Englewood Cliffs, N.J., Prentice Hall, 1970, p. 110.

23 Robert E. Cole, 'Japanese Workers, Unions, and the Marxist Appeal', *The Japan Interpreter*, vol. 6, no. 2 (Summer 1970), pp. 114–34, at p. 123.

24 Ezra F. Vogel, *Japan's New Middle Class: The Salary Man and his Family in a Tokyo Suburb*, Berkeley and Los Angeles, University of California Press, 1963.

25 See for instance the Imperial Rescript on Education, issued in 1890. Text in Arthur Tiedemann, *Modern Japan, a Brief History*, New York, D. Van Nostrand, 1962, pp. 113–14.

26 John W. Bennett and Iwao Ishino, *Paternalism in the Japanese Economy: Anthropological Studies of Oyabun–Kobun Patterns*, Minneapolis, University of Minnesota Press, 1963.

27 Clinton Rossiter (ed.), *The Federalist Papers*, New York, Mentor, 1961, pp. 77–84.

28 Harold D. Lasswell, 'Faction', *Encyclopaedia of the Social Sciences*, 1931, vol. 5, pp. 49–51.

29 J. A. A. Stockwin, 'A Comparison of Political Factionalism in Japan and India', *The Australian Journal of Politics and History*, vol. XVI, no. 3 (December 1970), pp. 361–74; Steven A. Hoffmann, 'Faction Behavior and Cultural Codes: India and Japan', *Journal of Asian Studies*, vol. XL, no. 2 (February 1981), pp. 231–54.

30 Akira Kubota, *Higher Civil Servants in Postwar Japan: Their Social Origins, Educational Backgrounds and Career Patterns*, Princeton, Princeton University Press, 1969, p. 72.

31 Ibid., pp. 59–91.

32 Eleanor M. Hadley, *Antitrust in Japan*, Princeton, Princeton University Press, 1970, p. 20.

Chapter 4 The American Occupation

1 The Americans were, for practical purposes, the sole effective occupying power, although there was a residual British Commonwealth presence; and two international bodies, the Far Eastern Commission in Washington and the Allied Council for Japan in Tokyo, were supposed to have some say in policy-making. In actual fact their influence was minimal.

2 Some Japanese politicians and intellectuals, notably on the left, argued that full sovereignty had not been restored by the terms of the peace settlement, and that in particular the Japan–US Security Treaty reduced the value of Japanese independence. This remained a major political issue over two decades, but opposition to the Peace Treaty as such quickly faded.

3 Much the most stimulating attempt to sort out these issues is Herbert Passin, *The Legacy of the Occupation of Japan* (Occasional Papers of the East Asian Institute, Columbia University), New York, Columbia University Press, 1968.

4 The most authoritative official source of Occupation policy is: Supreme Commander for the Allied Powers, *Political Reorientation of Japan, September 1945 to September 1948*, 2 vols, Westport, Connecticut, Greenwood Press, 1970 (reprint of original, published by US Government Printing Office, 1949). Worthwhile later analyses include: Kazuo Kawai, *Japan's American Interlude*, Chicago, Chicago University Press, 1960; Robert E. Ward, 'Reflections on the Allied Occupation and Planned Political Change in Japan', in Robert E. Ward (ed.), *Political Development in Modern Japan*, Princeton, Princeton University Press, 1968, pp. 477–535; and Passin, op. cit.

5 See for instance the following two critical accounts: Mark J. Gayn, *Japan Diary*, New York, W. Sloane Associates, 1948; W. MacMahon Ball, *Japan, Enemy or Ally?*, Melbourne, Cassell, 1948.

6 This abbreviation stands for Supreme Commander for the Allied Powers, the term used to designate the Occupation authorities as such. They were also sometimes collectively referred to as 'GHQ'.

7 *The Political Reorientation of Japan* comments that: 'the emperor is now no more than the crowning pinnacle of the structure, bearing no functional relation to the frame itself' (vol. 1, p. 114). For analyses of popular attitudes towards the emperor under the new dispensation, see Takeshi Ishida, 'Popular Attitudes Toward the Japanese Emperor', *Asian Survey*, vol. II, no. 2 (April 1962), pp. 29–39, and David Titus, 'Emperor and Public Consciousness in Postwar Japan', *The Japan Interpreter*, vol. VI, no. 2 (Summer 1970), pp. 182–95.

8 This was interpreted to mean 'civilians at the present time', and therefore not excluding those who had been members of the armed forces during or before the war.

9 See Solomon B. Levine, *Industrial Relations in Postwar Japan*, Urbana, University of Illinois Press, 1958.

10 Hans H. Baerwald, *The Purge of Japanese Leaders under the Occupation*, Berkeley, University of California Press, 1959.

11 Thomas A. Bisson, *Zaibatsu Dissolution in Japan*, Berkeley, University of California Press, 1954; Eleanor M. Hadley, *Antitrust in Japan*, Princeton, Princeton University Press, 1970.

12 The ceiling in Hokkaidō was twelve *chō*.

13 The best work on the land reform is R.P. Dore, *Land Reform in Japan*, London, Oxford University Press, 1959.

14 Kurt Steiner, *Local Government in Japan*, Stanford, Stanford University Press, 1965.

15 John M. Maki, *Court and Constitution in Japan*, Seattle, University of Washington Press, 1964.

16 Passin, op. cit., p. 9.

17 For an analysis of later attempts by the dispossessed landlords to obtain compensation from the Ikeda Government see Haruhiro Fukui, *Party in Power: The Japanese Liberal-Democrats and Policy-making*, Canberra, Australian National University Press, 1970, pp. 173–97.

18 Aurelia D. George, *The Strategies of Influence: Japan's Agricultural Cooperatives (Nokyo) as a Pressure Group*, unpublished Ph.D. thesis, Canberra, Australian National University, 1980.

19 Passin, op. cit., p. 27.

20 John W. Dower, 'Occupied Japan as History and Occupation History as Politics', *Journal of Asian Studies*, vol. XXXIV, no. 2 (February 1975), pp. 485–503.

21 *The Political Reorientation of Japan* glosses over the differences between the two systems. See the following comment: 'The device of parliamentary responsibility procures the answerability of the executive branch of government to the people through their duly elected representatives. In the United States this responsibility is enforced through direct election of the President and Vice President. In England and the continental democracies, the pattern is similar to that of Japan. In either case, the result is the same. The executive branch of government has no legal authority, excuse or justification for acting in defiance of the mandate of the people. Every public officer, every public employee is the agent and servant of the people' (pp. 115–16).

22 D.C.S. Sissons, 'Dissolution of the Japanese Lower House', in D.C.S. Sissons (ed.), *Papers on Modern Japan 1968*, Canberra, Australian National University, 1968, pp. 91–137.

23 Article 96 of the Constitution stipulates that amendment of the Constitution requires a concurring vote of two-thirds of all members of each House, followed by a simple majority of votes cast in a referendum of the people. The Constitution has not yet been revised in any particular.

24 For instance, in Australia between 1949 and 1972 and from 1975 the government was continuously in the hands of a coalition of the Liberal Party and the Country Party.

Chapter 5 Political Chronicle 1945–1981

1 The latter on the face of it sounds unlikely, but it was seriously argued by the late Professor Takayanagi Kenzō, who became chairman of the Commission on the Constitution set up in 1956. See Dan F. Henderson (ed.), *The Constitution of Japan: Its First Twenty Years 1947–67*, Seattle and London, University of Washington Press, pp. 71–88. Takayanagi was a leading supporter of the thesis that the Constitution had been introduced by a process of 'collaboration' rather than imposition.

2 See Hans H. Baerwald, *The Purge of Japanese Leaders Under the Occupation*, Berkeley and Los Angeles, University of California Press, 1959.

3 The main reasons seem to have been the elimination by the purge of most potential rivals with prewar political experience, the support given to Yoshida by a small band of former bureaucrats who were his protégés, and the absence of strong factional groupings within the Liberal Party. See H. Fukui, *Party in Power: The Japanese Liberal-Democrats and Policy-Making*, Canberra, Australian National University Press, 1970, pp. 40–1.

4 About 15 per cent of conservative Diet members at the 1949 election. Later, the percentage was to stabilize at about 25 per cent. Fukui, op cit., Appendix 1, pp. 272–3.

5 The new rules involved smaller constituencies and fewer members per constituency, and were less favourable to small parties, which had done well in 1946.

6 The Japanese name is Nihon Shakaitō. At this period the official English title was 'Social Democratic Party of Japan', an inaccurate translation chosen for political reasons. It was later corrected to 'Japan Socialist Party', which will be used throughout this book.

7 The Katayama Government actually brought in legislation to nationalize the coal mining industry, but the substance of the original proposals was drastically watered down to meet opposition within and outside the coalition.

8 Fukui, op. cit., p. 41.

9 For an account of the progressive reductions in reparations demands during the Occupation see Bruce M. Breen, 'United States Reparations Policy Toward Japan: September 1945 to

May 1949' in Richard K. Beardsley (ed.), *Studies in Japanese History and Politics* (University of Michigan Center for Japanese Studies, Occasional Papers, no. 10), Ann Arbor, University of Michigan Press, 1967, pp. 73–113. For a discussion of the reparations issue in Japanese relations with Southeast Asian countries after the Occupation, see Lawrence Olson, *Japan in Postwar Asia*, New York, Praeger, 1970, pp. 13–73.

10 *Daily Mail* (2 March 1949). MacArthur justified his advocacy of neutrality by expressing doubt about whether the Soviet Union either had aggressive intentions against Japan or would risk an attack in the knowledge of American deterrent power on Okinawa.

11 Japan entered into settlements with the last three countries at a later date.

12 Martin E. Weinstein, *Japan's Postwar Defense Policy, 1947–1968*, New York and London, Columbia University Press, 1971, p. 61.

13 Security Treaty between the United States and Japan, 8 September 1951, Preamble. The Peace Treaty also reaffirmed Japan's right of defence.

14 In 1954 the combined strength of the Self Defence Forces was less than 150,000 men.

15 This figure includes four seats held by the small left-wing Labour-Farmer Party (Rōnōto), which had seceded from the JSP in 1948.

16 In the general election of October 1952 the Liberals held 240 seats; in that of April 1953 they held 199.

17 In the February 1955 general election the Liberals retained only 112 seats.

18 For an interesting analysis of the Japan–USSR negotiations of 1955–6, stressing the ineffectiveness of the Japanese side during the negotiations because of factional conflict, see Donald C. Hellmann, *Japanese Foreign Policy and Domestic Politics: The Peace Agreement with the Soviet Union*, Berkeley and Los Angeles, University of California Press, 1969.

19 See D.C.S. Sissons, 'The Dispute over Japan's Police Law', *Pacific Affairs*, vol. 32, no. 1 (March 1959), pp. 34–45.

20 For details of the revisions to the Security Treaty and the issues involved, see chapter 12. For a detailed investigation of the Security Treaty crisis, see George R. Packard III, *Protest in Tokyo: The Security Treaty Crisis of 1960*, Princeton, Princeton University Press, 1966. For shorter discussions see Robert A. Scalapino and Junnosuke Masumi, *Parties and Politics in Contemporary Japan*, Berkeley and Los Angeles, University of California Press, 1962, pp.

125–53, and F. C. Langdon, *Japan's Foreign Policy*, Vancouver, University of British Columbia Press, 1973, pp. 7–21.

21 This required action by the Lower House Steering Committee and an affirmative vote in the plenary session, both opportunities for further Socialist obstruction.

22 The second vote was taken just after midnight, when the new session had just started, some fifteen minutes after the old one had been terminated.

23 In June 1960 the Socialist leader Kawakami Jōtarō, and in July Kishi himself, were injured by stabbing, in both cases by ultra-rightist individuals. In October 1960 the JSP chairman, Asanuma Inejirō, was assassinated in front of television cameras by a seventeen-year-old youth influenced by ultra-rightist groups. In February 1961 an ultra-rightist intending to kill the editor of the *Chūō Kōron*, a leading intellectual journal, wounded the editor's wife and killed a maidservant. Later the same year a rather amateurish plot to assassinate the whole Cabinet was discovered in time. Whereas the ultra-right has traditionally favoured individual assassination attempts, the left has not indulged in violence of this kind, preferring the mass demonstration, from which violence sometimes flows. Since the clampdown on student protest movements in the late 1960s, however, some extremist left-wing student groups have engaged in activities of a different stamp. Groups with variants on the name 'Red Army' in April 1970 hijacked a jet airliner to North Korea, in February 1972 took a woman hostage and kept police at bay for several days in a mountain lodge (causing three deaths), about the same time tortured fourteen of their members to death in a 'purge', and in May 1972 killed many people in a massacre at Lod Airport, Israel, on behalf of an Arab terrorist group.

24 In March 1959 the JSP secretary-general, Asanuma Inejirō, remarked in Peking that 'American imperialism is the common enemy of the peoples of Japan and China'.

25 The DSP has usually polled between 6 and 8 per cent of the vote and has ranged between 17 and 35 seats.

26 See James W. White, *The Sokagakkai and Mass Society*, Stanford, Stanford University Press, 1970.

27 The pace of its advance at that period can be seen from a comparison of the number of seats it has won in successive Lower House general elections: 1967: 5; 1969: 14; 1972: 38.

28 The Satō–Nixon Communiqué of November 1969 contained a reference to the security of South Korea being 'essential' to Japan's security, and the maintenance of peace and security in

the Taiwan area being 'most important' for the security of Japan. This drew a hostile reaction from China and was played down after a time in official comment.

29 For a discussion of Mishima, including translations of some of his most recent political writings, see *The Japan Interpreter*, vol. 7, no. 1 (Winter 1971), pp. 71–87.

30 Tachibana Takashi, 'Tanaka Kakuei kenkyū: sono kinmyaku to jinmyaku' (Tanaka Kakuei, his Money and his Men), *Bungei Shunjū*, November 1974, pp. 92–131.

31 For an interesting recent article analysing Tanaka's continuing political effectiveness within the LDP, see Tawara Kōtarō, 'Naze ima "Tanaka" na no ka' (Why Is It Now Tanaka?), *Bungei Shunjū*, August 1981, pp. 92–106.

32 Gerald L. Curtis, 'Domestic Politics and Foreign Policy', in William J. Barnds (ed.), *Japan and the United States: Challenges and Opportunities*, New York, New York University Press, 1979, pp. 21–85, at p. 50.

33 For an account of Japan–US negotiations at this period, see I.M. Destler, 'US–Japanese Relations and the American Trade Initiative of 1977: Was This Trip Necessary?', in Barnds, op. cit., pp. 190–230.

Chapter 6 The National Diet and Parliamentary Elections

1 *Nihonkoku Kempō* (The Constitution of Japan), article 42. Henceforth cited as 'Constitution'.

2 Constitution, article 43. See also article 44.

3 Constitution, article 45.

4 Constitution, article 46.

5 Constitution, article 48.

6 In contrast, the Senate (Upper House) of the Commonwealth of Australia has reinforced its separate identity by pioneering a system of parliamentary committees, and thus in a sense stealing a march on the House of Representatives.

7 The electoral system for the House of Councillors will be discussed below.

8 This section has profited from the following analysis of the legal–constitutional position of the National Diet: Kuroda Satoru, *Kokkaihō* (The Diet Law), Hōritsu Gakkai Zenshū (Collected Works of the Legal Academy), no. 5, Tokyo, Yūhikaku, 1968.

9 Constitution, article 55.

10 Constitution, article 57.

11 Constitution, article 58.

12 Constitution, article 58.
13 Constitution, article 16. This article grants a general right of petition, without actually specifying the Diet as their receiver.
14 Constitution, article 62.
15 Constitution, article 50.
16 Constitution, article 51.
17 Constitution, article 96. To revise the Constitution a two-thirds majority of the members of both Houses is required followed by a simple majority in a national referendum.
18 Constitution, article 69. It is now established that the Diet can be dissolved simply by application of article 7 of the Constitution, and does not require a vote of no-confidence to be passed.
19 Constitution, article 54. The double elections of June 1980 were only possible because the House of Councillors had come to the end of its term.
20 Ibid. The Yoshida Government convoked emergency sessions of the Upper House, in each case immediately after the close of a Lower House session, in August 1952 and in March 1953. The first lasted one day and the second three days. In both cases the object was to finish off business from the previous session, rather than because of anything that could reasonably be called a 'national emergency'. Kuroda, op. cit., pp. 74–5.
21 Constitution, article 59, para. 2. A majority of two-thirds of the members present is a less onerous requirement than the two-thirds of *members*, required to amend the Constitution.
22 Constitution, article 59, para. 3. On the other hand, where a bill originates in the House of Councillors and strikes trouble in the House of Representatives, the latter is not obliged to agree to a joint committee of both Houses, although the former may request this. *Kokkaihō* (Law No. 79, of 30 April 1947, as amended), article 84, para. 2. Henceforth cited as 'Diet Law'. See Kuroda, op. cit., p. 175.
23 Constitution, article 59, para. 4.
24 Constitution, article 60, para. 1.
25 Constitution, article 60, para. 2.
26 Kuroda, op. cit., p. 178.
27 Constitution, article 61.
28 See chapter 5. Langdon quotes the coal debate of 1962 as an instance where the Opposition was able to use delaying tactics in the House of Councillors to talk out a piece of legislation, which therefore lapsed at the end of the session and had to be revived in the next regular session. This would normally be impossible in the case of the budget – or of a treaty, although even here the

rigidity of session timetables can cause difficulties for governments. (See Frank Langdon, *Politics in Japan*, Boston and Toronto, Little, Brown and Co., 1967, p. 160.)

29 Constitution, article 67.

30 Constitution, article 52.

31 Diet Law, articles 2 and 10.

32 Diet Law, article 12, para. 2. Before 1955 as many as five extensions of one ordinary session were known.

33 Constitution, article 53.

34 Constitution, article 54, Diet Law, article 1, para 3.

35 Diet Law, article 12, para 2.

36 Diet Law, article 13.

37 Diet Law, article 68. The concept of 'non-continuity of sessions' is based on the principle that the Diet has existence only when it is in session and that there is no 'continuity of will' from one session to the next. This is one area where Meiji constitutional practice, itself derived from nineteenth-century German models, has influenced current practice. Kuroda, op. cit., pp. 65–7.

38 These include the presentation of large number of amendments, deliberate slowness by members in recording their votes (a practice known as 'cow walking') and obstructing the speaker.

39 Constitution, article 62.

40 Diet Law, article 56, para 1.

41 Diet Law, article 42. If they do not, their parties are given compensating weighting in the allocation of members on committees.

42 Diet Law, article 46.

43 Diet Law, article 25.

44 Kuroda, op. cit., p. 100. The principle here is one of 'winner takes all'. There are, however, a number of 'directors' (*riji*) appointed in each committee, and the Opposition parties obtain some of these positions even when they do not have the numbers to secure committee chairmanships.

45 Diet Law, article 45.

46 *Asahi Nenkan*, 1981, p. 215.

47 Ibid., p. 216.

48 Diet Law, article 51.

49 See Kuroda, op. cit., pp. 110–11. See Langdon, op. cit., pp. 166–7. Langdon comments that opposition interrogators in committee often 'treat the ministers like criminals in the dock'. Ibid., p. 166.

50 The highlights of a day's committee session where the Opposition has trenchantly interpellated leading government ministers

(especially the prime minister) are usually reported verbatim on the front pages of the leading newspapers in their evening editions.

51 See chapter 7 for a discussion of former government bureaucrats within the LDP.

52 *Kōshoku senkyohō* (Law No. 100 of 15 April 1950, as revised). Henceforth cited as 'Election Law'. For a description of the Law in English see Ministry of Home Affairs, *Election System in Japan*, Tokyo, Local Autonomy College, Ministry of Home Affairs 1970.

53 Japanese citizenship depends largely on having a father who is a Japanese citizen, and is not automatically conveyed by being born in Japan. Naturalization is possible in certain circumstances. *Kokusekihō* (Citizenship Law) (Law No. 147 of 4 May 1950, as revised). By the early 1980s this principle was under challenge, but the authorities were holding firm in its defence.

54 Election Law, articles 9–11.

55 The best work in English on elections in Japan is Gerald Curtis, *Election Campaigning Japanese Style*, New York, Columbia University Press, 1971. This book is based on an intensive study of the campaign of a single LDP candidate for the Lower House. See also Scott C. Flanagan and Bradley M. Richardson, *Japanese Electoral Behavior: Social Cleavages, Social Networks and Partisanship*. Sage Professional Paper, Series/Number 06-024, London and Beverly Hills, Sage Publications, 1977.

56 For description of *kōenkai*, see Curtis, op. cit., pp. 126–78, and Nathaniel Thayer, *How the Conservatives Rule Japan*, Princeton, Princeton University Press, 1969, pp. 87–110.

57 The Kōmeitō has made clever use of the national constituency through its parent body, the Sōka Gakkai. By dividing the country into several regions and instructing the Sōka Gakkai membership of a given region to vote for a particular Kōmeitō candidate, it has been able to minimize vote wastage and thus take almost optimal advantage of the sytem. See James W. White, *The Sokagakkai and Mass Society*, Stanford University Press, 1970, pp. 310–11.

58 Election Law, article 138.

59 Election Law, article 138, para 2.

60 Election Law, article 138, para. 3.

61 Election Law, article 139.

62 Election Law, article 199, para 2.

63 Election Law, articles 179–201.

64 Election Law, article 141.

65 Election Law, article 144.
66 Election Law, articles 152–166.
67 Election Law, article 167.
68 See Curtis, op. cit., pp. 153–8.
69 Part of the interest of Curtis's book lies in the fact that it describes the campaign of a 'new man'. Even here, however, the candidate in question had stood unsuccessfully for the same constituency at the previous election, and thus had had some years to build up his base of support.
70 *Asahi Nenkan*, 1981, p. 262.

Chapter 7 The Liberal Democratic Party

1 Michael Leiserson, 'Jimintō to wa renritsu seiken to mitsuketari' (The LDP as a Coalition Government), *Chūō Kōron* (August 1967), pp. 188–201.
2 The most famous of these is that of Ishida Hirohide, a one-time Labour minister and a leading figure in the progressive wing of the LDP, who predicted that demographic and educational changes would rob the LDP of its majority of votes by about 1970. Ishida Hirohide, 'Hoshu seitō no bijion' (Vision of the Conservative Party), *Chūō Kōron* (January 1963), pp. 83–97. An abbreviated translation may be found in the *Journal of Social and Political Ideas in Japan*, vol. II, no. 2 (August 1964), pp. 55–8.
3 See Shiratori Rei, *Seron, senkyo, seiji* (Public Opinion, Elections, Politics), Tokyo, Nihon Keizai Shimbunsha, 1972, pp. 73–131.
4 Nearly all Independents either join the LDP on election or are sympathetic to it. There are usually a few exceptions.
5 This is a complex issue and not all analysts agree with this conclusion, since the relationship between votes and seats is a difficult one to predict. For a contrasting view, see Ishikawa Masumi, 'Nihon no seiji no ima – 4' (The Present State of Japanese Politics – 4), *Asahi Shimbun*, 6 February 1981.
6 With the reversion of Okinawa to Japanese sovereignty in 1972, a further five seats were added.
7 Aurelia D. George, *The Strategies of Influence: Japan's Agricultural Cooperatives (Nokyo) as a Pressure Group*, unpublished Ph.D. thesis, Canberra, Australian National University, 1980.
8 See Haruhiro Fukui, *Party in Power: The Japanese Liberal-Democrats and Policy-Making*, Canberra, Australian National University Press, 1970, pp. 57–80 and 107–43; Nathaniel B. Thayer, *How the Conservatives Rule Japan*, Princeton, Princeton University Press, 1969, pp. 15–57.

9 For data on earlier elections, see tables in Fukui, op. cit., pp. 63, 276–7. In the 1972 election the average age was 56·7, the percentage of sitting members 85·6, the average number of times elected 5·5, and the percentage of university graduates 74·6. See first edition of this book, p. 102.

10 An illuminating account of *jiban* is given in Nobutaka Ike, *Japanese Politics: An Introductory Survey*, New York, Knopf, 1957, pp. 197–200.

11 Gerald L. Curtis, *Election Campaigning Japanese Style*, New York and London, Columbia University Press, 1971, p. 137.

12 Thayer, op. cit., pp. 88–103.

13 Fukui, op. cit., p. 99.

14 Fukui, op. cit., pp. 57–80.

15 Rei Shiratori, 'Revolt of the Middle Class Majority', *Oriental Economist*, August 1980.

16 For an evaluative survey of the literature in both languages, see Roger W. Benjamin and Kan Ori, *Some Aspects of Political Party Institutionalisation in Japan* (Institute of International Relations Research Papers, Series A-1), Tokyo, Sophia University, n.d. (1971?).

17 George O. Totten and Tamio Kawakami, 'The Functions of Factionalism in Japanese Politics', *Pacific Affairs*, vol. XXXVIII, no. 2 (Summer 1965), pp. 109–22.

18 Michael Leiserson, op. cit., and 'Factions and Coalitions in One-Party Japan: An Interpretation Based on the Theory of Games', *American Political Science Review*, vol. LXII, no. 3 (September 1968), pp. 770–87.

19 Fukui, op. cit., pp. 148–50.

20 Ibid., p. 128.

21 Other categories were (and are) sometimes distinguished, such as 'non-mainstream', 'middle-of-the-road' and 'neutral'.

22 'A Prime Minister will have a winning coalition in support of him if, by his distribution of rewards to the factions, he has kept the allegiance of enough of his old support coalition and earned the allegiance of enough of his old opposition that the two groups together constitute a majority of the electors in the party presidential elections.' Leiserson, 'Factions and Coalitions . . .', op. cit., p. 779.

23 Miyagawa Takayoshi (ed.), *Seiji Handobukku* (Political Handbook), Seiji Kōhō Sentā, 1980, pp. 194–5.

24 *Japan Times*, 12 March 1981.

25 *Seiji Handobukku*, pp. 194–5.

26 *Asahi Shimbun*, 26 March 1981.

27 The faction led by Kōmoto Toshio (who had inherited if from Miki Takeo, the original pioneer of the primary system) vigorously supported the retention of the system. Quite apart from party modernization, however, Kōmoto was no doubt motivated by the fact that he had devoted great energy to the creation of support among the party members at large. *Asahi Shimbun*, 26 March 1981.

28 Fukui, op. cit., pp. 138–9. Suzuki Zenkō is the latest in a long line of prime ministers to make such a declaration.

29 Arnold J. Heidenheimer and Frank C. Langdon, *Business Associations and the Financing of Political Parties*, The Hague, Martinus Nijhoff, 1968, pp. 140–205.

30 Ibid.

31 The People's Political Association reported its contributions to the LDP for 1979 as ¥10,050,916,320. *Seiji Handobukku*, p. 178.

32 For an earlier period, see Robert A. Scalapino and Junnosuke Masumi, *Parties and Politics in Contemporary Japan*, Berkeley and Los Angeles, University of California Press, 1962, p. 74.

33 Fukui, op. cit., p. 107.

34 'Tōsoku' (Party Rules), in *Waga tō no Kihon hōshin* (Basic Policies of our Party), Jiyūminshutō Kōhō Iinkai, 1981, articles 29–33.

35 Party Rules, articles 34–7.

36 Party Rules, articles 38–42.

37 Party Rules, articles 43–52.

38 Party Rules, articles 46–7.

39 Fukui, op. cit., pp. 81–106.

40 Party Rules, article 7. *Seiji Handobukku*, p. 179.

41 The secretary-general is appointed by the party president with the agreement of the chairman of the Executive Council, and his task, according to the party rules, is 'to assist the Party President and conduct Party affairs'. Party Rules, articles 7–10.

Chapter 8 The Structure and Process of Central Government

1 Hugh Patrick and Henry Rosovsky (eds), *Asia's New Giant: How the Japanese Economy Works*, Washington, D.C., The Brookings Institution, 1976.

2 Akira Kubota, in *Look Japan*, December 1980, pp. 25–7. *Asia's New Giant*, pp. 236–9.

3 Chalmers Johnson, 'MITI and Japanese International Economic Policy', in Robert A. Scalapino (ed.), *The Foreign Policy of Modern Japan*, Berkeley, Los Angeles and London, University of California Press, 1977, pp. 227–79.

4 T.J. Pempel and Keiichi Tsunekawa, 'Corporatism without Labor', in Philippe C. Schmitter and Gerhard Lehmbruch (eds), *Trends toward Corporatist Intermediation*, London and Beverly Hills, Sage Publications, 1979, pp. 231–70.

5 Ibid., pp. 266–7.

6 Ibid., pp. 246–57.

7 See C. Wright Mills, *The Power Elite*, New York, Oxford University Press, 1956. For a critique see Daniel Bell, 'Is there a Ruling Class in America?', in Daniel Bell, *The End of Ideology*, New York, The Free Press, 1962, pp. 47–74.

8 Haruhiro Fukui, 'Studies in Policymaking: A Review of the Literature', in T.J. Pempel (ed.), *Policymaking in Contemporary Japan*, Ithaca and London, Cornell University Press, 1977, pp. 22–59, at p. 38.

9 In March 1981 Prime Minister Suzuki established the Second Ad Hoc Committee on Administrative Reform (Dai niji rinji gyōsei chōsakai), under the chairmanship of the veteran business leader Dokō Toshio. In July it presented its first Report to the Prime Minister, recommending substantial cutbacks in government spending acrosss the range of its activities. *Asahi Shimbun*, 11 July 1981.

10 One writer maintains that this is a hangover from the Meiji Constitution, where all the ministries were regarded as equal before the emperor, and Cabinet as such did not have the constitutional power to control the ministries as it thought fit. Okabe Shirō, *Gyōsei kanri* (Administrative Control), Tokyo, Yūhikaku, 1967, pp. 89–97.

11 Okabe, op. cit., p. 99. See also Nathaniel B. Thayer, *How the Conservatives Rule Japan*, Princeton, Princeton University Press, 1969, pp. 186–7.

12 *Naikaku; Sōrifu* (The Cabinet and the Prime Minister's Office), Gyōsei kikō shirīzu no. 101, Tokyo, Kyōikusha, 1979.

13 *Bōeichō Setchi Hō* (Law No. 164 of 9 June 1954, as amended), article 62.

14 *Asahi Nenkan*, 1981, p. 224.

15 Ibid., 1971, p. 298.

16 Okabe, op. cit., pp. 100–1. According to Okabe, the Conference of Permanent Vice-Ministers sets a kind of rhythm for the central administration as a whole, since it generally meets twice a week, on the days before Cabinet meetings. Ibid.

17 Ōkurashō (The Ministry of Finance), Gyōsei kikō shirīzu no. 104, Tokyo, Kyōikusha, 1979.

18 Chalmers Johnson, op. cit. Sugimoto Eiichi (ed.), *Tsushōsan-*

gyōshō (The Ministry of International Trade and Industry), Gyōsei kikō shirīzu no. 108, Tokyo, Kyōikusha, 1979.

19 *Nōrinsuisanshō* (The Ministry of Agriculture, Forestry and Fisheries), Gyōsei kikō shirīzu no. 107, Tokyo, Kyōikusha, 1979.

20 *Gaimushō* (Ministry of Foreign Affairs), Gyōsei kikō shirīzu no. 103, Tokyo, Kyōikusha, 1979.

21 See Kiyoaki Tsuji, 'The Cabinet, Administrative Organisation, and the Bureaucracy', in *The Annals of the American Academy of Political and Social Science*, vol. 308 (November 1956), pp. 10–27, and in Japanese in the same writer's *Nihon Kanryōsei no kenkyū* (A Study of the Japanese System of Bureaucracy), Tokyo, Tōkyō Daigaku Shuppankai, 1970.

22 Principally the *Kokka Kōmuin Hō* (National Public Service Law): Law No. 120 of 21 October 1947.

23 Tsuji Kiyoaki, in Oka Yoshitake (ed.), *Gendai Nihon no seiji katei* (The Political Process of Modern Japan), Tokyo, Iwanami Shoten, 1958, pp. 109–25. A condensed translation into English is contained in the *Journal of Social and Political Ideas in Japan*, vol. II, no. 3 (December 1964), pp. 88–92.

24 Article 103 of the National Public Service Law provides that within two years following his retirement a civil sevant shall not join a profit-making organization with which his ministry has had a close relationship during the five years preceding his retirement. Section 3 of the same article, however, empowers the National Personnel Authority to waive this condition in particular cases. In practice it has given permission in the vast majority of cases. For instance, in 1980 it refused eight applications while accepting 228. *Japan Times*, 18 April 1981.

25 Akira Kubota, *Higher Civil Servants in Postwar Japan: Their Social Origins, Educational Backgrounds, and Career Patterns*, Princeton, Princeton University Press, 1969, pp. 154–9.

26 For figures, see *Asahi Shimbun* (evening), 31 March 1981. The generous emoluments and retirement benefits of former civil servants taking jobs in public corporations was criticized in a labour union report given publicity in 1981. *Asahi Shimbun*, 9 April 1981, and *Japan Times*, 18 April 1981.

27 Ino Kenji and Hokuto Man, *Amakudari kanryō: Nihon wo ugokasu tokken shūdan* (Descent from Heaven Bureaucrats: the Privileged Groups that Run Japan), Tokyo, Nisshin Hōdō, 1972, pp. 169–70.

28 Miyazawa Masayuki, *Seifu, Jimintō, zaikai* (The Government, the Liberal Democratic Party and the Financial World), Tokyo, Sanichi Shobō, 1970, p. 22.

29 Kubota, op cit., p. 78.
30 William K. Cummings, *Education and Equality in Japan*, Princeton, Princeton University Press, 1980. See especially chapter 8: 'The Examination Competition'. Since the most prestigious universities are national, not private, it would be a mistake to conclude that the children of wealthy parents opt in the first instance for private universities. A more accurate comment would be that children of less well-off parents, if they cannot get into Tokyo University, are sent to a private university as second-best, with the parents working hard to afford the fees.
31 'A Special Strength', *The Economist* (31 March 1973), p. 16.
32 So-called 'informal barriers' were a highly controversial matter, though it was uncertain how far the reluctance of foreign firms to exploit the Japanese domestic market was the result of their belief that such barriers existed, and how far the result of their actual presence.
33 See Chalmers Johnson, op. cit.
34 For an account of the groups formed to link business interests with Suzuki Zenkō, following his emergence as prime minister in 1980, see *Asahi Nenkan*, 1981, p. 334.
35 By law, political contributions have to be officially declared, but it is widely assumed that official declarations considerably understate total contributions.
36 On the attitudes of business groups to the possibility of coalition government in June 1980, see *Asahi Nenkan*, 1981, p. 334.
37 Higuchi Kōki, *Nihon no keieisha* (Japan's Managers), Nihon Rōdō Kyōkai, 1968, p. 60. See also Hiroshi Itoh (trans. and ed.), *Japanese Politics – An Inside View: Readings from Japan*, Ithaca and London, Cornell University Press, 1973, especially pp. 3–87.
38 Aurelia D. George, *The Strategies of Influence: Japan's Agricultural Cooperatives (Nokyo) as a Pressure Group*, unpublished Ph.D. thesis, Canberra, Australian National University, 1980. Michael S. Donnelly, 'Setting the Price of Rice: A Study in Political Decisionmaking', in T.J. Pempel (ed.), *Policymaking in Contemporary Japan*, Ithaca and London, Cornell University Press, 1977.
39 See William E. Steslicke, *Doctors in Politics: The Political Life of the Japan Medical Association*, New York, Washington and London, Praeger, 1973.

Chapter 9 The Politics of Opposition

1 See Table 20.
2 In March 1981 the Suzuki Government, despite the Prime

Minister's promises that he would pursue the 'politics of harmony', forced the budget through the Lower House in the absence of most of the Opposition.

3 See Robert E. Cole, *Japanese Blue Collar: The Changing Tradition*, Berkeley, Los Angeles and London, University of California Press, 1971.

4 For details see George O. Totten III, *The Social Democratic Movement in Prewar Japan*, New Haven and London, Yale University Press, 1966.

5 In the general elections of 1937 the Socialist Masses Party polled almost one million votes (nearly 10 per cent of the total vote), and won 37 out of 466 seats.

6 The most detailed work in English on the Japanese Socialist Movement from 1945 until the early 1960s is Allan B. Cole, George O. Totten and Cecil H. Uyehara, with a contributed chapter by Ronald P. Dore, *Socialist Parties in Postwar Japan*, New Haven and London, Yale University Press, 1966. See also *Journal of Social and Political Ideas in Japan*, vol. III, no. 1 (April 1965), passim.

7 Yamakawa remained active among left-wing socialists until his death in 1957, and a 'study group' led by his close ideological associate and follower, Professor Sakisaka Itsurō, remained a force within the Party, despite splits and defections, into the 1970s.

8 Indeed, during 1954 there was a short period when a minority conservative government was being shored up by the votes of the Right Socialists in the Diet.

9 For an extended discussion see J.A.A. Stockwin, *The Japanese Socialist Party and Neutralism: A Study of a Political Party and its Foreign Policy*, Melbourne, Melbourne University Press, 1968.

10 For instance, the argument about whether the JSP should be a 'class party' or a 'mass party' was dealt with by the use of a phrase that is translatable as 'a class-mass party'.

11 For a detailed analysis of this period, see D.C.S. Sissons, 'Recent Developments in Japan's Socialist Movement', *Far Eastern Survey*, March 1960, pp. 40–7, and June 1960, pp. 80–92.

12 J.A.A. Stockwin, 'Shifting Alignments in Japanese Party Politics: The April 1974 Election for Governor of Kyoto Prefecture', *Asian Survey*, vol. XIV, no. 10 (October 1974), pp. 887–99; Ellis S. Krauss, 'Opposition in Power: The Development and Maintenance of Leftist Government in Kyoto Prefecture', in Kurt Steiner, Ellis S. Krauss and Scott C. Flanagan (eds), *Political*

Opposition and Local Politics in Japan, Princeton, Princeton University Press, 1980, pp. 383–424.

13 As can be seen from table 14, the age structure of JSP Lower House Diet members is similar to that of their counterparts in the LDP. As with LDP members, a high proportion of JSP members are born locally, and are thus presumably able to utilize local connections for the purposes of being elected. Their educational level was however much lower, and in occupational terms (not stated in the table) trade unionists predominated.

14 The best book on the movement in English is James W. White, *The Sokagakkai and Mass Society*, Stanford, Stanford University Press, 1970. See also James Allen Dator, *Sōka Gakkai, Builders of the Third Civilisation*, Seattle and London, University of Washington Press, 1969.

15 The average age of *Kōmeitō* Lower House Diet Members at 50·2 years was slightly lower than that of the other parties (except for the New Liberal Club), but substantially higher than it had been a decade earlier.

16 For works in English on the JCP see Robert A. Scalapino, *The Japanese Communist Movement, 1920–1966*, Berkeley and Los Angeles, University of California Press, 1967; and Paul F. Langer, *Communism in Japan: A Case of Political Naturalisation*, Stanford, Hoover Institution Press, 1972.

Chapter 10 Some Problems of the Constitution

1 See Constitution, article 96.

2 For a lengthy and authoritative account see Robert E. Ward, 'The Commission on the Constitution and Prospects for Constitutional Change in Japan', *Journal of Asian Studies*, vol. XXIV, no. 3 (May 1965), pp. 401–29 (henceforth cited as Ward, 'Commission'). For a survey of the published documents of the Commission, which run to some 40,000 pages of Japanese text, see John M. Maki, 'The Documents of Japan's Commission on the Constitution', ibid., pp. 475–89.

3 This was also a theme of the 'United States Initial Post-Surrender Policy for Japan', issued as a presidential directive to General MacArthur on 6 September 1945. The issue was also complicated by an ambiguity in the Potsdam Declaration between coercive and voluntarist principles. See Robert E. Ward, 'The Origins of the Present Japanese Constitution', *American Political Science Review*, vol. 50, no. 4 (December 1956), pp. 980–1010, at p. 983 (henceforth cited as Ward, 'Origins').

4 Prince Konoe also busied himself with proposals for constitutional reform, but his efforts were repudiated by General MacArthur in circumstances that remain somewhat obscure. See Ward, 'Origins', and Theodore McNelly, 'The Japanese Constitution, Child of the Cold War', *Political Science Quarterly*, vol. 74, no. 2 (June 1959), pp. 176–95. A number of other revised constitutional drafts were produced by political parties and other groups.

5 McNelly, op. cit., pp. 183–4.

6 Supreme Commander for the Allied Powers, *Political Reorientation of Japan*, September 1945 to September 1948, 2 vols, Westport, Connecticut, Greenwood Press, 1970 (reprint of original, published by US Government Printing Office, 1949), vol. 1, p. 102.

7 Ward, 'Origins', p. 995. Yoshida, in his *Memoirs*, after pointing to the impending general election as a probable reason for haste, concludes: 'The fact remains, however, that there was a good deal of the American spirit of enterprise in the undertaking of such a fundamental piece of reform as the revision of the Constitution within two months of Japan's defeat; as for wishing to see that reform realised in so short a period as half a year or a year, one can only put it down to that impulsiveness common to military people of all countries.' Shigeru Yoshida, *The Yoshida Memoirs: The Story of Japan in Crisis*, translated by Kenichi Yoshida, London, Heinemann, 1961, p. 136.

8 Quoted in *Political Reorientation of Japan*, vol. 2, p. 421.

9 McNelly, op. cit., p. 184.

10 This account is that of Satō Tatsuo, who was a leading official of the Cabinet Bureau of Legislation, and closely involved with the constitutional drafting process, for part of the time as assistant to Matsumoto.

11 McNelly, op. cit., p. 187.

12 Whitney, on the other hand, has an account in which he boasts of telling the Cabinet members that he and his aides had been 'enjoying your atomic sunshine'. Major-General Courtney Whitney, *MacArthur, His Rendezvous with History*, New York, Knopf, 1956, pp. 250–2.

13 Kenzō Takayanagi, 'Some Reminiscences of Japan's Commission on the Constitution', in Dan F. Henderson (ed.), *The Constitution of Japan: Its First Twenty Years, 1947–67*, Seattle and London, University of Washington Press, 1969, pp. 71–88, at pp. 77–8. See especially footnote 13.

14 Ibid., pp. 76–82.

15 *Political Reorientation of Japan*, vol. 1, p. 105.

16 Ward, 'Origins', p. 996.

17 Ibid., p. 999.

18 Ibid., p. 1002.

19 Once the draft was published on 6 March, all critical comment in the press was suppressed. Kazuo Kawai, *Japan's American Interlude*, Chicago, University of Chicago Press, 1960, p. 52.

20 Ward, 'Origins', op. cit., p. 1001.

21 Ward commented in his 1956 article: 'Inconvenient constitutional provisions have too often tended to become simply a challenge to administrative ingenuity to invent ways of subverting their intent.' Ibid., p. 1010. Ward's view about the way in which the constitution was introduced has shifted considerably in his more recent writings, so that he is actually taken to task by Chalmers Johnson for accepting the Constitution as essentially the fruit of American-Japanese co-operation. Chalmers Johnson, *Conspiracy at Matsukawa*, Berkeley, Los Angeles and London, California University Press, 1972, p. 38. (See also his comment on p. 7.) The passage Johnson refers to is Ward, 'Reflections on the Allied Occupation and Planned Political Change in Japan', in Robert E. Ward (ed.), *Political Development in Modern Japan*, Princeton, Princeton University Press, 1968, pp. 477–535, at p. 511. Here Ward finds the Takayanagi 'co-operative' thesis has 'some plausibility', since 'there was more consultation by SCAP of Japanese sources than has generally been recognized', whereas in his 1965 article (Ward, 'Commission', pp. 408–9) he calls Takayanagi's stand in the Commission 'lonely', says that a 'long and convincing list of reasons' was adduced against it. His 1956 article (Ward, 'Origins') expresses in strong and critical terms an 'imposed constitution' thesis.

22 D.C.S. Sissons, 'The Pacifist Clause of the Japanese Constitution: Legal and Political Problems of Rearmament', *International Affairs*, vol. 37, no. 1 (January 1961), pp. 45–59, at p. 45. McNelly also quotes instructions received from Secretary of State Byrnes in October 1945, which left open the possibility of future armed forces for Japan. McNelly, op. cit., pp. 179–80.

23 At one point Cabinet attempted to have the clause relegated to the Preamble, but this was not acceptable to SCAP.

24 *Military Situation in the Far East* (Hearings Before the Committee on Armed Services and the Committee on Foreign Relations, United States Senate, Eighty-second Congress, first Session . . . Part 1), Washington, US Senate, 1951, p. 223. The relevant section is quoted in Sissons, op. cit., p. 45

25 Shidehara Kijūrō, *Gaikō gojūnen* (Fifty Years in Diplomacy),

Tokyo, Yomiuri Shimbunsha, 1951, pp. 211–13. Shidehara in effect claims responsibility for the peace clause, without specifically mentioning a meeting with MacArthur. He relates an encounter with a young man in a tram, who was emotionally haranguing his fellow passengers on the despair and destruction that the war had brought upon Japan. Shidehara contrasts this with the enthusiastic support which the people gave the Government in the Russo-Japanese War, and says this brought home to him how utterly people's attitudes to war had changed. He therefore decided, as prime minister, but unknown to others, that war and armaments should be banned in perpetuity. So far as he was concerned, the Constitution was not imposed by the Americans against the will of the Japanese.

26 Takayanagi, op. cit., pp. 86–8.

27 Sissons, op. cit., p. 46. For instance Yoshida, who was a Cabinet minister at the time, and later succeeded Shidehara as prime minister, thought it more likely that MacArthur suggested the peace clause to Shidehara, who may then have 'replied with enthusiasm'. *The Yoshida Memoirs*, p. 137.

28 Quoted in *Political Reorientation of Japan*, vol. 1, p. 102.

29 Sissons, op. cit., p. 47.

30 Ibid., p. 48.

31 Dan F. Henderson, 'Japanese Judicial Review of Legislation: The First Twenty Years', in Henderson, op. cit., pp. 115–40, at pp. 116–19.

32 A translation of the judgment is given in John M. Maki, with translations by Ikeda Masaaki, David C.S. Sissons, and Kurt Steiner, *Court and Constitution in Japan: Selected Supreme Court Decisions, 1948–60*, Seattle, University of Washington Press, 1964, pp. 362–5.

33 Ibid., p. 364.

34 For summaries of these two cases see Henderson, in Henderson, op. cit., pp. 127–38.

35 For a translation of and commentary on the decision, see John O. Haley, 'The Freedom to Choose an Occupation and the Constitutional Limits of Legislative Discretion', *Law in Japan: An Annual*, vol. 8 (1975), pp. 188–204.

36 For a translation of the judgment, supplementary opinions and opinions of the various Supreme Court judges in the Sunakawa case, see Maki, *Court and Constitution in Japan*, pp. 298–361. See also Kisaburō Yokota, 'Political Questions and Judicial Review: A comparison', in Henderson, op. cit., pp. 141–66, at pp. 146–52, and Yasuhiro Okudaira. 'The Japanese Supreme Court and

Judicial Review', *Law Asia* (Sydney, Journal of the Law Association for Asia and the West Pacific), vol. 3, no. 1 (April 1973), pp. 67–105. There is also interesting comment in Sissons, op. cit., p. 104.

37 Maki, *Court and Constitution in Japan*, pp. 305–6. The translator points out that a literal rendering of 'clearly obvious unconstitutionality or invalidity' would be 'unconstitutionality or invalidity that are extremely obvious at a glance', i.e. a stronger meaning than is easily turned into natural English.

38 Okudaira, op. cit., p. 104.

39 Quoted in ibid., p. 97. See also D.C.S. Sissons, 'Dissolution of the Japanese Lower House', in D.C.S. Sissons (ed.), *Papers on Modern Japan 1968*, Canberra, Australian National University, 1968, pp. 91–137.

40 Yokota, op. cit., p. 162. The Supreme Court in 1964 refused to intervene in a case where the issue was maldistribution of electoral districts, despite the fact that the maldistribution had become extremely acute because of shifts in population. Okudaira, op. cit., pp. 98–9 and 101–2.

41 Ibid., pp. 85–6. On the general issue of rights under the Constitution, see D.C.S. Sissons, 'Human Rights under the Japanese Constitution', in D.C.S. Sissons (ed.), *Papers on Modern Japan, 1965*, Canberra, Australian National University, 1965, pp. 50–69.

42 Okudaira comments that 'the enactment of such incitement clauses remains essentially a matter within the discretion of the legislature. If, for example, conscription should be introduced and found constitutional, there would be no legal obstacle whatsoever to the Diet's enacting penalties for inciting others not to register, not to undergo medical examination, etc.' Ibid., p. 87.

43 Maki, *Court and Constitution in Japan*, pp. 117–22; Okudaira, op. cit., pp. 88–9.

44 See Lawrence W. Beer, 'The Public Welfare Standard and Freedom of Expression in Japan', in Henderson, op. cit., pp. 205–38.

45 Maki, *Court and Constitution in Japan* pp. 70–83.

46 See Beer, op. cit., p. 228.

47 See ibid., p. 235; Maki, *Court and Constitution in Japan*, pp. 84–116.

48 Beer, op. cit., p. 228.

49 Nobushige Ukai, in Lawrence W. Beer (ed.), *Constitutionalism in Asia: Asian Views of American Influence*, Berkeley, Los Angeles and London, University of California Press, 1979, pp. 114–27.

50 Ibid., p. 126.

51 The Chief Justice of the Supreme Court is appointed by the

emperor (a formality designed to give him equal formal status with the prime minister) as designated by the Cabinet. The other Supreme Court judges are appointed by Cabinet. For an account of the organization of the Supreme Court, see Maki, *Court and Constitution in Japan*, Introduction, pp. xv–xlvi, and Okudaira, op. cit., pp. 78–80. For a wide-ranging account of the legal system in general see Arthur T. von Mehren (ed.), *Law in Japan: The Legal Order in a Changing Society*, Cambridge, Mass., Harvard University Press, 1963. For an account which is critical of the leading American analyses of the Japanese legal process for allegedly ignoring celebrated 'mistrials', see Chalmers Johnson, *Conspiracy at Matsukawa*.

52 For details see Okudaira, op. cit., pp. 80–2.

53 For accounts of the controversy over constitutional revision, see Ward, 'Commission', and Haruhiro Fukui, 'Twenty Years of Revisionism', in Henderson, op. cit., pp. 41–70.

54 Ward, 'Commission', p. 410. On grounds of international protocol, however, there was strong support for the designation of the emperor to be changed from 'Symbol of the State' to 'Head of State'.

55 Ibid., p. 416.

56 Ibid.

Chapter 11 Domestic Political Issues

1 Dore even argues that Japanese industry had a social democratic revolution after the war which in some respects left Japanese trade unions in a more advantageous legal position than British unions had achieved after decades of slow pressure. Ronald Dore, *British Factory – Japanese Factory: The Origins of National Diversity in Industrial Relations*, London, George Allen and Unwin, 1973, pp. 115–19.

2 E.S. Crawcour and Hiromi Hata, 'Japanese Labour Relations', in Peter Drysdale and Hironobu Kitaoji (eds), *Japan and Australia: Two Societies and their Interaction*, Canberra, Australian National University Press, 1981, pp. 236–53.

3 T.J. Pempel, *Patterns of Japanese Policymaking: Experience from Higher Education*, Boulder, Colorado, Westview Press, 1978.

4 This is often seen as a main reason why the LDP did so badly in the Lower House general elections of October 1979. See Chapter 5, p. 87.

5 See work being carried out in this area at the Australian National University by James B. Horne.

6 See Solomon B. Levine, *Industrial Relations in Postwar Japan*, Urbana, University of Illinois Press, 1958, pp. 140–5.

7 Between 1948 and 1952 it was simply the Public Corporation Labour Relations Law. A similar act was later brought down to cover employees in enterprises run by local authorities.

8 For a detailed discussion of the ILO Convention no. 87 issue in Japanese politics up to 1965, see Alice H. Cook, 'The International Labor Organisation and Japanese Politics', *Industrial and Labor Relations Review*, October 1965, pp. 41–57. An excellent full-length study is Ehud Harari, *The Politics of Labor Legislation in Japan: National–International Interaction*, Berkeley, Los Angeles and London, California University Press, 1973.

9 Cook, op. cit., p. 45. Another issue was that of the 'check-off', whereby public sector workers (like their private industry counterparts) were automatically enrolled as union members. This the Government wished to abolish so far as public sector workers were concerned.

10 For discussions of the issues dividing Nikkyōsō and the Ministry of Education, see *Journal of Social and Political Ideas in Japan*, vol. 1, no. 3 (December 1963), an issue devoted to 'Education in Japan'.

11 *Asahi Nenkan*, 1967, p. 459.

12 The main issue was the conditions under which workers in public corporations and similar bodies should be allowed to become full-time union officials. The legislation that went into effect in December 1966 provided that: (1) with permission from the authorities, a worker could become a full-time union official and retain his employment for no more than three years; (2) the period of absence from his job should not count towards his pension rights; (3) there was to be two years' grace before the system came into effect.

Sōhyō resistance was occasioned by the large number of union officials affected in some of its component unions. *Asahi Shimbun*, 12 December 1966.

13 See R.P. Dore, 'Textbook Censorship in Japan: The Ienaga Case', *Pacific Affairs*, vol. XLIII, no. 4 (Winter 1970–1), pp. 548–56.

14 See Henry DeWitt Smith II, *Japan's First Student Radicals*, Cambridge, Mass., Harvard University Press, 1972.

15 Pempel, op. cit., pp. 137–58.

16 Ibid., pp. 132–3.

17 Kurt Steiner, Ellis S. Krauss and Scott C. Flanagan (eds), *Political Opposition and Local Politics in Japan*, Princeton, Princeton University Press, 1980, p. 469.

18 For a comprehensive study of Japanese local government to the early 1960s, see Kurt Steiner, *Local Government in Japan*, Stanford, Stanford University Press, 1965. See also Steiner, Krauss and Flanagan, op. cit.

19 Nearly all the prefectures are called *ken*, but Hokkaidō, sometimes regarded as an underdeveloped frontier area, is called *dō* (province), Kyōto and Ōsaka prefectures are known as *fu* (untranslatable except as 'urban prefecture'), and Tokyo prefecture is called *to* (metropolis). There is no real difference of status or powers between the *dō*, *fu* or *ken*, but the Tokyo-*to* is in a sense a category of its own, as we shall see.

20 For a municipality to be designated a city, population must be over 50,000, it must provide public facilities 'suitable to a city', and the number of inhabitants engaging in 'industrial, commercial and other employment of an urban nature' must not be less than 60 per cent of the total population. Some exceptions can be made down to a population of 30,000.

21 At present there are six cities so designated: Kyōto, Ōsaka, Yokohama, Kōbe, Nagoya and Kitakyūshū.

22 See Steiner, op. cit., pp. 194–203.

23 *Chihō jichihō* (Law No. 67 of 17 April 1947, as amended), henceforth cited as 'Local Autonomy Law', articles 284–93. Another related meaning is the local development corporation, jointly established by two or more ordinary local public bodies. These are a rather new development of increasing importance. Local Autonomy Law, articles 298–319.

24 Local Autonomy Law, articles 294–7.

25 The urban equivalent of the *buraku* was the *tonarigumi* (neighbourhood association), but for the most part this has proved a less tenacious institution than the *buraku*.

26 These last include some offshore islands, which are administered as Part of Tokyo.

27 Local Autonomy Law, articles 281–3.

28 The special role of the ward assembly in selecting the ward head came about as a result of an amendment to the Local Autonomy Law in 1952. The Tokyo District Court in 1962 in effect declared the 1952 amendment unconstitutional on the grounds that the Tokyo wards were 'local public entities' in the sense of article 93 of the Constitution. This however was reversed in 1963 by the Supreme Court, which argued that the Tokyo wards were not the central focus of the lives of their inhabitants, since they were merged into another entity, the Tokyo Metropolis. Therefore article 93, with its provision about popular election of officials

of 'local public entities', was not relevant. Steiner, op. cit., pp. 122–6. For the circumstances leading up to the revision of the law in 1974, see Steiner, Krauss and Flanagan, op. cit., pp. 349–50.

29 Minobe won 3,655,299 votes; Hatano 1,935,694.

30 Steiner, Krauss and Flanagan, op. cit., p. 332.

31 Ibid.

32 Chong-do Hah and Christopher C. Lapp, 'Japanese Politics of Equality in Transition: The Case of the Burakumin', *Asian Survey*, vol. XVIII, no. 5 (May 1978), pp. 487–504.

33 Steiner, Krauss and Flanagan, op. cit., pp. 334–5.

34 Ibid., p. 329. The leading writer in English on Asukata and the politics of Yokohama is Terry MacDougall. See his chapter in Steiner, Krauss and Flanagan, op. cit., pp. 55–94.

35 See the excellent chapter on local politics in Kyōto by Ellis Krauss, in Steiner, Krauss and Flanagan, op. cit., pp. 383–424.

36 The location of polluting industries in Southeast Asian countries rather than Japan has caused some problems for Japan's image in Southeast Asia.

37 Takeshi Ishida and Aurelia D. George. 'Nōkyō: The Japanese Farmers' Representative', in Peter Drysdale and Hironobu Kitaoji (eds), *Japan and Australia: Two Societies and their Interaction*, Canberra, London and Miami, Australian National University Press, 1981, pp. 194–214.

38 Dore gives the following figures in his comparison of Japanese and British factories. The Hitachi Company spent 8½ per cent of total labour costs on 'housing, medical services, canteens, transport subsidies, sports and social facilities and special welfare grants other than pay during sickness'. In contrast , the median British firm of a group surveyed in 1968 spent 2½ per cent of its total labour bill on similar services, but including sick pay. Ronald Dore, *British Factory – Japanese Factory: The Origins of Diversity in Industrial Relations*, London, George Allen and Unwin, 1973, p. 203.

39 Very little has been written in English on Japan's welfare policies. For a rather dated account, see David E. Woodsworth, *Social Security and National Policy: Sweden, Yugoslavia and Japan*, Montreal and London, McGill-Queens University Press, 1977.

40 Susan J. Pharr, 'The Japanese Woman: Evolving Views of Life and Role', in Lewis Austin (ed.), *Japan: The Paradox of Progress*, New Haven and London, Yale University Press, 1976, pp. 301–27.

41 Hah and Lapp, op. cit. Thomas M. Rohlen, 'Violence at Yoka High School: The Implications for Japanese Coalition Politics of

the Confrontation between the Japanese Communist Party and the Buraku Liberation League', *Asian Survey*, vol. XVI, no. 7 (July 1976), pp. 682–99. Koreans were another disadvantaged minority, as were the remnants of the Ainu in Hokkaidō.

Chapter 12 Issues of Foreign Policy and Defence

1 I.M. Destler, Haruhiro Fukui and Hideo Sato *The Textile Wrangle: Conflict in Japanese–American Relations, 1969–1971*, Ithaca and London, Cornell University Press, 1979.
2 Whereas the English language version of the communiqué used the word 'alliance', the Japanese version used the words 'dōmei kankei', which mean 'alliance relationship'. The latter had a slightly vaguer connotation than the former.
3 Zenhōi gaikō.
4 Peter Drysdale and Hugh Patrick, 'Evaluation of a Proposed Asian–Pacific Regional Economic Organisation', Australia–Japan Economic Relations Research Project Research Paper No. 61, Canberra, Australian National University, 1979.
5 Alan G. Rix *Japan's Economic Aid*, London, Croom Helm, 1980.
6 See chapter 8, pp. 137–8.
7 For surveys of public opinion poll findings on these and related subjects, see Nishihira Shigeki, 'Yoron chōsa ni miru dōjidai shi' (Contemporary History Seen in Public Opinion Polls), *Jiyū*, September 1980–March 1981, especially no. 3 (November 1980), no. 5 (January 1981) and no. 6 (February 1981).
8 The Japanese units were withdrawn from these exercises after US vessels had allegedly damaged the longlines of Japanese fishermen.
9 He also said that it was upsetting for Self-Defence Forces personnel that the Government ruled out conscription because of an article in the Constitution banning 'slave-like bondage', and criticized the ruling doctrine of no preemptive attack in the face of a foreign threat.
10 Ōtake Hideo, 'Bōeihi zōgaku wo meguru jimintō no tōnai rikigaku' (The Intra-Party Dynamics of the LDP concerning an Increase in Defence Spending), *Asahi Jānaru*, 30 January 1981.
11 James W. Morley, 'A Time for Realism in the Military Defense of Japan', in Franklin B. Weinstein (ed.), *US–Japan Relations and the Security of East Asia: The Next Decade*, Boulder, Colorado, Westview Press, 1978, pp. 49–69, at p. 57.
12 Takuya Kubo, 'The Meaning of the US Nuclear Umbrella for Japan', in Weinstein, op. cit., pp. 107–25.

13 Morton H. Halperin, 'The US Nuclear Umbrella and Japanese Security', in Weinstein, op. cit., pp. 93–105.

14 For useful treatments of recent Japanese–American relations see William J. Barnds (ed.), *Japan and the United States: Challenges and Opportunities*, New York, New York University Press, 1979; Franklin B. Weinstein, op. cit.

15 See Martin E. Weinstein, *Japan's Postwar Defense Policy 1947–1968*, New York and London, Columbia University Press, 1971, pp. 95–100.

16 The Japanese word is 'mochikomi'.

17 *Asahi Shimbun*, 19 May 1981.

18 In the Preamble, and in articles IV and VI.

19 See Akio Watanabe, *The Okinawa Problem. A Chapter in Japan–US Relations*, Melbourne, Melbourne University Press, 1970.

20 F.C. Langdon, *Japan's Foreign Policy*, Vancouver, University of British Columbia Press, 1973, pp. 126–32.

21 What the Japanese left (particularly the Socialists) were protesting against was that normalization of relations between Japan and South Korea was likely to make reunification of Korea even more difficult than it was already was.

22 See Paul F. Langer, 'Japan's Relations with China', *Current History*, vol. 46, no. 272 (April 1964), pp. 193–8 and 244.

23 For a study in depth of LDP attitudes towards China see Haruhiro Fukui, *Party in Power: The Liberal Democrats and Policy Making*, Canberra, Australian National University Press, 1970, pp. 227–62.

24 This became known as 'Memorandum Trade' from 1968.

25 To be acceptable for trade with China, a firm could not trade with South Korea or Taiwan, invest in South Korea or Taiwan, export weapons for American use in Indochina or affiliate as joint ventures or subsidiaries of American firms in Japan. The rules do not appear to have been enforced with complete rigour, but none the less had the desired effect.

26 For a fuller account see J.A.A. Stockwin, 'Continuity and Change in Japanese Foreign Policy', *Pacific Affairs*, vol. 46, no. 1 (Spring 1973), pp. 77–93, at pp. 88–90. See also Chae-jin Lee, *Japan Faces China. Political and Economic Relations in the Postwar Era*, Baltimore, Johns Hopkins University Press, 1976.

27 Chae-jin Lee, 'The Making of the Sino-Japanese Peace and Friendship Treaty', *Pacific Affairs*, vol. 52, no. 3 (Fall 1979), pp. 420–45.

28 Japan claimed the two southernmost islands of the Kurile chain, and some small islands off Hokkaidō. The Soviet Union has at

times expressed willingness to return the latter on conclusion of a peace treaty, but Japan has held out for the former as well. On the history of the 1956 negotiations, and their political background in Japan, see Donald C. Hellmann, *Foreign Policy and Domestic Politics: The Peace Agreement with the Soviet Union*, Berkeley and Los Angeles, University of California Press, 1969.

29 Kazushige Hirasawa, 'Japan's Emerging Foreign Policy', *Foreign Affairs*, vol. 54, no. 1 (October 1975), pp. 155–72.

30 See Lawrence Olson, *Japan in Postwar Asia*, London, Pall Mall, 1970. Kunio Yoshioka, *Japanese Investment in Southeast Asia*, Honolulu, The University Press of Hawaii, 1978.

31 See Drysdale and Patrick, op. cit.

32 The 1981 budget provided for 7·6 per cent increase in defence spending over the previous year, and a further 7·5 per cent increase was envisaged by the Government for the 1982 budget.

33 J.A.A. Stockwin, 'Where is Japan Headed?', Australia–Japan Economic Relations Research Project Research Paper, Canberra, Australian National University, 1975.

Chapter 13 Conclusions and Dilemmas

1 See data on housing costs in the Tokyo area in *Asahi Shimbun*, 4 June 1981.

Further Reading

General Politics

The most up-to-date general text on postwar politics is Robert E. Ward, *Japan's Political System* (Englewood Cliffs, N. J., Prentice Hall, second edition, 1978). For an analysis based on theories of post-industrial society, see Taketsugu Tsurutani, *Political Change in Japan: Response to Postindustrial Challenge* (New York, David McKay, 1977). For detail on Japan's political sociology, see Joji Watanuki, *Politics in Postwar Japanese Society* (Tokyo, University of Tokyo Press, 1977); and Bradley M. Richardson, *The Political Culture of Japan* (Berkeley, Los Angeles and London, University of California Press, 1974). For general information on Japan's politics, history and culture, see *Encyclopedia of Japan* (Tokyo and New York, Kōdansha, forthcoming).

Historical Background

The following are good introductory texts: John W. Hall, *Japan: from Prehistory to Modern Times* (London, Weidenfeld and Nicolson, 1970), Richard Storry, *A History of Modern Japan* (Harmondsworth, Penguin, 1960); W.G. Beasley, *The Modern History of Japan* (London, Weidenfeld and Nicolson, third edition, 1981); and R.H.P. Mason and J.G. Caiger, *A History of Japan* (Cassell Australia, 1972). For a stimulating and controversial analysis of the formative period of the Meiji Constitution, see George Akita, *Foundations of Constitutional Government in Modern Japan, 1868–1900* (Cambridge, Mass., Harvard University Press, 1967). On twentieth-century history up to World War II, see Peter Duus, *Party Rivalry and Political Change in Taishō Japan* (Cambridge, Mass., Harvard University Press, 1968); Tetsuo Najita, *Hara Kei in the Politics of Compromise, 1905–1915* (Cambridge, Mass., Harvard University Press, 1967); and Gordon M. Berger, *Parties Out of Power in Japan, 1931–1941* (Princeton, Princeton University Press, 1977). For an interesting book combining social, economic and political history, see Gary D. Allinson, *Japanese Urbanism: Industry and Politics in Kariya, 1872–1972* (Berkeley, Los Angeles and London, University of California Press, 1975); and by the same author *Suburban Tokyo: A Comparative*

Study in Politics and Social Change (Berkeley, Los Angeles and London, University of California Press, 1979).

Social Background

Recent works on Japanese society include Ronald Dore, *Shinohata: Portrait of a Japanese Village* (London, Allen Lane, 1978); Thomas P. Rohlen, *For Harmony and Strength: Japanese White-Collar Organization in Anthropological Perspective* (Berkeley, Los Angeles and London, University of California Press, 1974); Hugh Patrick (ed.), with the assistance of Larry Meissner, *Japanese Industrialization and its Social Consequences* (Berkeley, Los Angeles and London, University of Calfornia Press, 1976); and Tadashi Fukutake, *Japanese Society Today* (Tokyo, Tokyo University Press, 1974).

The American Occupation

Considering its intrinsic interest and importance, it is surprising that no really scholarly book-length assessment of the Occupation has yet appeared in English. Many previously classified materials, however, are now available, and a good deal of research is being done on the Occupation period. Meanwhile, it it best to start with an authoritative statement of Occupation policy: Supreme Commander for the Allied Powers, *Political Reorientation of Japan* (2 vols, Westport, Connecticut, Greenwood Press, 1970 reprint of original, published by United States Government Printing Office, 1949). A good general book by a participant-observer is Kazuo Kawai, *Japan's American Interlude* (Chicago, Chicago University Press, 1960). For a stimulating 'thinkpiece' see Herbert Passin, *The Legacy of the Occupation of Japan* (Occasional Papers of the East Asia Institute of Columbia University, New York, Columbia University Press, 1968). The best study of a single area of reform is R.P. Dore, *Land Reform in Japan* (London, Oxford University Press, 1959). Two stimulating recent works are John W. Dower, *Empire and Aftermath: Yoshida Shigeru and the Japanese Experience, 1878–1954* (Cambridge, Mass., Harvard University Press, 1979) and Chalmers Johnson, *Conspiracy at Matsukawa* (Berkeley, Los Angeles and London, University of California Press, 1972).

Elections, Parties and Parliament

The best work on elections is Gerald Curtis, *Election Campaigning Japanese Style* (New York, Columbia University Press, 1971). On electoral behaviour, see Scott C. Flanagan and Bradley M. Richardson,

Japanese Electoral Behavior: Social Cleavages, Social Networks and Partisanship (London and Beverly Hills, Sage Publications, 1977). On parties (both prewar and postwar), see Haruhiro Fukui (ed.), *Encyclopedia of Political Parties in Asia and the Pacific* (New York, Greenwood Press, forthcoming), section on parties in Japan. On Parliament, see Hans H. Baerwald, *Japan's Parliament: An Introduction* (Cambridge University Press, 1974).

The Liberal Democratic Party

The best analysis is still Haruhiro Fukui, *Party in Power: The Japanese Liberal-Democrats and Policy-Making* (Canberra, Australian National University Press, 1970). Another informative discussion is Nathaniel B. Thayer, *How the Conservatives Rule Japan* (Princeton, Princeton University Press, 1969).

Policy-Making and Pressure-Group Politics

There have been a number of good policy-making studies since the early 1970s, including: John C. Campbell, *Contemporary Japanese Budget Politics* (Berkeley, Los Angeles and London, University of California Press, 1977); I.M. Destler, Haruhiro Fukui and Hideo Sato, *The Textile Wrangle: Conflict in Japanese–American Relations, 1969–1971* (Ithaca and London, Cornell University Press, 1979); T.J. Pempel, *Patterns of Japanese Policymaking: Experiences from Higher Education* (Boulder, Colorado, Westview Press, 1978); and T.J. Pempel (ed.), *Policymaking in Contemporary Japan* (Ithaca and London, Cornell University Press, 1977). Two interesting pressure-group studies are Donald R. Thurston, *Teachers and Politics in Japan* (Princeton, Princeton University Press, 1973) and William E. Steslicke, *Doctors in Politics: The Political Life of the Japan Medical Association* (New York, Washington and London, Praeger, 1973).

Political and Economic Organization

On this subject, see Ezra F. Vogel (ed.), *Modern Japanese Organization and Decision-making*(Berkeley, Los Angeles and London, University of California Press, 1975); G.C. Allen, *The Japanese Economy* (London, Weidenfeld and Nicolson, 1981); Hugh Patrick and Henry Rosovsky (eds), *Asia's New Giant: How the Japanese Economy Works* (Washington, D.C., The Brookings Institution, 1976); and Richard E. Caves and Masu Uekusa, *Industrial Organization in Japan* (Washington, D.C., The Brookings Institution, 1976).

The Opposition Parties

A very detailed work on the Japan Socialist Party in the postwar period is Allan B. Cole, George O. Totten and Cecil H. Uyehara, with a contributed chapter by Ronald P. Dore, *Socialist Parties in Postwar Japan* (New Haven and London, Yale University Press, 1966). On the Japan Communist Party see Robert A. Scalapino, *The Japanese Communist Movement, 1920–1966* (Berkeley and Los Angeles, University of California Press, 1967); and Paul F. Langer, *Communism in Japan* (Stanford, Calif., Hoover Institution Press, 1972). A standard work on the Kōmeitō and its parent organization, the Sōka Gakkai, is James W. White, *The Sokagakkai and Mass Society* (Stanford, Stanford University Press, 1970).

The Politics of Labour

A basic text, though now somewhat dated, is Solomon B. Levine, *Industrial Relations in Postwar Japan* (Urbana, University of Illinois Press, 1958) See also Robert E. Cole, *Japanese Blue Collar: The Changing Tradition* (Berkeley, Los Angeles and London, University of California Press, 1971) and, by the same author, *Work, Mobility and Participation: A Comparative Study of American and Japanese Industry* (Berkeley, Los Angeles and London, University of California Press, 1980). Another important study is Robert M. Marsh and Hiroshi Mannari, *Modernisation and the Japanese Factory* (Princeton, Princeton University Press, 1976). See also Ronald Dore, *British Factory–Japanese Factory* (London, George Allen and Unwin, 1973); and Ehud Harari, *The Politics of Labor Legislation in Japan* (Berkeley, Los Angeles and London, University of California Press, 1973).

The Constitution

There are many journal articles on the Constitution, but the following is perhaps the most useful: Robert E. Ward, 'The Commission on the Constitution and Prospects for Constitutional Change in Japan', *Journal of Asian Studies*, vol. XXIV, no. 3 (May 1964). A worthwhile collection of articles is to be found in Dan F. Henderson, *The Constitution of Japan: Its First Twenty Years, 1947–67* (Seattle and London, University of Washington Press, 1969). On the peace clause see D.C.S. Sissons, 'The Pacifist Clause of the Japanese Constitution: Legal and Political Problems of Rearmament', *International Affairs*, vol. 37, no. 1 (January 1961). On the Supreme Court and its power of constitutional review see John M. Maki, *Court and Constitution in Japan: Selected*

Supreme Court Decisions, 1948–60 (Seattle, University of Washington Press, 1964); and Itoh Hiroshi and Lawrence W. Beer, *The Constitutional Case Law of Japan: Selected Supreme Court Decisions, 1961–70* (Seattle, University of Washington Press, 1978).

Local Government and Politics

The standard work on postwar local government is Kurt Steiner, *Local Government in Japan* (Stanford, Stanford University Press, 1965). The same writer has co-authored an excellent recent study of what in the 1970s became a key focus of political activity and interest: Kurt Steiner, Ellis S. Krauss and Scott C. Flanagan (eds), *Political Opposition and Local Politics in Japan* (Princeton, Princeton University Press, 1980).

Foreign and Defence Policy

A number of worthwhile studies in this area have appeared since the early 1970s, though most of them are compilations of articles. See especially F.C. Langdon, *Japan's Foreign Policy* (Vancouver, University of British Columbia Press, 1973); Robert A. Scalapino (ed.), *The Foreign Policy of Modern Japan* (Berkeley, Los Angeles and London, University of California Press, 1977); I.M. Destler, Priscilla Clapp, Hideo Sato and Haruhiro Fukui, *Managing an Alliance: The Politics of* US-*Japanese Relations* (Washington, D.C., The Brookings Institution, 1976); Franklin B. Weinstein (ed.), US-*Japanese Relations and the Security of East Asia: The Next Decade* (Boulder, Colorado, Westview Press, 1978); William J. Barnds (ed.), *Japan and the United States: Challenges and Opportunities* (New York, New York University Press, 1979); Chae-jin Lee, *Japan Faces China. Political and Economic Relations in the Postwar Era* (Baltimore, Johns Hopkins University Press, 1976); and Alan G. Rix, *Japan's Economic Aid* (London, Croom Helm, 1980). For an unusual book which analyses aspects of Japan's foreign policy as well as domestic affairs by reference to Australia, see Peter Drysdale and Hironobu Kitaoji (eds), *Japan and Australia: Two Societies and their Interaction* (Canberra, London and Miami, Australian National University Press, 1981).

Journals etc.

Journals which regularly carry articles on Japanese politics include *Asian Survey*, *Japan Interpreter*, *Journal of Asian Studies*, *Journal of Japanese Studies* and *Pacific Affairs*. The *American Political Science Review* and other political science journals carry such articles from time to time. An invaluable source of information about what is happening in the field is the *Newsletter of Research on Japanese Politics*, published from Brigham Young University, Salt Lake City, Utah. For day-to-day information the English-language press in Tokyo is not entirely satisfactory, and the best source is the 'Daily Summary of the Japanese Press' (Tokyo, American Embassy, mimeo).

Index